JOURNAL FOR THE STUDY OF THE OLD TESTAMENT SUPPLEMENT SERIES
254

Sheffield Academic Press

1 and 2 Chronicles

Volume 2
2 Chronicles 10–36
Guilt and Atonement

William Johnstone

Journal for the Study of the Old Testament
Supplement Series 254

לבני אדם שׂר צבא
ולבתי חנה רופאה

כפי שהם מבינים מי שהם
כן הם מבינים מה שבספר הזה

Published by
Sheffield Academic Press Ltd
Mansion House
19 Kingfield Road
Sheffield S11 9AS
England

Typeset by Sheffield Academic Press
and
Printed on acid-free paper in Great Britain
by Bookcraft Ltd
Midsomer Norton, Bath

British Library Cataloguing in Publication Data

A catalogue record for this book is available
from the British Library

ISBN 1-85075-694-5

CONTENTS

ABBREVIATIONS

ANET	J.B. Pritchard (ed.), *Ancient Near Eastern Texts*
AV	Authorized Version
BBB	Bonner biblische Beiträge
BDB	F. Brown, S.R. Driver and C.A. Briggs, *Hebrew and English Lexicon of the Old Testament*
BHK	R. Kittel (ed.), *Biblia Hebraica*
BHS	*Biblia hebraica stuttgartensia*
BKAT	Biblischer Kommentar: Altes Testament
BZAW	Beihefte zur *ZAW*
C	Chronicles (1 and 2); 'The Chronicler', the assumed final editor/author of 1 and 2 Chronicles
CAH	*Cambridge Ancient History*
ExpTim	*Expository Times*
FOTL	The Forms of the Old Testament Literature
GKC	*Gesenius' Hebrew Grammar*, ed. E. Kautzsch, trans. A.E. Cowley
HB	Hebrew Bible
JPSV	Jewish Publication Society Version
JSOT	*Journal for the Study of the Old Testament*
JSOTSup	*Journal for the Study of the Old Testament*, Supplement Series
KBS	L. Koehler, W. Baumgartner, *Hebräisches und aramäisches Lexikon* (ed. J.J. Stamm *et al.*; Leiden: Brill, 3rd edn, 1967–90)
LBA	Late Bronze Age
NEB	New English Bible
NIV	New International Version
NRSV	New Revised Standard Version
OTG	Old Testament Guide
SJLA	Studies in Judaism in Late Antiquity
ST	*Studia theologica*
ZAW	*Zeitschrift für die alttestamentliche Wissenschaft*

2 Chronicles 10–36: Guilt and Atonement

In 1 Chronicles 1–9, the Chronicler (C) has propounded a problem and proposed a solution. The problem is the breakdown in the relationship between God and humanity, which C sketches in 1 Chronicles 1. The solution to that problem is to be provided through the vocation of Israel to holiness, that is, the rendering to God of all that is due to him, as laid down in the Law of Moses. This is made clear by the layout of the tribes of Israel in 1 Chronicles 2–8: the sacral tribe, Levi, stands in the centre (1 Chron. 6). Levi's role, focused in Jerusalem (1 Chron. 9), is to act as priest at the altar, musician in the liturgy, and doorkeeper and treasurer of the sanctuary; the Levite is thereby the preserver, teacher and monitor of Israel's practice of holiness. By this means, all duty owed to God is rendered to him and God's sovereignty over all is acknowledged.

In 1 Chronicles 10–2 Chronicles 9, C has presented the model of the monarchy of the house of David as the means whereby the sovereignty of God can be realized among all the nations of the world. The status of the king of the house of David has been expounded in sacramental terms. He sits on no merely human throne, but on the throne of the LORD: he is the visible expression in physical terms of the cosmic sovereignty of God (e.g. 1 Chron. 28.5). Likewise, the people of Israel are the LORD's host on earth, the counterpart in the physical sphere of the hosts of the LORD in the cosmic (e.g. 1 Chron. 11.9). The ark is the physical representation of the dynamic intervention of God on the field of battle; its resting in the Temple in Jerusalem is the symbol of victory attained (2 Chron. 6.41). Through David and Solomon, the ideal has been achieved: the kings of the earth pay their homage (1 Chron. 29.30; 2 Chron. 9.22-24).

These sacramental ideas belong to the 'Jerusalem' tradition of theology, as expressed particularly in Psalms (e.g. 'Psalms of Zion', such as Ps. 46) and in the prophet Isaiah (see the recurring echoes of the

'Immanuel theology' of Isa. 7.14, in C's work—for example, in 1 Chron. 11.9). An appropriate summary of the affirmations of this Jerusalemite theology, of the restoration of the primal relationship between God and humanity can thus be found in Isaiah (Isa.2.2-4; cf. 2 Chron. 33.15):

> In days to come the mountain of the LORD's house
> shall be established as the highest of the mountains...
> all the nations shall stream to it...
> 'Come, let us go up to the mountain of the LORD...
> that he may teach us his ways...'
> For out of Zion shall go forth instruction [Torah]...
> Nation shall not lift up sword against nation,
> neither shall they learn war any more.

C's account in 1 Chronicles 11–2 Chronicles 9 of the reigns of David and Solomon may be regarded as the casting into narrative form of these aspirations of Jerusalemite theology. He portrays the fulfilment of these hopes through them in the most ideal terms possible. The Temple, planned by David and built by Solomon as the resting place of the ark, is the ultimate expression of the pacification of the world. The sovereignty of God is acknowledged by Israel paying all that is due to him and by all the world bringing their tribute. The magnificence and wealth of the Temple, and the splendour of the court and throne of Solomon, maintained by these dues and tribute, are thus the outward sign of this universal recognition of the reign of God.

But, throughout, the conditional nature of the relationship between God and king has been recognized; the criterion has been obedient observance of the Law of Moses (e.g. 1 Chron. 22.12-13). Three times, in the fundamental areas of ark (1 Chron. 13), Temple (1 Chron. 17), and people (1 Chron. 21), David in his impulsiveness has shown himself negligent of the demands of the laws of holiness.

It is in connection with the last, David's census of the people in 1 Chronicles 21, that the nature of his relationship with God has changed. In the Law, when the people are mustered for action, there is a rite of prophylactic atonement, whereby the relationship between God and people, which is presupposed, is protected and maintained unimpaired (Exod. 30.11-16). It was the duty of the priests to maintain this unbroken, presupposed relationship through such rites as those of the Day of Atonement (cf. 1 Chron. 6.49). David, in violating this requirement of dedication, has threatened the relationship and immediately changed the nature of atonement. It is now no longer a matter of the prospective safeguarding of the existing relationship, but the retrospective restoration of the broken relationship, with all the cost of restoration that that breach entails. The guilt of David has resulted in the necessary correction of the balance between the house of David and the house of Levi: David's diminution in status and the growth of the status of the levitical priesthood (1 Chron. 29.22). The altar, where the holocausts of utter devotion and the communion sacrifices of unbroken fellowship had once been offered, has now been replaced by the altar marking the spot where the punishment of God's own people was arrested (1 Chron. 21.30–22.1).

Solomon has been presented as the flawless executor of the ideal (the Samuel–Kings source has been thoroughly screened—less than two fifths of it is used; see table in introduction to 2 Chronicles 1–9). True to his name (*š^{e}lōmô*), Solomon is the man of peace (*šālôm*, 1 Chron. 22.9), who is perfectly compliant (*lēbāb šālēm*, 1 Chron. 29.19), and under whom the whole system is completed (*šālēm*, 2 Chron. 8.16).

The remainder of C's work, in the second part of the narrative section in 2 Chronicles 10–36, is now to be taken up with the question of the capacity of the subsequent kings of the house of David to maintain this ideal realized under Solomon. There have already been premonitions of failure. C's task as an 'exilic' work is to understand that failure and to look beyond it to the conditions for the eventual recognition of God's sovereignty on earth, which will finally solve the problem of the relationship between God and humanity with which the work began.

These premonitions of failure have already been sketched in highly specific terms in the preface to the whole work, in the genealogies in 1 Chronicles 2–8, and in the account of the reign of the first king of all, Saul, in 1 Chronicles 10. Israel's ultimate failure in the monarchical period is now to be accounted for by the application of the theological concept of *ma'al*.

As has already been announced in the genealogical preface, *ma'al* is the defrauding of God of what is his due, not least as the giver of life in the land; this defrauding of God is the root cause of Israel's guilt and, ultimately, of Israel's forfeiture of that land (cf. 1 Chron. 2.7; 5.25; 9.1). The central significance of the term *ma'al* can be seen in its immediate reintroduction in this second part of the narrative section in the account of the reign of the first king after Solomon, his son Rehoboam (2 Chron. 12.2). It then recurs at critical points throughout the account of the succeeding reigns (2 Chron. 26.16, 18; 28.19 [twice], 22; 29.6, 19; 30.7; 33.19) down to the summary in 2 Chron. 36.14, in the reign of Zedekiah, the last of the Davidic kings. (For a fuller discussion of *ma'al*, see introduction to Volume 1.)

There are occasional moments when C broadens out his presentation so that the clear outline of his theology can be grasped. This is particularly the case in his account of that concluding reign in 2 Chron. 36.11-19 at the end of the work, when once more the significance of the whole is explained. A brief preliminary look at that final episode will help to keep the line of the argument of the whole clear.

In the account of Zedekiah's reign, the presentation of the specific details merges with more generalizing summary remarks. Zedekiah's downfall is caused at the surface level by his ill-advised political and military policy of revolt against the Babylonian power of the day. But this is merely symptomatic of deeper dynamics. In specific theological terms, Zedekiah has ignored the warning of Jeremiah and violated a solemn oath taken in the name of God (vv. 12-13; another cause of *ma'al*, according to Lev. 6.3, 5. For Jeremiah's view of Nebuchadnezzar as the LORD's servant see Jer. 25.9). But that failure too is broadened out: it is but the prime example of the general posture of resistance to God to be found throughout Zedekiah's reign (vv. 11-13). C's presentation then widens still further into a comment on the entire sweep of Israel's history: Zedekiah's reign is the culmination of a whole history of *ma'al*, in which the people at large are implicated (vv. 14-16).

> There is no justification in MT for separating vv. 14 and 15, as in the standard modern editions of the Hebrew Bible, *BHK* and *BHS*, and as in NRSV. The reason for the separation is that v. 14 seems to refer to Zedekiah's generation alone, whereas v. 15 to the whole sweep of history. But the personal pronoun 'them' in v. 15 refers to nothing other than 'all the leaders of the priests and the people' in v. 14. This is another example of C's 'timeless contemporaneity' (cf. introduction to Volume 1): all Israel, past and present, are swept up together into culpability and into the consequences of that culpability.

It is also in this final episode that C explains why this last third of his presentation (2 Chron. 10–36 contains 621 out of the total of 1765 verses of the whole work) is so long and complex. In it there is, of course, a reflection of the actual course of history, to which C is bound, but its very long-drawn-out character is itself testimony to the long-suffering patience and mercy of God. Throughout these reigns God has sent his messengers, above all his prophets, in the attempt to bring his people back. These messengers have been sent 'at the earliest opportunity and persistently' (2 Chron. 36.15) in warning and reproof, so that the people may be spared the consequences of their folly. But they have consistently rejected these divine messengers; their rejection of them is simply another feature of their hardened condition. At last God's patience is exhausted; the destroying force of his anger breaks out.

Two dominant features of this final episode will recur throughout the presentation of the reigns of the house of David in 2 Chronicles 10–36. On the one hand, the main part of the narrative will be taken up with the failure of the Davidic kings expounded in a great variety of ways, not least, as has already been argued, in terms of *ma'al*. On the other hand, C portrays the constant succession of prophets (and other emissaries) sent by God, as he strives with his people to prevent *ma'al* and its catastrophic consequences.

The importance of these two features is already clear from the regular pattern of the framework within which the account of each of these reigns is set. That framework includes, in principle at any rate, seven elements:

(1)   the age of the new Davidic king at his succession;
(2)   the length of his reign in Jerusalem;
(3)   the name of his mother;
(4)   evaluation;
(5)   the record of the rest of his deeds;
(6)   his death and burial in the city of David;
(7)   the succession of the next king.

There is one striking omission in this list of standard elements in the framework in C from the parallel list in Kings. In the Kings parallel after element (7) there is a cross-reference to the contemporary king of the northern kingdom (for the eleven kings after Rehoboam until the fall of the northern kingdom). This cross-reference is the standard means whereby Kings controls the chronology of the period in his presentation of the history of both north and south. For C, with his 'all Israel' focus centred on Judah, the history of the independent north is not relevant. Only once is the synchronism included (for Abijah in 2 Chron. 13.1), and that is because it contributes directly to the understanding of the course of the history of Judah as the surviving remnant of the true Israel. Relations with the house of Ahab have perforce to be considered in 2 Chronicles 18–24, but even those C exploits theologically to portray the house of Ahab as the archetype of wickedness (*rš'*), as contrasted with the righteousness of David (*ṣdq*; cf. on 2 Chron. 6.23).

The reigns of Amaziah and Uzziah (2 Chron. 25–26) give examples of the use, in principle, which C makes of this framework. Elements (1) to (3) introduce the reign in question in objective annalistic terms. Element (4), the evaluation, provides the trigger for the main narrative. It uses one or more incidents in the reign to justify the verdict on the king and thus varies greatly in length from a few verses to several chapters. Element (5), as will be argued in a moment, represents an uninterrupted strand of prophetic commentary on the reigns of the kings of the Davidic house, which complements the accounts of the intervention of prophetic figures in the course of events to condemn and warn in the exposition of element (4). Elements (6) to (7) conclude the account, again in annalistic style.

But C uses this stereotyped pattern with great freedom, both in its location in the narrative in question and in its completeness. Sometimes the annalistic material is gathered together at the end of the reign (as in the case of Rehoboam, 2 Chron. 12.13-16); sometimes C repeats material (for resumption mainly, most obviously in 2 Chron. 21.5, 20 and 27.1, 8; but also in more immediate contexts, 2 Chron. 22.1; 26.1, 3).

Element (1) is missing for Abijah and Asa (though the data for Asa are provided elsewhere in the narrative).

Element (2) provides the chronology for the period in historical terms.

Name of King	Reference	Length of Reign
1. Rehoboam	2 Chron. 10.1–12.16	17 years
2. Abijah	13.1–14.1a	3 years
3. Asa	14.1b–16.14	41 years
4. Jehoshaphat	17.1–21.1	25 years
5. Jehoram	21.2–22.1	8 years
6. Ahaziah	22.2-9	1 year
The Athaliah usurpation	22.10–23.21	6 years
7. Joash	24.1-27	40 years
8. Amaziah	25.1-28	29 years
9. Uzziah	26.1-23	52 years
10. Jotham	27.1-9	16 years

Name of King	Reference	Length of Reign
11. Ahaz	28.1-27	16 years
12. Hezekiah	29.1–32.33	29 years
13. Manasseh	33.1-20	55 years
14. Amon	33.21-25	2 years
15. Josiah	34.1–35.27	31 years
16. Jehoahaz	36.1-4	3 months
17. Jehoiakim	36.5-8	11 years
18. Jehoiachin	36.9-10	3 months, 10 days
19. Zedekiah	36.11-19	11 years

Here above all, C is firmly tied to historical realities. The sheer givenness of this succession of nineteen kings cannot be avoided by C, nor the 393 and a bit years that their reigns represent. He wrestles to make sense of the inescapable facts of Israel's past. But he is doing more: while this past experience is fully presupposed in all its calamitous actuality, he is seeking to generalize from the specifics of that experience to enable fundamental and enduring truths of the relationship of God with his people to be grasped for his own 'exilic' generation. Thus, as will be argued below, the raw data of this chronology are not the most important information for him: rather, it is the fifteen generations of the house of David from Rehoboam to Josiah, whose death marks the beginning of the exile, into which each of the four subsequent kings is led off.

The name of the mother, element (3), is given for most of the twelve kings from Rehoboam to Hezekiah (but not thereafter).

> The exceptions are Asa (the parallel in 1 Kgs 15.10, where Asa's mother is identified as a daughter of Absalom, is problematical), Jehoram and Ahaz (whose mothers are not recorded in Kings either). The note is omitted in the case of the seven last kings of Judah, from Manasseh to Zedekiah (though present in Kings). It may be that the name of the mother is given in connection with the question of purity of descent, and, therefore, of non-introduction of influences from the world of the nations into the nurture of the leader of the people of God. All the mothers of kings whom C records appear to have been native-born—as indeed were the mothers of the kings from Manasseh to Zedekiah, according to Kings—and therefore not responsible for the infiltration of foreign influences, apart from Rehoboam's mother, an Ammonitess, and Ahaziah's mother, the notorious Athaliah, daughter of Ahab, and wife of Jehoram.

Element (4), the evaluation of the reign in question and its exposition, is the heart of the matter; it provides the narrative core for the presentation of the reign of each king.

As far as the evaluation is concerned, these narratives need to be read in their entirety: the introductory framework element taken by itself can be misleading. Reigns may seem, at first sight, to be unreservedly commended in the formal evaluation (especially Asa and Uzziah in 2 Chron. 14.2; 26.4). In the parent text in Kings a qualification is introduced immediately by the adverb 'only' (*raq*); C may delay the introduction of the qualification (and may omit the adverb when he does introduce the qualification), so that he can present his narrative materials on the reigns in two (sometimes more) parts—one justifying approval, the other disapproval (see the qualification on Asa in 2 Chron. 16.12, and on Uzziah in 2 Chron. 26.16; the reigns of Jehoshaphat, Joash and Amaziah are similarly split, see at 2 Chron. 17.6; 24.2; 25.2; see also the reign of Jotham). The formal evaluation is omitted for only two kings, Abijah and Jehoahaz. In Abijah's case, MT introduces a strong paragraph marker between the two parts of the presentation of the reign; while the first part is strongly favoured, the second implies a negative judgment (see on 2 Chron. 13.21). For C, by Jehoahaz's time, the exile has already begun (see on 2 Chron. 35.25–36.4).

At first sight, a great range of variation is to be found in framework element (5), the record of further information on the reign in question (for thirteen out of the nineteen kings; nos. 5, 6, 14, 16, 18, and 19 are missing, but three of these—16, 18 and 19—disappear in exile; 6 dies in the North). The record of the kings' deeds is variously given as:

-   the words of a prophet (Shemaiah and Iddo for Rehoboam);
-   the commentary (midrash) of a prophet (Iddo for Abijah);
-   the vision of a prophet on the book of the kings of Judah and Israel (Isaiah for Hezekiah);
-   even just that a prophet 'wrote' the record (Isaiah for Uzziah);
-   the words of a prophet on the book of the kings of Israel (Jehu ben Hanani for Jehoshaphat);
-   the book of the kings of Judah and Israel (Asa, Amaziah, Ahaz; sometimes 'Israel and Judah'—Jotham, Jehoiakim);
-   the book of the kings of Israel including the words of the seers (Manasseh);
-   the commentary (midrash) on the book of the kings (Joash).

It is not clear what, precisely, is the nature of these records. The immediate impression is that there is a great variety. But it is also possible, is, indeed, more likely, that only one kind of writing is meant, namely, a prophetic commentary on the deeds of the kings of

Judah and Israel: the 'words of Iddo', for instance, is likely to be the same as the 'midrash of Iddo', which, in turn, is likely to be part of the 'midrash on the book of the kings'; the 'book of the kings' is part prophet-authored and contains theological evaluation, for example, on 'the abominations' of Jehoiakim, 2 Chron. 36.8. In that case, there is reference here to a single, written, definitive, theological commentary that has proceeded alongside the reigns of these kings, from beginning to end (it is notable that, in contrast to Kings, C never uses the purely secular formulation, 'the book *of the annals* of the kings...'); cf. the references to the 'canonical' authority of the prophets Gad and Nathan in 2 Chron. 29.25, and to Jeremiah's composition of a lament on Josiah in 2 Chron. 35.25, which also attained 'canonical' status (also, the letter written by Elijah to Jehoram in 2 Chron. 21.12). It is in harmony with this conclusion that it is said of Josiah, in especially honorific terms, that the remainder of his deeds was 'in accordance with what is recorded in the Law of the LORD'.

A further variation within the formulation of element (5) may confirm that an evaluative function is involved. The first phrase, 'the rest of the deeds of X', occurs in a variety of forms. Six times it appears as, 'The deeds, first and last, of X', four of these beginning, 'the rest of the deeds, first and last, of X' (2 Chron. 20.34; 25.26; 26.22; 28.26). But that last formulation is somewhat self-contradictory: 'the deeds, first and last' implies '*all* the deeds', while 'the rest of the deeds' implies only some. It is probable, therefore, that the Hebrew word *yeter*, translated 'rest', might be better translated 'the sum', 'the evaluation' (cf. the related word *yitrôn*, a key word in Ecclesiates, meaning 'lasting value', 'surplus'). It is striking that, when the phrase 'first and last' is not used, some other qualifying words are introduced: 'his ways and his words' (Abijah); 'and all his wars and his ways' (Jotham); 'and his acts of faithfulness' (Hezekiah and Josiah); 'and his prayer to his God and the words of the seers who spoke to him in the name of the LORD the God of Israel' (Manasseh); 'and his abominable practices which he performed and what happened to him' (Jehoiakim). In one case (Ahaz) both 'first and last' and 'and all his ways' are used.

Element (6) is missing with kings 14 and 16–19 (the last four presumably die in exile). The purpose of element (7) is to display the unbroken succession of the Davidic monarchy, passing directly from father to son. It is missing in the case of Joash, since the narrative itself is partly concerned with precisely the issue of securing the unbroken Davidic succession; it is not in the standard form for Amon (perhaps by textual error); the last four kings succeed irregularly in the pattern, son–brother–son–brother.

Within this annalistic framework C proceeds to narrate the respective reigns, the narrative being, essentially, an exposition of framework element (4). The presentation of the individual reigns shows enormous variation not only in length but also in content and arrangement. Yet a number of features regularly recur that illuminate C's two chief concerns, *ma'al* and the role of prophecy. C is interested above all in the attitude of the king of the day to the Temple and to the obligations implied and imposed by the Temple. Fundamentally, the Temple in Jerusalem, as resting place of the ark, expresses the peace of God established throughout the world and maintained by the rule of God's vicegerent on earth, the Davidic king. The kings of the earth are in principle the loyal subjects of the Davidic king, who bring him tribute in token of their recognition of his status. But, if the Davidic king is guilty of shortcoming in the discharge of his duty as representative and agent of the LORD on earth (sometimes expressed directly by the king's incapacitation through illness), the kings of these foreign peoples (including sometimes the northern kingdom) immediately reflect that disorder and disruption by revolt or even invasion. These invasions are not just punitive; in sacramental theology, when Israel fails in its vocation to be for the nations of the world that which they cannot themselves be, it is threatened by that act with forfeiture of its status and assimilation by that world of the nations, from whom it took its own origins.

The continuous written prophetic commentary on the reigns of the kings (element [5] of the framework) is complemented by the equally consistent intervention of the word of God to reprove and guide. A variety of agents is in fact used. Most typically it is the prophets themselves who are the 'messengers' of God (Shemaiah to Rehoboam; Oded to Asa; Micaiah ben Imlah and Jehu ben Hanani to Jehoshaphat; Elijah to Jehoram; Zechariah ben Jehoiada, among others unnamed, to Joash; an anonymous prophet to Amaziah; Isaiah to Hezekiah; Huldah to Josiah; Jeremiah to Zedekiah). But sometimes it is the priests (to Uzziah), occasionally the kings themselves (Abijah, Hezekiah). Sometimes it is a non-Judaean prophet (Oded to Ahaz), sometimes even a foreign king, who is not only God's instrument of punishment but even his spokesman (Neco to Josiah). Sometimes the agency is very generally stated (Ahaziah in 2 Chron. 22.7; Manasseh in 2 Chron. 33.10, 18). Only very occasionally is no such intervention recorded

(Jotham, Jehoahaz, Jehoiakim, and Jehoiachin: for the last three it is already too late).

The relative importance of these evaluative case-histories–expansions of framework element (4) for C can be seen from the space which he gives, especially initially, to the various reigns in comparison to Kings. The following statistics overlap the beginning and end of reigns because framework elements (1) and (2) are often in the same verse. The statistics for Judaean kings in Kings are sometimes a little difficult to unravel from those for northern kings. Columns 2 and 3 do not necessarily overlap in content: there is often wide divergence of materials.

Name of King	Number of Verses in C	Number of Verses in Kings
1. Rehoboam	59	36
2. Abijah	24	9
3. Asa	48	17
4. Jehoshaphat	102	51
5. Jehoram	20	10
6. Ahaziah	9	35
7. Joash (including Athaliah interregnum)	51	42
8. Amaziah	29	20
9. Uzziah	23	9
10. Jotham	10	8
11. Ahaz	28	21
12. Hezekiah	118	96
13. Manasseh	21	19
14. Amon	6	9
15. Josiah	61	51
16. Jehoahaz	3	4
17. Jehoiakim	5	10
18. Jehoiachin	3	11
19. Zedekiah	11	25

Down to Josiah C provides roughly half as much material again as Kings (609 verses to 433), while for the last four he provides less than half as much (22 verses to 50).

It has emerged at several points above that the treatment of the last four kings differs from that of the preceding fifteen in terms of details of framework and content. There is a highly significant reason for this, which is related to the overall chronology with which C is operating in his work. As argued in the Introduction to Volume I, C regards the exile as beginning with the death of Josiah, at the end of the forty-ninth generation from Adam; the last four kings, who all disappear in exile (contra Kings), thus belong to that exilic generation. The exilic generation, to which C himself and his audience belong, is the fiftieth generation to whom the Return of the eschatological jubilee is announced. As Lev. 5.14–6.7 provides him with an understanding of *ma'al* that merely heightens the predicament of Israel, so the reapplication of *ma'al* by Lev. 26.40-45, in the context of the legislation on the jubilee in Lev. 25.8–26.2, provides C with his ground of hope for the future. Beyond the failure of the royal house of David fitly to discharge its role as sacramental agent of God among the nations of the world (surely always an unrealistic hope), beyond the failure of the Temple rites to suffice to make atonement for the people, beyond even the forfeiture of the land itself, there lies the possibility of beginning even now, under the tutelage of the Levites, the life of holiness which is the proleptic experience of the eschatological jubilee about to dawn. C thus offers a critique of the 'Jerusalem' tradition of royal theology as represented by many Psalms and Isaiah, affirming its ideals but transposing its substance into the mode of levitical theology.

As the fiftieth generation from Adam, the 'exilic' generation have announced to them the definitive solution to the problem with which the whole work began.

Under Solomon all the means have been provided whereby Israel can attain its destiny as the agency through which the relationship can be realized that God originally intended to enjoy with humanity. Does Israel now succeed in fulfilling that destiny? In many ways Rehoboam's reign provides a paradigm of C's central theological idea: *ma'al*—unfaithfulness and its consequences.

With the accession to the throne of Solomon's son, Rehoboam, C begins to trace how the whole fabric of Israel's life starts at once to disintegrate. Rehoboam bears the programmatic name, 'the people have become enlarged' (or, 'may the people become enlarged'). But, with great irony, his fate is to see the immediate, drastic reduction of his people at the hands of his rival, Jeroboam ('may the people become many'), whose father's name, Nebat ('may he regard'), is added to stress his commoner status. Still worse, an Egyptian invasion brings a threat of destruction to the very gates of Jerusalem. In human terms, on the accession of Rehoboam the counter-forces to the reign of the house of David gain instant and almost overwhelming strength.

For Rehoboam's reign, as for Solomon's, C's account is highly selective. Only two main episodes out of the seventeen-year reign are recounted: the break-up of the kingdom right at the outset (2 Chron. 10.1–11.4); and the invasion of the Egyptian king in the fifth year (2 Chron. 12.2-12).

Once again C's purposes are made clearer by the ways in which he makes use of his source in Kings. C has only fifty-eight verses on the period as opposed to the ninety-eight in 1 Kings 12–14, though much of the latter is taken up with prophetic narrative. His perspective is wholly from the point of view of Jerusalem, for that is the seat of the royal house of David through which Israel is meant to be fulfilling its destiny. Affairs in the breakaway northern tribes are only of importance as they affect the ability of the remnant Israel centred on Jerusalem to fulfil its role.

Thus, most of the material on Jeroboam, the leader of the breakaway northern tribes, in 1 Kgs 12.25–14.20 is omitted: Jeroboam's actions to

ensure the independence of his state by city-building works; his setting up
of the sanctuaries at Bethel and Dan to counterbalance the Temple in
Jerusalem; the story of the prediction by a prophet from Judah of the
destruction of the sanctuary at Bethel, and the oracle from the prophet
Ahijah of Shiloh on the death of Jeroboam's son and the fate of his
dynasty. A principal function of the narrative in Kings is to explain 'the
sin of Jeroboam the son of Nebat' (1 Kgs 13.34), which runs like a
refrain down to 2 Kings 17. This is complementary to C's purpose and is
not reproduced by him.

Only echoes of this narrative remain in C: for example, the setting-up
of golden calves in the sanctuaries of Dan and Bethel, and the appointing
of a new group of clergy not from the Levites, in 2 Chron. 11.15.

Instead of the Kings material on Jeroboam, there is a long section in
2 Chron. 11.5–12.1 describing the measures Rehoboam took to consolidate his position in his now much reduced kingdom in the south.

C also slightly adjusts the sequence of the material in the parent text in
1 Kings in connection with the second incident he records of the reign. He
holds back the annalistic data in 1 Kgs 14.21 and links them with 1 Kgs
14.29-31 at the end of his account. The intervening narrative from Kings
telling of the invasion by the Egyptians is thus brought into greater prominence by being placed in 2 Chron. 12.2-12.

The Break-up of the Kingdom (2 Chronicles 10.1–11.4)

Right at the outset of Rehoboam's reign, the kingdom so assiduously
united by David, and so successfully made the focal point of the
nations of the world by David and Solomon, falls apart.

The reason is two-fold. On the surface there is the political ineptitude of the new king; but this brings into play at the deeper level the
hidden but inescapable theological factor.

The immediate cause of the trouble is the incident retold in almost
identical terms from 1 Kings 12: Rehoboam refuses his people's
request that he should lighten the burdens that Solomon his father has
laid upon them. Rehoboam consults first the elders and then his
younger contemporaries. He rejects the lenient advice of the seasoned
elders who had served under Solomon, and follows the harsh advice
of the inexperienced youngsters. The decision is a disastrous misjudgment in straightforward political terms.

But all this has happened because there is an inexorable theological
factor deeply embedded in the course of events. This turn of events
arises from God himself (2 Chron. 10.15): it happens in order to fulfil

the word spoken by the prophet Ahijah from Shiloh to Jeroboam.

The narrative is, however, not easy to understand within the context of C's presentation, for C has not reproduced from 1 Kings 11 the grounds for the people's grievances, nor the incident in which the prophetic word was communicated to Jeroboam. Furthermore, there are good reasons why C should not have reproduced that narrative, for in certain basic respects it runs counter to his own presentation.

At first sight there appears to be here also a deeply disturbing theological problem: Rehoboam goes to Shechem and by his action precipitates, like an automaton, what God has already announced beforehand through his prophet; yet Rehoboam is held accountable for the consequences of the action. This seems to be an example of the insoluble mystery of how human freedom is curtailed by divine omnipotence and fore-knowledge, yet of how, paradoxically, humanity is still held responsible for its actions.

The narrative, however, shows the mechanism by which all this is brought about. God does not act arbitrarily or out of blind omnipotence or maliciousness to destroy his own purpose by removing his own installed royal house. As the spores of dry rot are present constantly by the million to invade even the most imposing building if the necessary conditions of neglect are present, so the fabric of the life of human society begins to be destroyed if the basic principles of its maintenance are violated. As far as both Kings and C are concerned, the most basic principle is theological, though it is rather different in each.

In Kings, the initial blame attaches to Solomon himself. In 1 Kings 11 there is the catalogue of misdeeds and misjudgments that marred the declining years of Solomon's reign: pre-eminently the foreign marriages leading to the introduction of foreign religious cults into Jerusalem. This leads directly to the use of the figure of the 'tearing away' of the kingdom (1 Kgs 11.11-13), which is solemnly enacted by the prophet Ahijah tearing up his new cloak into twelve pieces, ten of which he gives to Jeroboam, symbolically representing the transfer to him of the ten northern tribes (vv. 26-40). The chief political grievance, so far as his people was concerned, and which prepared the ground for Jeroboam's popular support, was the forced labour that Solomon had imposed on the people of the northern tribes.

None of this is applicable in C's account. No shadow has lain across his presentation of Solomon's reign. No foreign wives have been

attributed to Solomon except one, Pharaoh's daughter, and in his relationship with her he has observed the utmost propriety so far as his
religion is concerned (2 Chron. 8.11). No heterodox religious practice
has been thinkable for such a compliant agent of the divine will. No
enslavement of his people had been perpetrated by him—indeed, he
has been explicitly cleared of any such accusation (2 Chron. 2.2, 17,
18).

In C's presentation, however, fundamental theological factors
remain absolute and the divine word through the prophet to Jeroboam
still stands. But how do these relate to C's account of affairs? The
catalyst in the situation for C is Rehoboam's unawareness or neglect of
the theological implications of his status as Davidic king in Jerusalem,
not his insensitivity to the needs of his people.

One significant adjustment by C of the underlying text at the outset
may explain his view of the matter. In 1 Kgs 12.3 it is the whole
qāhāl, the sacral assembly of all the laity in Israel (1 Chron. 13.2),
which addresses Rehoboam: reformation of the Solomonic regime is
what is required. In C the word 'sacral assembly' is dropped
(2 Chron. 10.3): what takes place at Shechem is not an approved
assembly of the whole community for some divinely instigated purpose. Rather, it is an unauthorized secular gathering, without theological validity. Rehoboam's failure was not merely in the surface
matters of human relations, or of indecisiveness (he needs three days,
v. 5, to give his answer), or of ineptitude in listening to the younger
advisers at the expense of the older; it was in going to Shechem in the
first place. It was sheer presumptuousness that 'all Israel' should seek
to 'make king' (*himlîk*) the one who was in any case the rightful
successor of his father to the throne of David.

> Other examples of 'making king' can be contrasted: 1 Chron. 12.31, 38;
> 23.1; 28.4: 29.22: 2 Chron. 1.8, 9, 11; 11.22; 21.8; 22.1; 23.11; 26.1;
> 33.25; 36.1, 4, 10.

Rehoboam had no need to leave his seat of government, where he
exercised rule in the name of the LORD, to go to a northern regional
city of doubtful loyalty to all that Jerusalem stood for, in order to
answer for himself. It was sheer perfidy on their part that they should
summon Jeroboam as the champion of their cause against the king.
Why should Rehoboam have to go to answer the challenge of a rival,
let alone one who had been a fugitive from his father's own justice? It
was sheer impertinence on their part that they should seek to dictate

the terms on which he should exercise his rule; that they should bargain with him about the terms on which they would be prepared to be his loyal subjects.

C's presentation is, then, that Rehoboam should never have left Jerusalem to go to Shechem (compare other disastrous departures from Jerusalem, 2 Chron. 18.2; 22.5; 35.20; and see 2 Chron. 16.2; 25.17; 28.16; 32.31). By going there he shows himself inadequate, and having got there he shows himself inept. Not having sought first the kingdom of God, all these things are taken away from him. That Rehoboam's failure is fundamentally a theological matter is to be made explicit by C's later comments—all additional to his Kings source—in 2 Chron. 12.1-2 at the crucial moment of the transition from the close of this incident to the opening of the next: he and all Israel with him 'abandoned the Law of the LORD'; in so doing, they 'defrauded the LORD'.

A number of points of detail serve to emphasize the significance of the occasion. The whole scene is a parody of courtly behaviour that serves to point up the illicit nature of the incident. In the complaint of the people there is a play in v. 4, already present in Kings, between the noun 'yoke' and the preposition 'upon': 'our *yoke* ['*ullēnû*]...*upon* us ['*ālênû*]'. The play on 'yoke' and 'upon' is continued in v. 9. The smart young advisers recast this in v. 10 into a neatly turned couplet, where the words are counterpointed at the end of each phrase: 'Your father made heavy *our yoke* but you make [it] light from *upon us*'. They then suggest a reply in which they pair the words in each half line, 'my father loaded *upon you* a heavy *yoke*, but I shall add *upon...your yoke*'. The rhetorical force is increased by the addition of the two vivid figures: 'my little finger is thicker than my father's thighs'; 'my father castigated you with whips; but I with scorpions' (where, incidentally, Rehoboam is made to concede the rightness of the people's complaints). The apparent aptitude of the young men as advisers, for whom elegance and force of expression were prerequisites, is thus underlined by their rhetorical skills. The figures, however, merely emphasize their boorishness and callousness. In his reply to Jeroboam and all the people, all Rehoboam can do is to parrot the replies in which his young mates have schooled him—if not worse.

It is tempting to emend the text v. 14, 'I will make heavy your yoke' to 'my father made heavy...', as in Kings. This is what v. 10, the parallel in v. 14b and the strong contrastive, 'but I...', with which the second

half of the couplet begins, would lead us to expect. As it stands, however,
it does fit well enough into the context: it makes Rehoboam exculpate
Solomon, thus *not* following to the letter the advice of the youngsters; but
this merely implicates himself still further in guilt.

Other apparently trivial adjustments of the text in C point to the
unseemliness of the comportment of king and counsellors. Rehoboam
allows an inappropriate intimacy between himself and his advisers.
The elders, as mere advisers to the divine plenipotentiary, are indeed
downgraded: whereas in Kings they had stood '*with* the presence of
Solomon', here they merely stand 'in' his presence (v. 6). That is how,
too, the young hotheads begin (v. 8). But soon they are allowed
greater intimacy. By v. 10, Rehoboam's young companions continue
the familiarity with the king they had enjoyed while he was still
prince: he does not have the understanding of his new role to make the
transition from 'Prince Hal' to 'King Henry'. They now converse
openly *with* him, whereas in Kings they had more deferentially
addressed him. They give him the words which he then communicates
to the people. The distance from the reprehensible acts of the people is
reduced by the dropping in v. 10 of the disparaging '*this* people' of
the Kings source.

In v. 7, C cannot bring himself to reproduce the Kings text, 'If
today you become the servant of this people and serve them and
answer them [kindly] and speak to them good words...', which would
imply the subordination of the Davidic king to the people. He substitutes acceptable, if vague, advice: 'If you will be ['today' omitted
because it is to be his constant demeanour] for good for this people
and will be favourably disposed towards them and speak to them good
things...' 'Be favourably disposed towards' is at least the technical
vocabulary of the divine acceptance of sacrifice: God's anointed ought
to share the divine graciousness towards his people. 'The good things'
(cf. 1 Chron. 16.34) that ought to be the happy experience of God's
people, are picked up again, but only in the heavily modified form in
which they have been realized by the end of Rehoboam's reign, in
2 Chron. 12.12. In 2 Chron. 19.3 they are defined in terms of the
blessing that results from 'seeking the LORD', the positive form of
avoiding *ma'al* (cf. 1 Chron. 10.13-14).

> C's lack of interest in the circumstances of Jeroboam's emergence as the
> populist champion is evident in a number of details.
>   For the Kings narrative the location of his showdown with Rehoboam
> is significant. Shechem lies in the hill country of Ephraim close to the

border with Manasseh (Josh. 17.7; 20.7). It is precisely the forced labour of Ephraim and Manasseh, 'the house of Joseph', of which Solomon had put Jeroboam in charge (1 Kgs 11.28).

The details of Jeroboam's flight to Egypt do not concern him. In v. 2, he omits 'still' from the 'Now he was still in Egypt' of Kings; for the words of Kings, 'Jeroboam had stayed in Egypt', C reads, 'Jeroboam had returned from Egypt'.

C's reader is now well prepared for the comment that all this was a turn of events controlled by God himself (v. 15). Given Rehoboam's status as the LORD's representative on earth reigning from Jerusalem, his going to Shechem was by that action a forfeiture of his standing. The incident marks a catastrophic reverse in the role of the one people of God who together had had a destiny for the world of the nations. So far from being the focus for hope of restoration, Israel itself is now plunged into division and weakness. Once again the restart to the divine purpose, even through the Davidic house, has been aborted.

Again, one should probably attribute significance to changes, no matter how apparently slight, from the underlying text. In C the turn of events is *God*'s doing, that is, the Deity in his international, indeed cosmic, form. Kings reads simply the domestic, national, 'the LORD'. The more domestic role of God in the word spoken by Ahijah of Shiloh to Jeroboam son of Nebat as it affects Israel is marked by C by the insertion of 'the LORD' at the beginning of the next clause.

In Samuel–Kings the fact that Ahijah came from Shiloh is significant. It had had a sanctuary traditionally associated with the ark of the covenant (see the cycles of stories in 1 Sam. 1–4, not reproduced by C). If the house of David, which had removed the ark to Jerusalem, was not fulfilling the expectations of the northern region, where more appropriately could the voice of prophetic protest be raised than in Shiloh?

Verses 16 and 17 mark diverging responses. Each begins with a strongly marked subject: 'As for all Israel' (v. 16) is contrasted with 'As for those Israelites who lived in the cities of Judah' (v. 17).

This sharp contrast by means of *casus pendens* is C's contribution. Kings begins its parallel to v. 16, 'When all Israel saw that the king...'

'All Israel' rejects the king of the house of David (v. 16). In truth, two tribes are left; but if one section secedes, all are implicated. The ideal is shattered. The reason given is that the king would not listen to an illicit demand. Had the ideal held, there would have been an intuitive understanding between the divine representative and his people, a wholesome realization of potential and quality of life and fulfilment of

destiny. But the impossibility of maintaining throughout the succeeding generations such a utopian regime as C has portrayed for David
and Solomon is evident even in the stating of it. The necessity for the
function of the Levites in the midst begins to come more sharply into
focus.

> Again, there is a slight change in C's formulation: whereas Kings reads,
> 'the people returned the king a word, saying...', C omits 'a word', per-
> haps thus altering the sense of the verb to 'the people *rejected* the king,
> saying...'

The vocabulary that the people use for their rejection of the Davidic
house comes from two sources. The first ('What share do we have in
David? We have no inheritance in the son of Jesse') is derived from
the conquest and settlement of the promised land: it is used of the
allotted share of territory in the land which is passed down as heritable property within the family (e.g. Deut. 10.9, cf. Josh. 13.7). So
far as the northern tribes are concerned, this is the definitive break
(cf. Gen. 31.14): they have freed themselves and their heirs from any
allegiance to the house of David. By stressing David's commoner origin ('son of Jesse'), they make him of no more significance than
Jeroboam ('son of Nebat').

The second ('to your tents, Israel') is the vocabulary of secession
backed up by military force (it is used by the Benjaminite Sheba
against David, 2 Sam. 20.1). The tents are the war camp. It is not that
the northern tribes intend to invade the south, but that they are in
readiness to defend their independence by force of arms against any
attempt to reconquer them—such as Rehoboam immediately feels
himself obliged to undertake (2 Chron. 11.1).

> C personalizes the resolve of every individual male Israelite by adding
> '*each one* to your tents...'

'Now look to your house, David' is probably not a threat of invasion
from the north but a statement that the north will now abandon the
south to its own fate. Every fraternal bond has been severed. But
there is a deeper menace: the divine promise of a '*house* for David',
which was precisely the theme of 1 Chronicles 17, has by Israel's
intransigence also been laid under threat.

By contrast, the Israelites who live in the cities of Judah accept
Rehoboam as king (v. 17). The term 'Israelites', rather than
'Judaeans', is presumably deliberately chosen to indicate that they

remain the loyal rump of the true Israel. 'Rehoboam reigned over them': in Judah there is no *making* of him king, that is, no presumptuous attempt to make him what he already is, as in v. 1, which, by implication, had turned out to be a questioning of his status.

Rehoboam immediately seeks to impose his authority (v. 18). The luckless Hadoram, Jeroboam's one-time superior in charge of the forced labour, is sent to try to enforce his rule. Hadoram is stoned to death by the populace. His fate is to be understood not simply as a lynching by an irate mob, but as a deliberate judicial act in which the whole community takes part and for which it shares responsibility (e.g. Deut. 21.21; 2 Chron. 24.21). The break away of the north is absolute and is given a veneer of legal respectability.

> The Hadoram of the text appears in Kings as Adoram (as in 2 Sam. 20.24) and is presumably identical with the Adoniram of 1 Kgs 4.6; 5.14. If these are all the same individual, then, having been in office already under David, he must have been well advanced in years—Jeroboam's erstwhile senior colleague among the forced labour supervisers, in fact. The venerability of this, the senior superviser, and his possible authority over Jeroboam, availed Rehoboam nothing. But again, such historical speculations are of little moment for C.
>
> The reason for the variety in his name is not clear. 'Adoniram', 'my lord is great', is straightforward Hebrew; Adoram is presumably a shortened form of it. Hadoram may be one of C's intentional distortions, relating the name to the Canaanite deity Hadad, the proper name of Baal. At any rate, the only other bearers of the name in C are foreigners (1 Chron. 1.21; 18.10): is C implying that Hadoram had become assimilated to foreign ways and got no more than he deserved?
>
> C indicates that it was the northern Israelites only, not the 'all Israel' of Kings, who were responsible for the death of Hadoram.

Only with a supreme effort is Rehoboam able to extricate himself from Shechem and escape by chariot ignominiously to Jerusalem (there is an ironical use of the intensive reflexive conjugation of the theme term 'be strong' in David's encouragement of Solomon [1 Chron. 22.13; 28.20; cf. 2 Chron. 32.7]: here Rehoboam summons all his strength—to flee). The whole episode, which had begun in impropriety and continued in farce, ends in humiliation.

The MT matches the finality of the last sentence of the chapter (v. 19) by placing it in a single stark paragraph by itself:

> 'Thus Israel has been in revolt against the house of David to this day'.

No sooner is Solomon dead, than the house of David encounters failure; the breach has never been healed; reconciliation is still awaited.

Rehoboam, having retired to Jerusalem, takes stock of the situation (2 Chron. 11.1). His first reaction is to send an army to crush the rebels. As is indeed his prerogative as king of the house of David, he now summons a *qāhāl*, a sacral assembly, of the choicest warriors of the Israel that is left, 'the house of Judah and Benjamin'. The role of these warriors should be to fight the LORD's battle for the LORD's anointed. What more just cause could there be than to restore the Davidic monarchy to its proper sphere of authority?

> The formulation in 1 Kgs 12.21, 'Rehoboam assembled all the house of Judah and the tribe of Benjamin', does not satisfy C: all that are left belong together in the one 'house' (as indeed Kings reads in the parallel to v. 3), that is, the one Israel that survives. It is in line with this concept of 'all Israel' remaining within the surviving 'house' of Judah that C suppresses the whole of the preceding verse (1 Kgs 12.20)—how 'all Israel' had made (*sic*) Jeroboam king over 'all Israel' and how only Judah was left to the house of David.
>
> One can only assess the significance of the numbers mustered— 180,000—by comparison with other military forces (cf. table at 1 Chron. 5.18). Thus, in 2 Chron. 14.8, for example, the numbers which Asa, Rehoboam's grandson, can command—580,000—are more than three times greater (not to mention the doubling of these under his great-grandson, Jehoshaphat, to 1,160,000 [2 Chron. 17.14-18]). Numbers clearly indicate theological acceptability.
>
> At the end of v. 1, C reads 'to restore the *kingdom* to Rehoboam'; Kings reads, '…the *kingship*…' C's is the superior reading for his purpose: Rehoboam had not lost his kingship, only the greater part of his kingdom. C omits the last phrase in Kings, 'Rehoboam, *son of Solomon*', presumably for abbreviation.

Rehoboam is thwarted in his intention by another prophetic voice, Shemaiah (v. 2; MT emphasizes the intervention of the prophetic word by placing vv. 2-4 in a separate paragraph). Nothing further is known of Shemaiah: he appears in the Hebrew Bible only here (and in the parallel in Kings) and in the next chapter, 2 Chron. 12.5, 7, 15. But his name, 'the LORD has heard', is a suitably absolute theological comment on events.

> Perhaps even Shemaiah's name is intended in this context to mean the imperative 'hear the LORD'—which indeed the people at last do at the end of v. 4. There may also be intended a deliberate contrast with 'the king did not hear the people' of 2 Chron. 10.15, 16.

C changes 'the word of *God*' (1 Kgs 12.22) to 'the word of *the*
L*ORD*': once again, the word is of immediate, intimate significance for
Israel and its ideal role. This is emphasized at the end of v. 3, where, for
the 'to all the house of Judah and Benjamin and the rest of the people' in
Kings, C reads, 'to all Israel in Judah and Benjamin': what is happening
in Judah is in principle an expression of the destiny of the whole people of
God.

Only the commissioning of Shemaiah is described (vv. 3, 4a), not his
actual delivery of the message to the *qāhāl* (that is presupposed by
v. 4b).

Shemaiah's oracle in v. 4a is very tersely formulated (for structure
cf. 1 Chron. 17.4-14): a straightforward command, introduced by the
'messenger formula', and the reason for the command. Rehoboam
should not 'go up', that is, launch a military campaign, against the
north. The ground for this oracle is, as is usual in C (and also, in this
case, in Kings), not military but theological (cf. 1 Chron. 10). It is not
a question of calculating the relative strengths of the opposing armies
or of working out appropriate strategies. Deeply embedded in the
course of events are theological factors: all that has happened has
inevitably happened because of the violation of the fundamental principles of the Davidic monarchy on which the unity of the people has
depended. The north remain the 'brothers' of the south; but mere
force of arms cannot reunite the people. Thus, instead of the 'each
man to his tent' of the call to defensive arms in the north (2 Chron.
10.16), it is 'each man to his house', each to return to the ordinary
constructive affairs of life.

Lest there be any confusion that the north might have a monopoly on the
claim to be called 'Israel', C omits the wording of Kings, 'the Israelites',
after 'your brothers'.

C's last phrase, 'they turned back [or, even, 'repented'] from advancing against Jeroboam', underlines the historic elements in the decision and
avoids the repetition of 'they repented to go, according to the word of the
L*ORD*' that is found in Kings.

Rehoboam accordingly turns to consolidate his position in Jerusalem.

Rehoboam's Measures to Consolidate his Position
(2 Chronicles 11.5–12.1)

This passage, though it is divided by topic into three sections 2 Chron.
11.5-12; 13-17; 18-12.1, is linked together by the resumption of the

main theme of the first section—the fortified cities—in the third section (v. 23; MT has only two sections: 2 Chron. 11.5-12; 2 Chron. 11.13–12.1). The main point is to illustrate how wise practical measures are nullified by personal failing, in this case the violation of the Torah of Deuteronomy.

1. First, there are physical measures (vv. 5-12). C is again at pains to contrast the outward appearance and the inner reality. Rehoboam affects the status that his position as descendant of the house of David requires and goes to all the lengths that prudence suggests to secure that position. But the observance of mere outward form cannot compensate for lack of genuineness of substance.

Thus, in v. 5, Rehoboam 'takes his seat as king'—the same vocabulary used, for example, of Solomon as successor to David in 1 Chron. 29.23. Naturally, as befits the Davidic king, his seat is in Jerusalem. As Solomon had done (cf. 2 Chron. 8.5, where the same technical term for 'fortified city' is used), so Rehoboam now sets about the defence of the realm (vv. 6-10). Jerusalem, situated almost at the frontier with the breakaway state, stands exposed to the threat of invasion from the north. Rehoboam strengthens the Judaean heartland of his kingdom by rebuilding fifteen fortresses in a double ring. The inner ring, more or less hugging the central hill country, goes down on the east from Jerusalem, via Bethlehem, Etam and Tekoa, turns on the south through Bethzur and continues up on the west through Socoh and Adullam. The outer ring defends the southern and western flanks: it runs across the south from Gath, through Mareshah to Ziph, and doubles back to dominate the western lowlands from Adoraim in the south, through Lachish, Azekah and Zorah right up to Aijalon again on the northern frontier [Grollenberg, Map 13]. The catalogue is completed by Hebron, the main stronghold in the south of the country; with Jerusalem, it binds the whole system together. The list is rounded off in v. 10 by a phrase matching the opening in v. 5: 'fortified cities'. 'Benjamin' is included as part of the surviving kingdom, though none of these fortified cities is actually situated within its bounds.

> All of these, with the exception of Adoraim, Lachish and Azekah, have already occurred in C. Some will figure later (2 Chron. 14.9; 20.20; 26.6; 28.18, etc.). Many of them, like Bethlehem, Adullam, Hebron, have appeared in connection with earlier exploits of the Davidic house (1 Chron. 11.1, 15, 16, etc.). Perhaps more significantly, many occur in the genealogical section in 1 Chronicles 2–8 (2.24, 42, 45; 4.3, 4, etc.):

these places are part of the elements that belong to the very constitution of the people of God (cf. the use of the technical term for registering the members of the community in the works of Rehoboam's official prophetic biographers in 2 Chron. 12.15). The strategic importance of these places is graphically illustrated by Lachish and Azekah which figure in the 'Lachish Letters', the dramatic correspondence, discovered in 1935, about the loss of the western lowlands in the early 580s to the Babylonians (*ANET*, pp. 321-22).

The 'strengthening'—a key term as in v. 16—of the fortifications of these cities involves also men, supplies and armaments (vv. 11-12). It is part of the prerogatives of the Davidic king to install 'prefects' (so already David, 1 Chron. 13.1; 26.24; 27.16). As the Davidic king is himself the 'prefect' of God (1 Chron. 11.2; 2 Chron. 6.5), so these officials are the king's representatives and agents in his kingdom.

Appropriately enough, therefore, they are charged with the task of stocking these fortresses with provisions: corn, wine, and oil. Again a word is used that is of central significance in C's presentation: 'storehouses'. It is the storehouses in the Temple that provide the index of Israel's fulfilment of its obligations towards God (cf. 1 Chron. 9.26); the royal storehouses can be held to discharge an analogous function with regard to the people's fulfilment of their obligations towards God's representative on earth, the Davidic king (cf. 1 Chron. 27.25). The weapons listed are 'shields and spears', the basic items of the infantryman's defensive and offensive armour (cf. 1 Chron. 5.18).

As the sequel is about to make clear, however, all these measures can avail nothing if there is theological corruption at the heart of the regime.

2. Religious measures follow (vv. 13-17). At first, it seems that Rehoboam is aware of the need to maintain the religious core of his rule: the priests, and the Levites from all over the country, present themselves to him in Jerusalem. The initiative, however, hardly comes from Rehoboam: the presence of the Levites is the inevitable consequence of the secession of the north; they come as the dispossessed. Jeroboam's affirmation of political independence has brought with it necessary religious consequences: having rejected the Davidic house with its claims to divine regency on earth, he has no choice but to expel the Levites who serve in the name of that LORD who is worshipped in the Temple in Jerusalem. Verse 14 thus describes, with

great poignancy, how these northern Levites have had to abandon their 'pasture grounds and ancestral holdings', that is, have had to give up their symbolic witness to the ideals of pastoral existence in the midst of the northern tribes (cf. 1 Chron. 6.54-81; for 'holdings', the ideal stake in the land to be restored in the jubilee, cf. 1 Chron. 9.2; Levitical holdings in Judah have hitherto been exclusively priestly, 1 Chron. 6.54-65). For the north to remain independent this expulsion has to be permanent: it is an act not just of Jeroboam, but also of his 'sons', not just of the founder, but also of the dynasty.

C uses the language of rejection (v. 15) that he has introduced in 1 Chron. 28.9 (cf. 2 Chron. 29.19): the rejection of the Jerusalemite priesthood and debarring of the Levites is the signal violation and denial of the rights of God by Jeroboam, which can only confirm the downfall of his kingdom. Jeroboam is the Saul of the north—and there is to be no David.

The full horror of Jeroboam's self-invented religion, which comprehensively replaces the worship of the LORD and thus denies the rights of God, is detailed (v. 15). It involves the appointment (the verb as in 1 Chron. 6.31) of an alternative priesthood of Jeroboam's own devising; worship on the 'high places', those sanctuaries on physical heights, natural or man-made, in the landscape that were believed to represent the cosmic dwelling places of the gods, the would-be rivals of the God of Israel (cf. 2 Chron. 14.3); and the worship of calves and goats, the animal representations under which these gods are portrayed, a system of idolatry in which deity is submerged within the natural world in the hope of controlling and manipulating it.

> In v. 15, C has adapted 1 Kgs 12.32b. He adds 'goats', which would appear refer to the fertility cults condemned in Lev. 17.7. 'The calves which he had made' are added from 1 Kgs 12.32a and refer to the 'golden calves' which Jeroboam had set up in his new royal sanctuaries of Bethel and Dan and which he had acclaimed as the gods which had delivered Israel from Egypt.

The infringement of God's prerogatives could not be starker. Yet in this disaster there is still hope for the true Israel that remains in Judah. It is very striking how this structure for the preservation of the surviving rump of the people of Israel corresponds to the presentation of Israel in the genealogical section in 1 Chronicles 2–8: the outer limits of the people are defined by the tribes of Judah and Benjamin and at the heart of this people the Levites function. Even within its drastically reduced compass, the kingdom retains the outline of the authentic Israel of God and still has the potentiality of becoming the agency of God's purpose in the world.

Thus there is a possibility for the continuation of Israel's life in ideal terms (vv. 16-17); Israel's destiny is still in principle realizable. The vocabulary of v. 16 is extraordinarily freighted with theological significance.

- Those gathering in Jerusalem follow 'after' the priests and Levites, not just arriving in their wake, but in terms of obedience. Under the supervision of the Levites they can fulfil their obligations to God.
- They come 'from all the tribes of Israel': although it is only a partial participation, they come, nonetheless, from the ideal twelve tribes, even including those in Jeroboam's breakaway state.
- In contrast to the vocabulary of rejection, C now uses the vocabulary of commitment: all 'who put their minds to it'. He has already used this turn of phrase in connection with according God his rights in 1 Chron. 22.19, the climactic verse in David's exhortation to the community leaders at the time of the preparation for building the Temple and the designation of Solomon.
- The key term 'seek' is used (*bqš*; cf. 1 Chron. 16.11), that is, to consult God and acknowledge his claims in all matters.
- Here, as in 1 Chron. 21.19, C uses the twin designation 'the LORD God': all that is implied by deity is acknowledged and operative. The special application to the destiny of the people is recognized by the completion of the phrase, 'the LORD God of Israel'.
- In contrast to the rejection of the LORD's priests in the north, those gathering in Jerusalem 'sacrifice': the implication of the vocabulary is that they offer communion sacrifices. On this basis of oneness with God reaffirmed, they seek to acknowledge God's prerogatives in the whole of life.
- By all these actions the generation of Rehoboam show their faithfulness to their national destiny as laid down by their founding fathers: the God whom they worship is now designated as 'the LORD, the God of their ancestors' (cf. 1 Chron. 5.25). The ancestors here, one may assume, are in the first

instance David and Solomon (cf. v. 17), but behind them lies
the Torah of Moses (2 Chron. 12.1).

In this way, Rehoboam's reign is confirmed. The first verb, 'they
strengthen' (v. 17), is the key term, *ḥzq*, used of the accession of support for the Davidic house (cf. for David himself in 1 Chron. 11.10;
of Solomon, 2 Chron. 1.1). Indeed, for the people's support, C uses
the two verbs 'to strengthen', addressed elsewhere to the successor as
encouragement to carry on and bring to realization the mission of his
predecessor (so already in 1 Chron. 22.13; 28.20 of David to
Solomon). It is notable that C uses first the general term, 'the kingship
of Judah': it is the eternal reign of the house of David that is the
essential. Only then does the holder of the office of the day,
Rehoboam, merit mention, and then only as 'the son of Solomon', the
legitimate successor of David. Thus the remnant kingdom 'walk in the
way of David and Solomon' (cf. 2 Chron. 6.16): they follow their
practices and so perpetuate their ideals. But this, C ominously records,
continues for a bare three years.

3. Rehoboam's amours (2 Chron. 11.18–12.1). As in the account of
David (1 Chron. 14.3-7; cf. Solomon, 2 Chron. 8.11), a note on the
royal court follows the beginnings of international recognition (even
if, in this case, it is only the limited recognition of some sections in
the north). The court is an outward expression of the king's standing.
The invasion of Shishak, which follows (2 Chron. 12.2-12), may then
be interpreted as an attempt by the foreign power to neutralize this
perceived threat of the growing status of Judah (cf. the invasions of
the Philistines in the matching place in David's reign, 1 Chron. 14.8-
17).

It is not clear that C explicitly connects Rehoboam's amours, his
eighteen wives and sixty concubines, with his falling away from the
Law of the LORD, just implied and about to be made explicit in
2 Chron. 12.1. After all, it is the collective disloyalty of the whole
people along with the king that is mentioned in 2 Chron. 11.17 (*'they*
walked in the way of David and Solomon for three years').

> It is tempting to follow LXX in v. 17 and read the singular verb, '*he* (i.e.
> Rehoboam himself) walked in the way of David and Solomon for three
> years'. Certainly in 2 Chron. 12.1, the singular verb is used: '*he* forsook
> the Law of the LORD', though there too 'all Israel with him' is added.

Yet the connection is at least implied (certainly MT combines 2 Chron. 11.13–12.1 in one subsection and no other explanation of how the king fell away is offered).

The fact that Rehoboam could not possibly have conducted all these affairs within 'three years' is neither here nor there in C's 'timeless contemporaneity': the chronology of his reign given in 2 Chron. 12.13 (he was forty-one at his accession) and the fact that his sons are old enough to take charge of the fortresses (v. 23) imply that the marriages had been contracted long ago in the past. If the last phrase of v. 23 means, 'but he demanded a horde of wives' (as the text actually runs, contra NRSV), the connection is indeed explicit. The law in question is, then, the law governing the conduct of the king in Deut. 17.17, 'he shall not make many wives for himself', which also gives the reason for such legislation: 'lest his heart turn away'.

Certainly, C is making more of Rehoboam's love life than that of any other figure with whom he deals in his whole work. He is the only king to whom concubines are attributed in the entire narrative section from 1 Chronicles 10–2 Chronicles 36. The catalogue of wives contrasts with C's restrained treatment of David's marriages (cf. 1 Chron. 14.3, where the concubines in the parallel in 2 Sam. 5.13 are omitted, though they have been noted in 1 Chron. 3.9). As has been noted above, C passes over in discreet silence the prodigious harem of Solomon recorded in 1 Kgs 11.3, beside which Rehoboam's would pale into insignificance. Of Rehoboam's successors, only his son Abijah (fourteen wives, twenty-two sons, sixteen daughters, 2 Chron. 13.21) has any such comment passed upon him (cf. the quite oblique reference to the 'wives' of his great-great-grandson Jehoram in 2 Chron. 21.14).

The text is not clear as to how many of Rehoboam's wives are actually being mentioned by name. The first marriage is introduced in the straightforward narrative tense in v. 18, 'Rehoboam married a wife, Mahalath...' The subsequent marriage to Maacah in v. 20 begins with an emphatic contrast: 'But after her...', as if only one had previously been mentioned. But v. 18 seems to include two wives, though the second is not distinguished from the first by a conjunction. Neither of the wives of v. 18—if two there be and the second is not a correction of the first—is mentioned elsewhere in the Hebrew Bible.

The parentage given for the wives in v. 18 shows how closely Rehoboam kept within the family circle for his brides: he marries a

first cousin (Solomon's half-brother's daughter) and a first cousin
once removed (David's oldest brother Eliab's daughter).

> Jerimoth, the father of Rehoboam's first wife, has not been included
> elsewhere by C in his list of David's nineteen sons, more than half by
> named wives, in 1 Chron. 3.1-9 (unless Jerimoth is a corruption of
> Ithream, David's sixth son). Are we to assume that he was, therefore, the
> son of one of David's 'other wives', mentioned in the by-going in
> 1 Chron. 14.3? If so, her inferior origin may be being alluded to.

Taking the text in v. 20 at face value, Rehoboam's favourite wife,
Maacah, is yet another first cousin (the daughter of Solomon's half-
brother, Absalom).

> In 2 Chron. 15.16 and its parallel in 1 Kgs 15.13, however, she is the
> mother of Rehoboam's grandson, Asa, and thus the wife of Rehoboam's
> son, Abijah. That is supported by 2 Chron. 13.2, where Abijah's moth-
> er's name is given as 'Micaiah daughter of Uriel of Gibeah'.

In contrast to David, where marriage was an instrument of potential
influence, Rehoboam's contacts are introverted within his own family.

The proportion of Rehoboam's sons and daughters—twenty-eight
sons and sixty daughters—may also imply imperfection (contrast, e.g.,
1 Chron. 25.5 and the family of David 1 Chron. 3.1-9, as well as
more widely in the Hebrew Bible, Job 42.13, 'seven sons and three
daughters', being perhaps the most celebrated case).

The list of Rehoboam's sons includes only one mentioned elsewhere—Abijah, his successor-to-be (2 Chron. 12.16–14.1). It may be
that Rehoboam's choice of Abijah as his heir apparent, for no better
reason than that his mother, Maacah, was his favourite wife, is meant
to function as another illustration of his arbitrary exercise of power.
It may also be yet another example of Rehoboam's lack of judgment:
C may have in mind the chicanery of Maacah's father, Absalom,
recorded in 2 Samuel 13–19, and the fact that Maacah would be called
after her foreign Aramaean mother. Yet it is striking that C uses once
more his established convention of centrality to express importance—
Abijah is the middle son of seven (see, for example, the position of
David in 1 Chron. 2–4, of Levi in 1 Chron. 2–8, and of Solomon in
1 Chron. 3.1–9). If Abijah is a substitute for an older brother, then
here is another example of C's motif of restart after unsuccessful initial start. Even within the sharply reduced circumstances of Rehoboam's reign the potentiality for realizing destiny remains, as Abijah's
name, 'the LORD is my father', implies.

C certainly regards Rehoboam's subsequent actions with regard to Abijah and his sons with favour, so far as they go. In this case, 'he acted with understanding' (v. 23): he distributed some of his twenty-eight sons round the territory of Judah and Benjamin to take charge of the fifteen regional fortresses specified in vv. 6-10 (a Davidic regime indeed!) and provisioned them (a similar action is attributed to Jehoshaphat in 2 Chron. 21.3), and appointed Abijah as their *nāgîd* ('leader'). The title no doubt refers to Abijah's immediate responsibilities of supervising his brothers (see the use above in v. 11), but, since David and Solomon had once borne it (see 1 Chron. 11.2; 17.7; 29.22), it also carries the overtone of the high office of Davidic monarch that he is destined to hold.

But this wisdom, which Rehoboam manifests towards the security of his realm, contrasts with his folly in chasing after numerous wives. Thus (2 Chron. 12.1), almost as soon as Rehoboam's kingdom has been secured and he shows every promise of fulfilling the hopes invested in him, he destroys the true foundation of his rule: 'he abandoned the Torah of the LORD—and all Israel with him'. C uses his by now standard key terms in this summary theological verdict on Rehoboam: the 'establishing' of the kingdom should be the continuation of the destiny of the house of David as inaugurated by David (for the key term, *kûn*, see 1 Chron. 14.2); his 'being strong' is the characteristic of the successor (cf. 2 Chron. 11.17); 'abandon' is one of the standard terms in the vocabulary of rejection (cf. 1 Chron. 28.9); the Torah has already been recognized as the foundation for the life of the people in 1 Chron. 16.40; 22.12; 2 Chron. 6.16; 'all Israel' is the essential focus of the discussion (cf. 1 Chron. 11.1).

3. *The Assault on Rehoboam by the Egyptians* (*2 Chronicles 12.2-12*)

This section falls into three parts (so MT):

1. vv. 2-4: the invasion;
2. vv. 5-8: the prophetic word;
3. vv. 9-12: the penalty mitigated.

The section is framed by the key term, 'strength' (root *ḥzq*; cf. 2 Chron. 11.17): 2 Chron. 12.1, 'when he became strong'; 2 Chron. 12.13, 'so the king Rehoboam became strong'. The fundamental issue in the section is thus, 'wherein does strength lie?' The previous section in 2 Chron. 11.5–12.1 has shown how Rehoboam has done all in his power to 'establish himself'; the present section shows how all that counts for nothing, if there is neglect or rejection of God's claims.

> This section incorporates material from 1 Kgs 14.25-28, but with substantial additions: vv. 2a, 9-11 are virtually identical with the Kings material; vv. 2b-8, 12 completely independent. These independent verses contain key elements of C's concepts. The added vv. 2b-8 are framed by the repetition of 1 Kgs 14.25b in vv. 2a and 9a, 'Shishak the king of Egypt came up against Jerusalem'.

1. *The Invasion (2 Chronicles 12.2-4)*

The consequences of the denial of God of his rights do not take long to appear. It is in Rehoboam's fifth year that the blow falls. Judah is invaded by the Egyptian Pharaoh, Shishak.

Shishak is identified by Egyptologists as Shoshenq I, founder of the twenty-second 'Libyan' Dynasty and dated to the third quarter of the tenth century BCE.[1] The precise reason for his invasion of Palestine is a matter for conjecture: was Shoshenq coming to support Jeroboam, who had been a refugee from Solomon at his court, against Rehoboam? Or, since the list of Sheshonq's conquests in his triumphal inscription in the temple of Amun at Karnak includes the names of cities in Jeroboam's kingdom, had Jeroboam in some way provoked his former protector? The intricacies of international politics, the reasons for military expeditions, and the explanation for events at the level of human history are not C's concern. As the prophetic interpretation of the event in the next section makes clear, the Pharaoh is, in C's view, but the instrument of the LORD's anger (v. 7). He cites the historical reference from 1 Kings 14 in order to provide his own theological interpretation.

The disaster has not happened by chance: it is because 'they have defrauded the LORD' (v. 2b). Here for the first time since the account of the death of Saul (1 Chron. 10.13; cf. 1 Chron. 2.7), the key term *ma'al* used. The specifics of the *ma'al* are not fully drawn out: Rehoboam's failure to prevent the breakaway of the northern kingdom and the amours of Rehoboam are the factors supplied by the immediate context. Whatever the factors, the luckless populace at large are inextricably enmeshed in the failures of the Davidic king.

---

1.   *CAH*, III, pp.534-49, pl. 174.

The Egyptian host (v. 3) is fearsome alike in its size and in its alien nature. The significance of the size—1200 chariots, 60,000 horsemen and an uncountable host of infantrymen—can only be gauged from other comparable statistics (cf. table at 1 Chron. 5.18 and 1 Chron. 19.7; e.g. 1 Chron. 18.4, for the 1000 chariots and 7000 horsemen and 20,000 infantrymen that David captured from the Aramaean power of Zobah, or 2 Chron. 1.14 for Solomon's 1400 chariots and 12,000 horsemen). Equally terrifying must have been the exotic appearance of this host: the Libyans, correctly reflecting the ethnic origin of the regime; Sukkiim, traditionally (LXX) troglodytes from north Africa; and Cushites, the Nubians, from south of the first cataract on the Nile.

Precise information about factual details is not of first moment. The fundamental point is again theological. Israel's destiny is to realize on behalf of the nations of the world what they themselves are incapable of—the relationship with God first envisaged in Adam. When Israel fails to be in herself what she is intended to be, she is exposed to incursion by the ruthless forces of the world of the nations, and reverts to the condition of those from among whom she took her origin. So far from Israel being the source of blessing, the forces of destruction pour into the land. It is hardly accidental that Cush, father of Nimrod, numbered here among the invaders, is one of the emblematic sources of military destruction from the threatening world of the nations mentioned already in 1 Chron. 1.8-10.

C includes an important detail (v. 4): Shishak invades Judah all the way to Jerusalem. All Rehoboam's careful defensive measures, represented by the double ring of fortresses round the Judaean heartland, manned under the leadership of his own sons, are completely unavailing—not because of Shishak, but because of the theological rottenness at the heart of the regime. The section ends with an ironical contrast: whereas in 2 Chron. 11.1 Rehoboam 'came to Jerusalem' to consolidate his position, it is now Shishak who 'came to Jerusalem' to threaten the very existence of Rehoboam's rule.

2. The Prophetic Word (2 Chronicles 12.5-8)
Shemaiah the prophet, who has already intervened to prevent Rehoboam from launching hostilities against the north (2 Chron. 11.2-4), again makes explicit the theological factor in events. In the midst of all this 'coming', he too 'comes' (v. 5), as the effective agent and

spokesman for God. Where the Davidic king is out of tune with the purpose of God, there inevitably God must speak and act (as has happened already, even for David, 1 Chron. 17.4; 21.10). But it would have been better if such speaking and acting had been unnecessary.

Again, there is a grim irony in the depiction of the circumstances of the audience—the king and his officials—whom Shemaiah addresses. Whereas such an audience had 'gathered' (again a key word, cf. 1 Chron. 11.1) in, for example, 1 Chron. 23.2 in enthusiastic commitment for the setting up of the institutions of the kingdom that would enable them to realize the great tasks to which David was summoning them, here they gather out of fear at the prospect of the destruction of the last vestige of that kingdom.

Shemaiah's oracle consists of two parts (cf. 1 Chron. 17.4-14). It is expressed in the language of the law-court: first the verdict of guilty is pronounced by God; then sentence is passed. 'You have abandoned me', is God's verdict on Israel's conduct; the charge has been substantiated. Here again the vocabulary of rejection is used, as in 1 Chron. 28.9; 'abandon' is the opposite of 'seek', failure in which was the emblematic guilt of Saul (1 Chron. 10.13-14). The sentence passed by God is the automatic counterpart of the guilt, '*I have abandoned you to the power of Shishak*': inevitable demotion by God from the realm of privilege; and permission to the world of the nations to invade and to destroy by assimilation. There is no half-way position: either God and his people are in complete harmony or they are in total disharmony. There can be no accommodation. God must be accorded his exclusive rights in full; any shortfall must be made up. (This is not a doctrine of retribution but a corollary of sacramental thinking, see the Introduction to Volume 1.) But it is at this point that the graciousness of God becomes evident. The sentence is not irrevocable though the penalty must be paid.

The leaders of the people and the king admit their guilt (v. 6); they abandon any self-righteousness (they 'humble themselves', as in the situation envisaged by Solomon in 2 Chron. 7.14) and acknowledge the justice of God's action (cf. 1 Chron. 18.14). In response, God relents (v. 7). He again sends a two-fold message: he accepts the acknowledgment of guilt; he suspends the full payment of the sentence. The acknowledgment of guilt ('they have humbled themselves') uses the vocabulary of Lev. 26.41, one of the key passages on *ma'al*: it marks the first step on the costly road back towards rehabilitation (see on 2 Chron. 7.14). The sentence is only mitigated: 'I will not destroy them' uses the techical term for God's punitive action in the 'negative Passover' after David's presumptuous census in 1 Chron. 21.12, 15; 'I will allow a few of them to survive as a remnant'. What that few is, is defined in the next phrase, 'my fury will not be poured out on Jerusalem' (though ultimately it will be, 2 Chron. 36.16; cf. 28.9; 34.21, 25): the fifteen fortresses have gone; only Jerusalem, the central focus of God's rule on earth through the house of David, is spared being ravaged—and even that by no means escapes unscathed, as the next section makes clear.

Once the relationship with God has been broken, the damage endures. There is no cheap grace. The way to restoration is costly—as C is now setting out in his work to portray. The immediate effect is, therefore, that Israel 'will become slaves' to the Pharaoh (v. 8). For a people who traced their origin to an act of deliverance from slavery to Egypt, the overtones and associations of this phrase are startling. Now, in the very first generation after the realization of the ideal of the regency of God on earth of the Davidic house, even in the land they have been given as their own, as their badge of freedom, they have been reduced once more to the status of slaves in Egypt. But Egypt is only a representative power: Israel has become in principle the victimized subjects of the whole world which it is their mission to restore. The point of the stark either–or of acknowledgment of God or rejection by him made at the beginning of the section is thus forcefully made once more at the end, this time in the language of slavery: 'they are going to become their slaves so that they will learn what it is to be my slaves or the slaves of the kingdoms of the lands' (the root *'bd* [cf. 1 Chron. 28.9] repeated three times). The either–or is made clear by a pun between the last verse of this section and the first verse of the next: Israel's choice is clear—it is either 'the kingdoms of the lands' (*maml^{e}kôt hā'^{a}rāṣôt*) or 'the treasuries of the king' (*'oṣ^{e}rôt hammelek*): either subjection to foreigners or loyal acknowledgment of God represented by the payment of all that is due to him.

> The identification of such a pun here may sound far-fetched. It is strengthened, however, by the fact the word for 'treasuries' is written 'defectively' (unlike 1 Kgs 14.26), thus giving it a consonantal outline even closer to that of the word for 'lands'.

3. The Penalty Mitigated (2 Chronicles 12.9-12)

The first phrase of v. 9 resumes v. 2a, thus marking the end of the long explanation C has inserted into his parent text on the consequences of *ma'al* (cf. v. 2b). The invasion of Shishak is now accounted for in the light of *ma'al* and its implications.

The cost of *ma'al* in physical terms is stated: once *ma'al*—the defrauding of God in the symbols in kind of the dedication of life or in that life itself—has been committed lasting damage has been inflicted. There is no cheap grace, no easy restoration. Shishak plunders not just the 'storerooms' of the Temple and of the king, but the 'treasures' themselves. As C has been at pains to point out, the treasures are the index of the people's faithfulness in the observance of their obligations to the LORD and to his vicegerent, the Davidic king (see, e.g., 1 Chron. 9.26; 26.20-26; 27.25-29). The co-ordination of 'the house of the LORD' and the 'house of the king' is especially notable: the realm of the divine and that of his human counterpart are simultaneously impaired. Since the contents of the storehouses are the tokens of the people's loyalty, their physical removal is the expression of the alienation that has taken place between God and people; their loss registers the debt they have incurred; their irreplaceability marks the lasting damage that has been inflicted.

> A small, but significant, adjustment from the parent text in 1 Kgs 14.26 occurs in v. 9: Kings reads, '*and* everything he took', as though it were additional to the treasures of God and king. C reads an apposition without the conjunction—the treasures of God and king *are* everything.

Shishak not only strips these treasuries; he removes the golden shields made by Solomon (2 Chron. 9.16; cf. 1 Chron. 18.7; 2 Chron. 23.9).

> Kings is here more emphatic adding '*all* the shields'.

These shields, too, are symbolical. They represent the offensive and defensive capability of the nations of the earth, the powers of chaos that threaten the stability of God's regime exercized through Israel, and the exposure of Israel to invasion by these powers and their assimilation by them rather than their transformation of them. But, laid up in Temple and palace as the tribute and tokens of recognition paid by the leaders of the nations of the world to Solomon, they acknowledge God's status as the overlord of the nations of the world and their status as his vassals; the shields become the symbols of the peace on earth imposed by the LORD as the sovereign over all. Their removal thus symbolizes the rejection of this claim to sovereignty, subordination and the taking over of this claim by the gods of the victorious Egyptians. The irony and the pathos must be felt in all their acuteness: the dominion of the LORD, once expressed by the deliverance of his people from Egypt, is now challenged at the gates of the LORD's own citadel by the very Egyptians themselves.

But the penalty is mitigated (v. 10). The acknowledgment by the people of their *ma'al* allows the tempering of the effects of their guilt. Rehoboam is able to replace the looted golden shields with bronze ones. Again, the symbolism, this time of the metals (as elsewhere, notably Dan. 2.31-45), is striking: the baser metal expresses the now only debased standing that Rehoboam, because of his folly, can claim as the LORD's representative and agent among the kings of the earth. Rehoboam retains his title 'king', but another 'king' has imposed terms upon him: Israel's kings are now 'once and future' kings; for the present he is but a shadow of the true substance of the position that he has inherited.

Rehoboam is given constant, bitter reminder of his devalued standing (v. 11). 'As often as' he goes in solemn procession as the LORD's representative from his palace into the temple, these brass bucklers are on parade. The impairment of his position is permanent and he is not allowed to forget it.

The shields are in the care of his 'guard', literally, 'runners': the word expresses the constant readiness of these attendants, specially appointed to guard access to the king, to execute his command with the utmost speed. They are rapid response troops, trained to kill (good examples are given in 1 Sam. 22.17; 2 Kgs 11.4-8—as non-sacral agents they have been suppressed in the parallel in 2 Chron. 23). Here one gets the impression that these 'keepers of the king's house', so far from expressing the king's power as the potentate sallying forth, now keep watch on the king himself: 'whenever the king came, they would come' (that last verb not in the Kings parallel). Under Solomon these shields were kept in the 'house of the forest of Lebanon'—the chamber where the vassals sought audience, paid homage, and received judgment (2 Chron. 9.15-16). Now, under Rehoboam, such is the insecurity that the guards keep these shields in their own guard-room (Ezek. 40 is the other context in the Hebrew Bible where the word is used). So far from Rehoboam being the free exponent of the system, he is now trapped by it.

Verse 12 is a summary verse, resuming in particular the vocabulary of vv. 6 and 7 (and thus of the end of the Holiness Code in Lev. 26), in order to reinforce the central theological point. The first step in the restoration of one guilty of *ma'al* must be the acknowledgment of guilt in defrauding God, as the prelude to paying full satisfaction. Rehoboam has at least taken that first step in rehabilitation: 'he humbled himself' (the first king of Israel of whom that is said in C; compare 2 Chron. 32.26; 33.12; 34.27). The gracious response of God is the mitigation of the punishment (he did not 'destroy them completely'): the fifteen fortresses may have fallen but in Judah there were still 'good things'. For this apparently vague term, see above under 2 Chron. 10.7: it was used in the advice of the elders at the beginning of Rehoboam's reign to express the well-being of Israel under the enlightened rule of the Davidic king through the avoidance of *ma'al*. What had been the true destiny of the people under Rehoboam's rule is now realized only in heavily modified terms.

Concluding Theological Verdict on Rehoboam
(2 Chronicles 12.13-14)

MT separates off vv. 13-14 as the theological summary on Rehoboam's reign.

> In 1 Kgs 14 the parallel verses (vv. 21-22) come before the material C has used in 2 Chron. 12.2, 9-12.

The narrative has accounted for how Rehoboam received his position as Davidic king in Jerusalem and the manner in which he discharged his responsibilities. The translation, 'established himself' (v. 13, NRSV), might suggest that there has been a fundamentally presumptuous element in his kingship, as in the charge against Jeroboam in 2 Chron. 13.8. But, as noted above (2 Chron. 11.17), the verb *ḥzq* is a thematic term that is also used of Solomon in 2 Chron. 1.1: there is no question about Rehoboam's right to his status as Davidic monarch, only about what he did with it (the same root, though in a different conjugation, has been used of Rehoboam's activities in establishing his position and maintaining the security of his realm in 2 Chron. 11.11, 12, 17; see the noun in 12.1). Thus, again, C insistently uses the title 'the king' with Rehoboam's name (he does not need to be called 'Solomon's son' as in the Kings parallel); he reaffirms that Davidic Jerusalem is his capital (rather than 'Judah' as in Kings), and states with all curtness, 'he reigned': Rehoboam has every right to his position.

The second half of v. 13 is a straight quotation from Kings (probably so marked as such by the introductory conjunction *kî* in the Hebrew, correctly not rendered by NRSV). It is as though C were saying, 'The following are the annalistic data handed down to us; I have already explained in my theological terms how it worked out'.

C retains the inherited theological comment on Rehoboam's capital: it is the place chosen out of all the tribes of Israel where the LORD has placed his Name (cf. 1 Chron. 13.6).

But the citation of the Kings text has a particular appropriateness for C's purpose: it brings the name of the LORD into sharp contrast with the name of Rehoboam's mother, Naamah ('lovely one'), the Ammonitess. No explanation has been offered by C of how a son of Solomon should have a foreigner as his mother (for his presentation of Solomon as the ideal successor of David, C has not reproduced the material on Solomon's foreign marriages from 1 Kgs 11.1). But it can hardly be doubted that the traditional view of guaranteeing purity of descent—or the reverse—through the mother is functioning here: Rehoboam was foredoomed; his own foreign mother was an agent of introducing into her son's reign contamination from the world of the nations that it was the very destiny of Israel to resist and overcome (elsewhere, when Israel is discharging its true role, the Ammonites appear as defeated enemies and vassals of Israel; see 1 Chron. 18.11; 19.1–20.3).

But in v. 14 C deviates from his source: whereas Kings states that '*Judah* did what was evil', here it is Rehoboam himself (indeed consistently hereafter throughout the Kings narrative itself as well as C it is the king himself who is personally appraised). As anointed Davidic king, Rehoboam bears full and sole responsibility. The text states baldly, 'He committed the evil' (omitting the 'in the eyes of the LORD' of Kings). It is evil in an absolute, qualitative sense (not merely quantitative, as in the parent text, where it is defined as more provocative than that of any previous generation). This evil is then defined in terms of C's key concept, *ma'al*. Rehoboam has been a new Saul: he has not 'fixed' (the thematic term, *kûn*, 1 Chron. 14.2) his heart to seek the LORD, precisely the vocabulary used of Saul in 1 Chron. 10.13-14 with all its implications of defrauding God and, in consequence, of surrendering status.

Concluding Annalistic Comment (2 Chronicles 12.15-16)

Even in the bare annalistic material borrowed from the parent text C cannot forbear to make theological comment. The changes are significant. 1 Kings 14.29 reads, 'as for *the rest* of the affairs of Rehoboam *and everything that he did,* are they not *those* recorded *in the account of the daily events of the kings of Judah?'* C changes the words and phrases italicized. The actions of Rehoboam, 'first and last', a merismus to express everything from beginning to end, are now under theological scrutiny: they are recorded not in the secular annals of the royal chancery but in the record of two prophets, Shemaiah, who has already been introduced in 2 Chron. 11.2, and Iddo (only here and 2 Chron. 13.22—unless he is the same figure as Jedo in 2 Chron. 9.29). These correspond to the prophetic records already met in the case of David (1 Chron. 29.29, Samuel, Nathan and Gad) and Solomon (2 Chron. 9.29, Nathan, Ahijah and Jedo; see Introduction to 2 Chron. 10–36). These overlapping streams of prophetic writing express the word of God, continuously accompanying the decisions and actions of his royal representative, in guidance and in warning, and now written with canonical force to provide guidance for future generations.

The text of C adds somewhat obscurely that this prophetic record was 'for the purposes of enrolment'. Many (e.g. RSV, but not NRSV) have regarded the expression as simply a secondary addition to the text. But, if the text is sound, it adds an ominous note: elsewhere in C, the expression concerns the rights of groups to be enrolled in the people of Israel itself or for a specific status or function within it—or the forfeiture of that right (for example, 1 Chron. 5.1 on the forfeiture of Reuben of the rights of the first-born). In this light, the expression shows that this theological commentary on the course of events is not that of a detached observer; it is instrumental is shaping the future. It implies evaluation of what has happened even in the first generation of the disruption as beginning the process of qualifying or disqualifying those concerned in the events for participation in the true Israel (cf. 1 Chron. 9.1, where it is used in connection with those with an entitlement to belong to the Israel even though now in exile because of their *ma'al*).

The last phrase of the verse, 'the wars of Rehoboam and Jeroboam continued the whole time', shows what is at stake: the unity of the one people has been permanently fractured, disabling its ability to realize its destiny; the battle for the restoration of the identity of the true Israel has begun.

C intensifies the struggle by reading 'wars' for 'war', as in 1 Kgs 14.30, and depersonalizes by dropping 'between'.

The account of the reign of Rehoboam concludes with the last two elements of the standard form of the annalistic framework.

The major difference from the Kings text is that here Rehoboam's successor is called 'Abijah', whereas in Kings he is called 'Abijam'. An explanation for this change (unless there is textual error in Kings or C) may lie in the fact that in the next chapter Abijah appears as an eloquent apologist for Jerusalemite orthodoxy against Jeroboam, the usurper of the northern kingdom. As such, it is only appropriate that he bears an impeccably orthodox name, 'the LORD is my father', rather than 'Yam [the Canaanite sea-god] is my father' of the Kings version.

There are other insignificant differences from the Kings parallel: some repetitions in the Kings text are suppressed (the name of Rehoboam's mother, which has just been given in v. 13, and the fact that he was buried 'with his ancestors in the city of David').

2 CHRONICLES 13.1–14.1A: THE REIGN OF ABIJAH

The account of Abijah's brief reign is set within an annalistic framework (vv. 1-2a, 22-23; cf. Introduction to 2 Chron. 10–36). It is focused almost exclusively on one incident—a battle with Jeroboam, the founder of the breakaway northern kingdom (vv. 2b-20)—in which Abijah shows exemplary reliance upon God. The remaining verse (v. 21) on his extensive harem may stand duty for framework element (4), the evaluation of the reign, and explain why, despite his exemplary trust, Abijah's reign was so short.

> MT divides the material into two major sections, vv. 1-20 (subdivided vv. 1-3a, 3b, 4-5, 6-9, 10-20), and 2 Chron. 13.21–14.1. But, since 14.1b refers to the next reign, it is considered with the reign below.

The bulk of the chapter is C's own material (chiefly vv. 3-21, but also other elements; the Kings parallel [1 Kgs 15.1-8] is much briefer—only eight verses to C's twenty-three): it provides a 'prophetic midrash' (v. 22), dramatizing the theological factors at work in the relations between the remnant of the Davidic dynasty centred on Jerusalem in Judah and the new schismatic regime in the north.

The annalistic framework begins with an element unique in C—a cross-reference to the reign of the contemporary king in the north (v. 1a): Abijah's accession to the throne took place 'in the eighteenth year of the king, Jeroboam'. The reason for its inclusion is that the information is of direct relevance to the topic of this chapter. It introduces the two protagonists: Abijah, with his rights as the sole legitimate Davidic ruler of the Kingdom of Israel, and Jeroboam, with his pretensions to be king of an independent state in the north. Jeroboam's pretensions are gaining in substance: he has outlived Rehoboam, the first legitimate successor of Solomon; he is termed 'king'; and the extent of the kingdom of Rehoboam's successor is defined as merely Judah.

> It may be that, by the addition of an 'and' with its change of grammatical construction between the two parts of v. 1, C subtly modifies any implied

equation of the status of the two kings. The cross-reference can be thereby linked—in syntax, at any rate, despite the chapter, verse and paragraph division—to what goes before: the date now refers to the chronological fact of when Abijah became king in place of his father, rather than to the more theologically sensitive fact of when he became king over Judah.

The name of Abijah's mother (v. 2a) is quite different from that given in Kings (and contradicts also C's own information in 2 Chron. 11.20): Micaiah ('who is like the LORD?'), daughter of Uriel ('my light is God'), as opposed to Maacah, daughter of Absalom. The name given here stresses the theological orthodoxy of her background. So, too, of her place of origin: Gibeah is presumably the town of that name in Benjamin. She is thus no importer of foreign theology, unlike Rehoboam's Ammonite mother. Rehoboam's marriage to her also represents a diplomatic act of binding the non-Judaean part of the southern kingdom closely to the crown.

Verse 2b introduces the main incident in the reign which C wishes to record: 'there was a battle between Abijah and Jeroboam'.

Again, the differences between C and Kings are significant. 1 Kgs 15.6 reads 'Rehoboam' for Abijah, perhaps by textual error; Abijah's reign is certainly the matter in hand. On the other hand, C's text is identical with 1 Kgs 15.7b, which he may simply have promoted to this point.

Kings adds at the end, 'all the days of his life': the single engagement here, 'a battle', is understood there as 'war' (cf. v. 3a, which MT links with vv. 1-2 as the end of the sub-paragraph). That is certainly not the point that C wishes to make. While Rehoboam was locked in war with Jeroboam throughout his reign—and that was an indication of his ineffectiveness—Abijah, as C is about to show, in one decisive engagement demonstrates the superiority of his position theologically and, therefore, militarily. It is a single decisive 'battle', not a long, drawn out war of attrition in which he is involved.

The evaluations of Abijah–Abijam are very different in Kings and C. Whereas C is presenting him as a case study of a king in harmony with Davidic theology, for Kings he simply followed the evil practices of Rehoboam and was tolerated only for David's sake. Kings dismisses Abijam in eight verses; no incident from his reign is recorded, only annalistic data and negative theological comment.

Abijah in person organizes his forces (v. 3a; the same expression is used only once again in the Hebrew Bible [1 Kgs 20.14]). His crack troops are described in the same way as those used by David and Jehoshaphat (1 Chron. 12.1, 8; 2 Chron. 17.13; compare 1 Chron. 1.10: these are the forces of the LORD ranged against the disruptive forces of the world). The numbers involved, 400,000, are presumably grossly exaggerated (for comparative figures see table at 1 Chron. 5.18).

What is more important here is the relative proportion of these Judaeans to those deployed in the field by Jeroboam: exactly half the number of Jeroboam's force of 800,000.

> For effect, MT places v. 3b in a sub-paragraph by itself. The subtle vow-elling of the word 'army' in v. 3a produces a suitable balance: not 'with an army *of* warriors' but 'with an army: *namely*, warriors...'

With but half the human resources, Abijah is about to demonstrate the superior strength of his position, sustained as he is by the promises attached to the Davidic house (cf. 1 Chron. 14.15; 2 Chron. 14.11; 20.15). This is the fundamental point C wishes to make.

The place (v. 4) where the encounter takes place, Mt Zemaraim ('twin-peaks' [KBS]), is significant. In Josh. 18.22, the only other context were Zemaraim occurs in the Hebrew Bible (assuming it is the same place), it is a city assigned to Benjamin. But there it is listed next to Bethel, normally regarded as the southern frontier of the northern kingdom; here Zemaraim, too, is identified as in the 'hill country of Ephraim'. It seems that Abijah has massed his troops on the frontier just threateningly enough to provoke Jeroboam into armed response.

From this vantage point Abijah delivers a speech in which he expounds the role of the house of David (vv. 4-12; the logistics of how Abijah could make himself heard in the open air to such a throng do not concern C). It is notable that, as the legitimate Davidic king, he himself possesses the authority to be his own spokesman and, more to the point, spokesman on behalf of God: the opening summons, 'He arose...and said, 'Hear me'' (v. 4), is precisely the formulation that was used of David himself in 1 Chron. 28.2 (compare the authoritative 'Hear me' of other approved Davidic kings, Jehoshaphat [2 Chron. 20.20] and Hezekiah [2 Chron. 29.5]; see also the prophets in 2 Chron. 15.2; 28.11). It is striking that, in the paragraphing of the MT, vv. 4 and 6 both begin new paragraphs with the same word, 'and he arose', in the one case Abijah and in the other Jeroboam: it is as though v. 4 begins the definitive response of the Davidic house to Jeroboam's insurrection.

Abijah's audience, too, is significant. He addresses Jeroboam and 'all Israel'. Presumably by that 'all', he is including not only the followers of the upstart monarch of the north (contrast v. 16, where, when the reference is to the north alone, the 'all' is missing) but also his own men as well. The significance of 'all Israel' is made clear by the emphasis on Israel twice in v. 5: the LORD is identified as the 'God of Israel' and David is the one who has been given 'kingship over Israel for ever'. The combined armies of Israel are the hosts of the LORD to carry out his purpose on earth; here, in bitter irony, they are drawn up against one another in potentially self-destructive conflict.

The structure of Abijah's speech is accusation about past and present behaviour (vv. 5-12a), followed by appeal (v. 12b). The accusation falls into a number of subsections. First, there is the general accusation that the north know very well that they are flouting the divine order about the ruling house of Israel (v. 5). Then follows a denunciation of specific actions: the rebellion led by Jeroboam against Rehoboam in the immediate past (vv. 6-7); the present attempt to continue that rebellion, which is, however, but the surface expression of their deeper revolt against the sovereignty of God (vv. 8-9). That revolt against God is then contrasted with Judah's faithfulness in religious institutions and practices (vv. 10-11), which must now be vindicated on the field of battle (v. 12a).

Abijah does not mince his words from the outset. The rhetorical question with which he begins (v. 5), 'Ought you not to know...?', functions as a strong affirmation, 'You know very well...' The fundamental theological premiss is stated in trenchant, unambiguous terms (and with emphatic word order): 'It is the LORD the God of Israel who has given kingship to David over Israel for ever—to him and to his sons by a covenant of salt.' It is a moment of appeal to the basic traditions of the whole people (cf., e.g., 1 Chron. 11.2; 17.16-17).

The phrase, 'covenant of salt', carries with it a broad range of allusion. Salt, as an essential element of diet, is a permanent requirement in sacrificial ritual (see Lev. 2.13, where it is sprinkled on the cereal offering as 'the salt of the covenant of your God'; Ezek. 43.24). It thus carries with it the associations and connotations of sacrifice itself: devotion to God, and atonement and fellowship with him. The phrase, 'covenant of salt', is also used in connection with the priests' irrevocable rights of participation in sacrifice (Num. 18.19): it expresses legitimacy, permanency and privilege of status. Applied to the house of David, the phrase thus conveys irrevocable, sacral status: the Davidic kings are those whom God has bound to himself by solemn, unbreakable, covenant (cf. 2 Chron. 6.14; 21.7) to enjoy an unparalleled privilege of access and intimacy with him, as his indispensable representatives on earth. All that the north knows full well.

Again, with all directness, Abijah then turns to the immediate past history (vv. 6-7). Despite his presence in direct confrontation, Rehoboam speaks of Jeroboam in the third person to expose him to particular humiliation in front of his troops and uses his patronymic, 'son of Nebat', to stress his lack of Davidic descent. It is this fellow, a mere slave to his master, who, without a scrap of legitimacy, has led a rebellion against Solomon, son of David; Abijah cites the names of the two founders to impart every legitimacy to Rehoboam. (The word 'to rebel', *mrd*, C will use once again in his work—of Zedekiah against Nebuchadnezzar in 2 Chron. 36.13.)

Abijah now proceeds to expose Jeroboam as the antithesis to David (v. 7). 'There gathered themselves to him' his supporters: the same verb is used as in 1 Chron. 11.1 for those who 'gathered' to support David. Only this time it is 'empty men of the worthless class' who do so. They then 'encouraged one another' against Rehoboam: the verb chosen is the intensive reflexive of the verb of encouragement used by David to Solomon (1 Chron. 22.13; 28.20; cf. 2 Chron. 11.17). Rehoboam was too young (aged forty-one, according to 2 Chron. 12.13!) and tender-hearted (the characterization is that of Solomon by David in 1 Chron. 22.5; 29.1) to 'pit himself against them': the verb takes up the standard verb of the Davidic king establishing himself or of the kingdom being established, thanks to him (1 Chron. 11.10).

Abijah then turns to address the northern army directly with scorn and rebuke (v. 8). 'Now *you* are planning to pit yourselves against [the same vocabulary as is used of Rehoboam in v. 7] the kingdom of God in the hand of the sons of David'. The choice of expression in that last phrase is as far-reaching as in 1 Chron. 28.5, where the throne of David is equated with the throne of God: the kingdom is God's kingdom; revolt against the Davidic king is revolt against God.

The scorn turns to sarcasm: 'Sure, you are a mighty host [the term is now to be used frequently by C of the rabble of the world's forces, massed in threat against the Davidic house, 2 Chron. 14.11; 20.2, 12, 15, 24; 32.7] and with you [the preposition as in 1 Chron. 11.9] are the golden calves [referred to in 2 Chron. 11.15] which Jeroboam made for you as gods.' The specific point of the narrative now unfolds, as the sequel makes clear: the futility of reliance on any power but God's. No matter how great the forces arrayed against them may appear to be in number or in ideology, and even though outnumbered two to one, the true Israel cannot be defeated.

Explicit charges now follow (v. 9, introduced by a rhetorical question as in v. 5). As in 2 Chron. 11.14-15, they have expelled the Levites from the north and rejected the Aaronic priesthood in Jerusalem, the system to ensure holiness which was the purpose of the elaborate scheme prepared by David in 1 Chronicles 22–27. They have replaced them by any individual not of the priestly family who can come up with the appropriate sacrifices to qualify for service in sanctuaries. There they officiate in the name of deities that do not even exist.

The vocabulary for ordination to priesthood ('fill the hand') has already been met in 1 Chron. 29.5. The sacrifice for the consecration of the priesthood in Exod. 29.1; Lev. 8.2 is one bull, as a sin or purification offering, and two rams (one as a whole burnt offering, the other for the consecration rites), not seven as here. But no matter how far in their religious zeal they exceed the required sacrifices, they can be to no avail. Apostate religion focused on gods that are 'no gods', no matter how zealously pursued, can in itself bring no benefit to its practitioners but only provoke the ire of God.

Here again is the vocabulary of rejection from the semantic field of *ma'al* (1 Chron. 2.7): the verb 'to expel' is used once again in C (2 Chron. 21.11) where it refers to Jehoram's actions in driving Judah away from the worship of the LORD. In so doing the northern kingdom has forfeited its status as part of the people of Israel. They have become, in a significant phrase, 'like the peoples of the lands': they have become conformed to the world of the nations, the transforming of which was their vocation.

Verse 10 begins with an emphatic personal pronoun, 'As for us', to contrast with the 'you' of v. 8 (the contrast is strengthened in MT by the opening of a new sub-paragraph, which continues the rest of the action down to v. 20, thus combining confession of faith with deliverance in battle). There is an equally emphatic claim, to contrast with the accusation of self-invented religion in the north: '*The LORD is our God*'. And the system of priest and Levite, of Temple and the daily offices of Temple worship bequeathed by David, which celebrates and maintains in cult and liturgy the order of the universe, is preserved intact in Jerusalem (vv. 10b, 11; for the items mentioned see especially 1 Chron. 28.13-16; 2 Chron. 2.4; 4.7, 8, and for the system as a whole, 'the charge of the LORD', 1 Chron. 23.32). The vocabulary of rejection is firmly countered: 'we have *not* forsaken the LORD our God' (v. 10a; cf. 1 Chron. 28.9). But that is contrasted with the statement at the end of v. 11: 'but *you have* forsaken him'.

Finally, Abijah turns to the present critical moment (v. 12a). What are the forces on the battlefield? To the outward eye Judah is outnumbered two to one. But, in the light of the theology outlined in vv. 5, 10-12, Abijah affirms, 'God is with us [contrast v. 8] at the head'. With the cosmic power of God expressed sacramentally through a loyal Davidic house in the lead no force on earth can resist them. Whether by few or by many, God can bring victory (cf. v. 3). The realization of victory is, therefore, a matter of invoking the power of God: the trumpets once blown on the field of battle and blown at the installation of the ark have only to be blown now to actualize that victory already won (cf. 1 Chron. 13.8; 15.24, 28; 16.6, 42; 2 Chron. 5.12-13). The overwhelming blast of the trumpets, sounded against the north, announcing the arrival of God on the field of battle, is enough to spread panic and force submission.

Abijah closes with the plea to the north (v. 12b). Calling them with pathos, 'Sons of Israel', he summons them to realize their true identity. He warns them solemnly not to engage in battle, for to do so is nothing less than to fight with the LORD, the God of their own fathers (1 Chron. 5.25). If they persist, they cannot succeed (another thematic term, cf. 1 Chron. 22.11).

Abijah's plea falls on deaf ears. So far from heeding, Jeroboam seeks to press home the apparent advantage of superior numbers by dividing his forces and hemming Judah in from front and rear (v. 13). In response, Judah's only recourse is to cry to the LORD (v. 14; cf. 1 Chron. 5.20). The priests sound the trumpets and the people raise the festal shout (v. 15). In that moment, with sacramental instantaneousness, God routs the North (he 'smites' them as in a negative exodus, 1 Chron. 21.17; cf. 2 Chron. 21.14, 18). They are delivered into Judah's hands; five eighths of them are slain (v. 17).

It is vain to speculate how in physical or psychological terms such a rout could have happened. It is all an inevitable consequence of the theology C expounds. If not willingly, then against their will, Israel must submit (the key word, 'humble oneself, acknowledge' [cf. 2 Chron. 7.14], opens v. 18). The corollary for Judah is that they are indeed 'strengthened' (the key word already used in v. 7, cf. 1 Chron. 22.13) because they have relied (a new term, to be used a number of times later in C, 2 Chron. 14.11; 16.7-8) on the LORD, the God of their fathers (the last phrase a deliberate contrast to the north's resistance in v. 12): those, who by divine choice and personal commitment are in harmony with the purpose of God, do not passively 'stand still' as spectators of the deliverance of God but 'take their place', swept up into the action of God (see 2 Chron. 20.17; for similar deliverances in the Hebrew Bible one might think of the exodus [Exod. 14] or the fall of Jericho [Josh. 6] or Samuel's confrontation with the Philistines [1 Sam. 7]).

Abijah drives the advantage home (v. 19). The outcome is the acquisition of territory from the north, the beginning of the rolling back of the frontier of the illegitimate state. In physical terms the acquisition may seem modest, but the symbolical significance is great: the first of the three places mentioned is Bethel with its 'daughter' settlements. Its new sanctuary, dedicated to the non-gods referred to in v. 9, provided one of the two foci for the pretensions of the upstart regime; its capture makes a fundamental theological statement in the divine trial of strength, which has been the major subject of this chapter.

The second city listed, Jeshanah, is otherwise unknown, but is perhaps to be related to Shen (Mandelkern, s.v.) referred to in 1 Sam. 7.12 in the vicinity of Mizpah, which in turn appears in the same list as Zemaraim (v. 4) in Josh. 18.21-28. The third city, Ephron (if that is the correct reading and identification) is actually listed within the territory of Judah to the west of Jerusalem in Josh. 15.9 (compare the town of Ephraim [2 Sam. 13.23] and Ophrah [Josh. 18.23] [Grollenberg, s.v.]).

C concludes the incident in v. 20 by noting succinctly, in line with his theological presentation, Jeroboam's subsequent powerlessness and death at the hand of God (again the vocabulary of the negative exodus; cf. v. 15). The expression 'to be powerless' is again highly theological: it is the opposite of that used in wonderment by both David and Solomon that they have been empowered by God to plan for and to build the Temple (1 Chron. 29.14; 2 Chron. 2.6).

> According to the chronology of 1 Kgs 14.20; 15.9, Jeroboam actually survived Abijah by two years.

Verse 21 resumes C's edition of the annalistic framework (MT places 2 Chron. 13.21–14.1 in a separate paragraph). The opening phrase, 'So Abijah was established', uses the thematic term now familiar from

Solomon onwards (2 Chron. 1.1). In this narrative it has been counterpointed with the attempt of others to establish themselves (v. 8) at
the cost of Abijah, the Davidic dynasty, and, ultimately, God's own
purpose.

C now offers a note on Abijah's marriages without comment either
in approval or disapproval. He allows the statistics to make their own
impact, fourteen wives, by whom he was blessed with twenty-two sons
and sixteen daughters. On balance, the judgment is probably meant to
be adverse. The restrained way in which C has dealt with the courts of
David and, especially, Solomon (1 Chron. 14.3-7; 2 Chron. 8.11), and
the unfavourable judgement implied on Rehoboam's amours (2 Chron.
11.18-23), suggest a negative view. The brevity of the reign also
requires an explanation. In that case, the evaluation of Abijah by C in
two contrasting sections corresponds to his presentation of the remaining reigns of the House of David, even those of Hezekiah and Josiah
(2 Chron. 32.24-31; 35.20-24; compare discussion of framework element [4] in Introduction to 2 Chron. 10–36). The abrupt switch from
'being established' to acting foolishly is paralleled, for example, in
2 Chron. 18.1.

> An implied negative judgement would match the negative evaluation given
> for Abijam in 1 Kgs 15.3.

Clearly, given Abijah's short three-year reign, these marriages had
been contracted long before he came to the throne: it is not said what
age he was when he began his reign, but he had been old enough
during his father's lifetime to be put in charge of a fortress and to be
the leader of his brothers as regional commandant (2 Chron. 11.22).

For the continuous prophetic commentary on the reigns of the kings
including now 'the ways and the words of Abijah' (v. 22) one
is directed to the work of Iddo, the otherwise unknown prophet who
has already had a hand in commenting on the reign of Rehoboam
(1 Chron. 12.15; it seems to be immaterial whether he is referred to
as 'seer' or 'prophet').

The burial 'in the city of David' (2 Chron. 14.1a) serves at least to
note the unbroken continuation of the line of David as rulers of an
independent state (contrast 2 Chron. 36.4-20, where such a note is
lacking).

2 CHRONICLES 14.1B–16.14: THE REIGN OF ASA

C divides the forty-one year reign of Asa into a number of sub-periods by inserting his own chronological system :

1. for ten years the land is 'quiet' (2 Chron. 14.1b);
2. there is an invasion of the Cushites (2 Chron. 14.9);
3. for the twenty years from years fifteen to thirty-five 'there is no war' (2 Chron. 15.10, 19);
4. there is an invasion by the northern kingdom in year 36 (2 Chron. 16.1); in year 39 Asa falls terminally ill (2 Chron. 16.12);

Thus, the chronological pattern is 10–5–20–5.

While the overall chronology of the reign is derived from Kings, none of these internal chronological subdivisions by C is found in Kings. The parallels to Kings (1 Kgs 15.9-24) are mainly annalistic materials, which are broken up in 2 Chron. 14.1b-3a; 15.16-18; 16.1-6, 11-14, with some rearrangement, abbreviation, and many variations in detail.

Within the clarity of this chronological pattern, C traces an equally clear theological pattern. He is reflecting on by now familiar ideas: the peace within Israel, and in Israel's relations with the world of the nations, that is symbolized by the resting of the ark in the Temple in Jerusalem. He does this in four 'movements':

1. the establishment of peace (2 Chron. 14.1b-7);
2. the defence of peace (2 Chron. 14.8-15);
3. the consolidation of peace (2 Chron. 15.1-19);
4. the forfeiture of peace (2 Chron. 16.1-14).

The major MT divisions are:

2 Chron. 14.2-7;
2 Chron. 14.8–15.9, subdivided into 2 Chron. 14.8a; 8b-11; 12-15; 15.1-7; 8-9;
2 Chron. 15.10–16.14, subdivided into 2 Chron. 15.10-19; 16.1-5; 6; 7-14.

The main difference in the MT division of the material is that the events from year fifteen to the end of the reign are combined in one section.

1. *The Establishment of Peace (2 Chronicles 14.1b-7)*

C states his theme right at the outset: 'the land was quiet for ten years' (2 Chron. 14.1b).

> This statement comes in place of the note on the length of the reign, standard element (2) of the framework within which these reigns are set (see Introduction to 2 Chron. 10–36). Element (2) does not appear until C's final resumption of the framework in 2 Chron. 16.11-14, where it is embedded in element (5), the note on the record of the deeds of king Asa.

What 'quiet' means here is defined in v. 6 as 'absence of war' (cf. 1 Chron. 22.9). How this ideal state of peace is realized is the subject of the first section.

Peace was achieved (v. 2) because Asa ('he heals' [?; KBS]) did 'what was good and upright in the eyes of the LORD his God' (the forms of the divine name express both the special relationship of God with Israel and his universal deity; cf. 1 Chron. 17.16-17).

> C adds 'what was good' (cf. 1 Chron. 16.34), presumably to contrast Asa with Rehoboam who 'did what was evil' (2 Chron. 12.14): Asa's reign continues to undo the harm that Rehoboam caused.
>
> C uses 'his God' instead of the 'like David his father' of Kings. The comparison with David is indeed occasionally retained by C elsewhere (negatively for Ahaz in 2 Chron. 28.1; positively for Hezekiah in 2 Chron. 29.2 and for Josiah 2 Chron. 34.2), but the point at issue here is the king's ability to exercise rule on behalf of God both within Israel and within the world of the nations.

The narrative immediately proceeds to explain what this 'good and upright in the eyes of the LORD' is.

Asa's specific reforming measures are listed in vv. 3-5. They involve both positive and negative steps: the positive in v. 4, to place again God's law and commandments at the centre of life, is framed by the negative in vv. 3 and 5a, to destroy the competing systems of belief and practice.

Fundamentally, Asa's aim is to restore the system achieved under David and Solomon: to accord recognition to the LORD, the God of their fathers (cf. 1 Chron. 5.25) through the way of life focused on the Temple in Jerusalem and to resort only to him for guidance and support (v. 4). C uses his standard vocabulary: 'to seek the LORD'. The thematic term *drš*, as in 1 Chron. 10.13-14, is the opposite of the thematic term *ma'al*, the defrauding of God.

The reversing of the deadly effects of *ma'al* involves specific reforming measures: the abolition of non-Israelite, sometimes pre-Israelite, religious institutions.

> 'Foreign altars' occur here for the first time (see 2 Chron. 33.15 for the removal of foreign gods in Manasseh's reformation). Kings is more domestic: 'the idols which his fathers had made'.

The regional sanctuaries on the 'high places' are removed and with them the incense burners and the symbols of male and female deities, the stone pillar and the wooden post (these are now to figure largely in C's presentation of the later monarchy: 2 Chron. 17.6; 19.3; 24.18; 31.1; 33.3, 19; 34: 3, 4, 7). The high places (cf. 2 Chron. 11.15) are the local representations of the cosmic mountain where the Canaanite god in question was assumed to dwell; the possession of a dwelling place by a god constitutes rivalry with the LORD, an infringement of his sole deity. Israel, therefore, could tolerate only one sanctuary on one mountain, the Temple on Mount Zion, the representation on earth of the cosmic dwelling place of the one cosmic deity.

> The Kings list of cultic institutions removed by Asa is quite different: it begins with male prostitutes. At no point in his work does C refer to male prostitutes (mentioned by Kings in 1 Kgs 14.24; 15.12; 22.46; 2 Kgs 23.7; see also 2 Chron. 15.8, where the word is again avoided despite the echoes of 1 Kgs 15.12 in the passage). This is presumably because the word concerned, *qādēš*, is derived from the same root as 'holiness', one of the central concerns of C's work (cf. 1 Chron. 6.49) but is not to be allowed in any way to contaminate it.

It is thus, v. 5b, that the opening statement in v. 1b has come about.

The cycle of ideas is once again plain in vv. 6-7. The ark resting in the Temple at the centre of the land is the expression of the divine pacification of the earth (the complex of ideas has already been explored, especially in 1 Chron. 22.9 in connection with Solomon the man of peace—the word here—and, therefore, Temple-builder). But peace is not an invitation to passivity. The wording of v. 6 is striking: '*because* the land is at peace' and 'the Lord has given rest', works to strengthen the defence of the realm are undertaken. In accordance with C's sacramental theology, whereby Israel's life is the out-ward expression of the sovereignty of God, this pacification finds appropriate physical expression in the rounding out of settlements and in well ordered defences. As under Solomon (2 Chron. 8.5), Rehoboam (2 Chron. 11.5) and, later, Jehoshaphat (2 Chron. 17.2; 21.3), fortresses throughout the country are rebuilt (the ideological nature of the writing here is perhaps indicated by the fact that no place names are actually given). Asa's actions are crowned with success because they are in tune theologically with the system which he represents (the key terms, *drš*, again, and 'succeed' as in 1 Chron. 22.11).

2. *The Defence of Peace (2 Chronicles 14.8-15)*

As the LORD's host, the nation is in a state of perpetual mobilization (cf., e.g., 1 Chron. 27.1-15). Thus, at the same time as securing the territory through the construction of fortresses, Asa re-equips the army: 300,000 infantrymen from Judah (MT places these in a separate sub-paragraph) and 280,000 bowmen from Benjamin (v. 8; for the idealized statistics and for the equipment, see 1 Chron. 5.18). These are the 'valiant warriors' whose task it is to vanquish the tyrants of the nations (for *gibbôr*, 'warrior/tyrant', see 1 Chron. 1.10).

The wisdom of Asa's care for defence and battle-readiness is soon borne out and his resolve as the LORD's vicegerent on earth tested. An invasion is launched on Judah from the world of the nations in stylized terms (v. 9; for the key word, *yṣ'*, cf. 1 Chron. 1.12). It is launched from Egypt, that nation of the nations of the world which was Israel's original enslaver. It is a 'Cushite' army. Geographically, the Cushites come from Nubia; they are listed with Egypt among the sons of Ham in 1 Chron. 1.8. But, more importantly, archetypally Cush is the father of Nimrod, the first warrior to spread chaos through the world of the nations (1 Chron. 1.9): here is a recrudescence of the primordial threat to the order that God conceived for relations between himself and human society. Zerah, the leader of the invaders, bears a Hebrew name (e.g. 1 Chron. 2.6) meaning 'arising' presumably from the soil, that is, a native; here it may be meant to indicate an insurrectionist.

The Cushite invading force is daunting and overwhelming enough but appreciably more modest than that which Rehoboam had to face in 2 Chron. 12.3 (one million infantry as opposed to an uncountable throng; 300 chariots as opposed to 1200, not to mention 60,000 cavalry; and representing only one section of the much more comprehensive Egyptian army; for the statistics, see 1 Chron. 19.7). Perhaps the reason for the smaller size is that on this occasion it is 'merely' a matter of testing, whereas the invader in Rehoboam's time was a punitive force launched at the very heartland of Judah and threatening its very existence because of the proven failure of Rehoboam to have faith in his own position as Davidic ruler.

The object of attack now is 'only' Mareshah, a peripheral town in the south-west lowlands, but, significantly enough, one of Rehoboam's garrison towns (2 Chron. 11.8; and to be the place of origin of a prophetic protest under Jehoshaphat, 2 Chron. 20.37). The valley of Zephathah in the vicinity of Mareshah (v. 10), where Rehoboam engages the invader, may be equated with Zephat, the original name of Hormah (Judg. 1.17).

In the conduct of the battle, Asa behaves with exemplary devotion and dependence on the rule of God (v. 11). As approved Davidic ruler, he speaks directly to God without need of mediator (cf. Abijah in 2 Chron. 13.4-12). It is not on their own account but on God's account and in his name that they are undertaking the task. As under Abijah, the numbers involved have no bearing on the rights of the matter (2 Chron. 13.3; cf. 1 Chron. 14.15); God has no respect for the mighty merely as such. Asa's orthodoxy is couched in suitably standard vocabulary: his cry for help in the heat of battle (Jehoshaphat, 2 Chron. 18.31; 20.9; Hezekiah, 2 Chron. 32.20; cf. 1 Chron. 5.20); his reliance (2 Chron. 13.18); his description of the invading force as an unruly throng (2 Chron. 13.8); and his appeal to God against the self-assertion of these mere humans who are God's own enemies (2 Chron. 13.20).

In response to this appropriate demeanour on the part of Asa, it is the LORD himself who routs the invader before his king and people (v. 12; the language of the exodus, the first deliverance from Egypt, is used, cf. 2 Chron. 13.15). It is because the fear of the LORD has fallen on the whole area that none can withstand them (v. 14; cf. 1 Chron. 14.17). As in the case of Abijah (2 Chron. 13.19), Asa and his troops are then swept up into the LORD's victory. They press home the advantage by pursing the invaders to the south-western frontier at Gerar (see the boundary of the land of Canaan as defined in Gen. 10.19). They totally annihilate those who have thus presumptuously sought to infringe the peace of the land and the rule of God; there are no survivors ('life', like health, belongs to the sphere of the Lord's blessing, just as death and disease are the instruments of punishment; cf.the conclusion of the Asa narrative in 2 Chron. 16.12). They reap the spoils of the towns over the whole area, even down to the animals of the grazing-grounds (see the model case on the East Bank in 1 Chron. 5.19-22).

In sacramental Davidic theology, the armies of Israel, if dedicated to him in the exemplary fashion of Asa, *are* the hosts of the LORD; their war-camp becomes his war-camp (v. 13; cf. 1 Chron. 12.22). With order once more imposed on relations with the nations of the world, Asa and his army can, as the climax of the incident, return in peace to Jerusalem (v. 15), where the ark still rests. The expected dedication of the spoils of victory is recorded in the next section, 2 Chron. 15.11, 18.

3. *The Consolidation of Peace (2 Chronicles 15)*

The next section describes the appropriate response to God's reassertion of victory. By renewal of the covenant between God and people there is renewal of peace.

The returning victors (MT appropriately links 2 Chron. 15.1-9 with 2 Chron. 14.8-15) are met by a prophet (of whom nothing is known beyond this chapter). He bears a programmatic name: Azariah ('The LORD has helped', picking up the verb used in Asa's petition in 2 Chron. 14.11), son of Oded ('He [the LORD] has restored'; the verb is used in Pss. 146.9; 147.6; a prophet of that name figures in 2 Chron. 28.9). His inspiration is described in terms of possession by the 'spirit of God': the spirit is medium of revelation to David 1 Chron. 28.12; and to prophets, 1 Chron. 12.18; 2 Chron. 18.20; 24.20; see 1 Chron. 5.26.

Azariah's speech is divided into three sections: a statement of fundamental principle (v. 2), which provides him with a framework for a review of the past (vv. 3-6), and for the encouragement with which his speech closes (v. 7).

MT throws the statement of principle into great prominence by placing it with v. 1 in a separate sub-paragraph; the second and third parts are then combined in a further sub-paragraph (vv. 3-7).

Azariah opens his speech with the call for attention already noted in Abijah's speech in 1 Chron. 13.4. He addresses the king, specifying by name the two main elements of his kingdom, Judah and Benjamin. But that leads to the point: the kingdom is in principle to be expanded to all Israel and for that expansion continued unwavering loyalty to God is required.

He states the fundamental sacramental principle at the outset with all clarity (v. 2b): 'The LORD is with you [the 'messianic' preposition, 1 Chron. 11.9] when you are with him; if you seek him [the key term, *drš*, 1 Chron. 10.13-14], he will be be found by you; if you forsake him [the antonym of *drš*, cf. 1 Chron. 28.9], he will forsake you' (cf. 2 Chron. 24.20b).

> This is one of the fullest expressions in the whole work of the sacramental principle, which is well caught in St Augustine's prayer, alluded to in Introduction to Volume 1: 'From whom to be turned is to fall, to whom to be turned is to rise, and in whom to stand is to abide for ever'.[1]

As the LORD's host, cosmic power and earthly power should meet in Israel; in Israel's ideal form, the two sides of the one reality, the unseen and the seen, are brought to perfect, harmonious expression. By unreserved commitment to God, Israel becomes what she is intended to be. Any failure is by that failure to forfeit that status.

The prophet turns to a review of the past (vv. 3-6): for many years, Israel (it is not clear whether he is referring to the northern kingdom only or to the whole people, but the description favours the first) has gone without a true God, a teaching priesthood and a law (v. 3). Disorder at the heart of Israel has as its inevitable corollary disorder among the nations. When Israel fails in its responsibility to the Gentiles, the peace required for ordinary human activity ('going out and in') is lost; anarchy reigns for 'all the inhabitants of the lands'; feuds erupt between states and even towns (vv. 5-6). It is only adversity sent by God himself, and the confusion into which he has thrown them, that has brought them back to their senses (v. 4; the vocabulary in v. 4b picks up the statement of principle in v. 2, with the synonym for *drš* used in 1 Chron. 16.10-11; for the educational force of adversity, see 1 Chron. 21.13; 2 Chron. 6.28; there is a play in this section on the words 'anarchy' [*mᵉhûmōt*, v. 5] and 'confuse' [*hmm*, v. 6] and the word for the chaotic 'horde' of the nations [*hāmôn*] in 2 Chron. 14.11).

If there is a specific reference intended, the adversity must be

---

1. E. Milner-White and G.W. Briggs, *Daily Prayer* (Oxford: Oxford University Press; Harmondsworth: Pelican, 1959 [1941]), p.173.

during the reign of Jeroboam and the defeat he suffered at the hand of Abijah. But it may just be a generalized truth.

In the light of these warning examples, the prophet concludes with an exhortation (v. 7). It begins with an emphatic personal pronoun, sharply contrasting the present generation with the past: 'But as for *you*, be strong' (the same root as 'being established' as used by David to Solomon [1 Chron. 22.13; etc.]). The vocabulary of encouragement used here does not occur elsewhere in C (not, at least, in quite this sense; for the first phrase, contrast 1 Chron. 21.15): 'Let not your hands be slack; for there is a reward for your work.' The last phrase coincides with Jer. 31.16. The cross-reference is highly apt. In Jeremiah, it expresses the expectation of return and restoration of the deportees of the northern kingdom after exile. The same thought is not far distant here: it is part of the mission of Judah to re-establish the united kingdom of Israel under the one Davidic ruler. In that task Judah will need all the perseverance it can muster.

Asa responds in model terms (vv. 8-9). He does indeed 'establish himself' (the intensive reflexive conjugation of the verb 'be strong' used in v. 7 but also the stock verb of the successor to the throne taking possession of the kingdom [2 Chron. 1.1, etc.]). He removes 'the abominations' from his territories, these being defined, in terms that match the greater Judah of v. 2, as Judah, Benjamin and the territories newly annexed from the North (presumably those annexed by his father in 2 Chron. 13.19, since Asa himself has not been credited with any such conquests).

> What the 'abominations' are (the same word as used of the pollutions of the sanctuary in Dan. 9.27, etc.), is not revealed. After the reforms undertaken at the beginning of the reign, it comes as a surprise that there still remain measures requiring to be taken in Judah. As pointed out above in connection with 2 Chron. 14.3, in the parallel in 1 Kgs 15.12 the reference is to male cultic prostitutes.

The reforming zeal in removing the pollutants throughout the country, both at the beginning of his reign and now, is matched positively by the restoration of the altar in the Temple court in Jerusalem.

> There is no explanation as to why or how the altar needed 'renewal'. Is the case similar to 2 Chron. 7.7 where the existing altar is inadequate in size and has to be extended in anticipation of the huge number of sacrifices about to be offered?

The scene for consolidation of peace for the future is set by the incorporation of two further features: the sacrifice of some of the spoils won in the campaign against the invading Cushites in thanksgiving for the past; and renewal of the covenant in prospect for the future.

For the rededication, Asa 'gathered' (v. 9; the thematic term as in 1 Chron. 11.1, though now in the active conjugation) the complete population that he now controls. These come both from the residents of his heartlands of Judah and Benjamin and from the émigré population from the north, Ephraim and Manasseh, attracted by the evident divine blessing that has accompanied his reforming zeal (Simeon is also specified, with a separate preposition 'from', though that had long been subsumed under Judah [cf. the association in 1 Chron. 6.65]; the same association of Ephraim, Manasseh and Simeon recurs in 2 Chron. 34.6).

Following the response and initiative of the king, the people as a whole now respond (vv. 10-15; the relevant verbs are now all in the plural). They gather (the same verbal root as at the beginning of v. 9) in Jerusalem at the beginning of the third month of Asa's fifteenth year (v. 10).

> No explanation is given as to why the event takes place in the third month, whether because, practically, it takes that time to gather the populace, or because it takes the celebrations well clear of passover in the first month and any passover observation of the second month, such as is referred to in 2 Chron. 30.2 on the occasion of a similar summons to the north.

As under a new David or a new Solomon, they sacrifice 700 cattle and 7000 sheep of the spoils taken at Gerar (v. 11; for the statistics, see the table at 1 Chron. 29.21; the ten to one ratio recurs in the Passover victims in 2 Chron. 35.7, 9, contrast 2 Chron. 35.8). In contradistinction to the archetypal act of *ma'al* committed by Achar in 1 Chron. 2.7, they offer the fruits of victory to God, the giver of victory.

> It is explicitly said, however, that only *some* of the spoils of war were dedicated; is there a hint here of a less than perfect devotion?

They enter the covenant 'to seek' (the thematic verb, *drš*, again) the LORD, the God of their fathers (v. 12; cf. 1 Chron. 5.25): their theological tradition in both its relational and its cosmic terms is reaffirmed with full commitment (for the combination of 'heart and soul', see the model cases in 1 Chron. 22.19; 28.9). It is enjoined with absolute stringency on all, young and old, male and female, on pain of death (v. 13): only total devotion can enjoy the answering blessing of God. For similar stringency see 2 Chron. 34.30 in connection with Josiah.

> Echoes in v. 13 of the intolerance of totalitarian regimes send a shiver down the spine of the modern reader. But, as in the use of war imagery (cf. at 1 Chron. 5.22), the absoluteness of the language must be allowed to stand: in the ideal presented, it is assumed that the whole community is of one mind and, because it is of one mind and—the basic proviso—is perfectly in harmony with the purpose of God, is in a position to express the undivided will of God on earth.

With festal shout and acclamation acknowledging God's dominion (cf. 1 Chron. 15.28), they bind themselves by oath (the only other passage linking 'covenant' and 'oath' in C is 1 Chron. 16.15-16 of God's covenant with the patriarchs). By ram's horn and trumpet (see again 1 Chron. 15.28, the only other place in C where ram's horn occurs), they (priests and Levites must be implied) announce the action of God.

'Judah rejoiced over the oath' (v. 15; for 'joy', cf. 1 Chron. 12.40): the restriction to Judah may simply be that that is the name meantime for the rump state of the true Israel in waiting. It may, however, imply the joy of Judah, as the remnant, over those from the north who are now coming to join them to swell the ranks of the people committed to the traditional Davidic theology. 'With all their pleasure' (cf. 2 Chron. 10.7 for the related verb denoting favourable disposition), they seek the LORD. In response, God 'is found' by them, a vague phrase but corresponding to the promise relayed through the prophet in v. 2 (cf. v. 4). The conditions for the maintenance of peace have been fully met.

The summary in v. 15b again defines peace in terms of 'rest', the key word, with the implied cross-reference to the Temple as the resting of the ark. It is notable that thirteen out of the twenty-seven religious uses of 'covenant' in C relate it explicitly to the ark. This peace is 'on every side': the dominion of God is recognized universally, inside and outside the kingdom.

With vv. 16-18, C returns to materials derived from 1 Kgs 15.13-15, the continuation of the list of Asa's reforming measures, which he had broken off in 2 Chron. 14.3. They fit well enough here in C's account of the second phase of Asa's reforms (there is no hint in Kings that the reforms should be assigned to two periods). This is especially true for the third of the reforms (v. 18), the dedication of the 'holy things': C's narrative of phase two of Asa's career, the expulsion of the Cushite invaders and the bringing back of the spoils from Gerar (2 Chron. 14.8-15), at least gives an explanation (lacking in Kings) of what these holy things might have been, certainly as far as Asa's 'holy things' are concerned. There is no indication in the narrative of what his father Abijah's 'holy things' might have been, apart from the standard fulfilment of the requirements of the laws on holy offerings (cf. 1 Chron. 23.28).

The king's mother (v. 16) seems to have played a vital role in the transition of the rule from father to son (standard element [3] in the annalistic framework is testimony to that; see also the powerful status of Maacah in 2 Chron. 11.21 and the decisive role of Athaliah in 2 Chron. 22.10–23.21). Thereafter, she appears to have retained honorific status as queen mother. It is, therefore, a striking breach of etiquette—and perhaps even a threat to his own position, given the other possible claimants to the throne (2 Chron. 13.21)—that Asa should remove his own mother from her position. It is a powerful statement of his priorities: his power-base lies fundamentally in his religious orthodoxy, not in court arrangements or intrigues. Maacah forfeits her position (after v. 13, is fortunate to escape with her life, if indeed she did) because she has been instrumental in setting up a statue to the female consort of Baal. This object, doubly objectionable (etymologically the word means 'horrific') both in itself as an idol and as an encouragement to a rival theological system, Asa cuts down (it was presumably a wooden object; see 2 Chron. 28.4), crushed (an addition by C) and burns in the Kidron valley, presumably as a means of conveying away in the stream the polluting influence (cf. 2 Chron. 29.16; 30.14; Deut. 21.1-9).

> C omits the complicating annalistic note in 1 Kgs 15.2, 10 that Maacah was the daughter of Absalom (cf. 2 Chron. 11.21-22 and its incompatibility with 2 Chron. 13.2).
>
> The underlying text of v. 17 ('the high-places were not removed') presents a problem for C, since it would contradict 2 Chron. 14.5. C neatly solves the issue by adding 'from Israel', that is, the north. The notice then gives additional grounds for elevating Asa's theological orthodoxy ('his heart was sound [again the pun with 'Solomon', 1 Chron. 29.19] all his days';) over against the apostate north.

A particularly vital manifestation of that theological soundness for C is Asa's dedication of the spoils of victory to God (contrast 1 Chron.

2.7 and see the importance of the treasuries of the Temple as the index of according to God all that is due to him, for example, 1 Chron. 9.26). These are 'holy things', not just holy in themselves as dedicated to God, but as a representation of the general posture of dedication in the whole of life.

All of these reforming measures, which have brought the whole of Judah's life back into focus on the Temple—the place where the ark rests from war and the place where the tokens of Israel's dedication are laid up—have their appropriate counterpart for C in a twenty-year period of peace (v. 19).

> C's chronology is here fundamentally different from that of Kings. According to 1 Kgs 15.33, Baasha, Asa's adversary from the north, about to be introduced in 2 Chron. 16.1, came to the throne of the north in Asa's third year and reigned for twenty-four years. All through this period, there was continual war between north and south (1 Kgs 15.16, 32), that is, from Asa's third until his twenty-seventh year. In C's view, by contrast, Asa suffers no hostilities from Baasha until his thirty-sixth year, when, on the Kings chronology, Baasha would have already been dead for nine years (cf. 1 Kgs 16.8).

4. *The Forfeiture of Peace (2 Chronicles 16.1-14)*

What takes thirty-five years to secure is lost in five. The trial of strength between the status of Jerusalem and the pretensions of the north cannot be indefinitely postponed. In C's theological periodization of Asa's reign, it was only in his thirty-sixth year (v. 1) that Baasha (a shortened form of 'Baal has heard'? [KBS]), the king of the north, launches an attack on the south.

> Baasha occurs in C only in 2 Chron. 16.1-6: the extensive materials in 1 Kgs 15.27-30 on Baasha (e.g. his destruction of the House of Jeroboam) C omits, as usually in the case of data on the north which are not of immediate relevance to the course of events in the south.

The physical threat from Baasha looks real enough (v. 1). He blocks the northern access route to and from Judah by building a fortress at Ramah (according to Josh. 18.25, situated on the northern frontier of Benjamin). The same expression of 'coming and going' as has been used of normal life in 2 Chron. 15.5 is again used here, though now no doubt with the overtone of ability to undertake military expeditions (cf. 1 Chron. 1.12; 14.15).

It is now (v. 2) that Asa makes his fundamental theological error. Instead of relying on the inherent strength of his position as Davidic king, he seeks to secure his safety in the crisis by hiring the help of the Aramaean king of Damascus. To hire this help he has to raid not only his own treasury, but the Temple treasury itself. Nothing could more dramatically express Asa's abject failure to trust in the validity of his own theological system. The very holy things that have just been dedicated (2 Chron. 15.18) in recognition that it is God who delivered him from the Cushites are now paid as inducement to another foreign king to come and rescue him!

The Aramaean king's name, Ben-hadad, adds theological point. 'Baal', the term for the Canaanite god most frequently referred to in the Hebrew Bible as the chief rival of the LORD, is in fact merely a title, itself meaning 'lord'. The proper name of the deity who bore this title was Hadad. The Aramaean king's name means, then, 'son of Hadad': theologically his position as ruler of Damascus is exactly analogous to that of the Davidic house in Jerusalem as 'son of the LORD' (cf. Ps. 2.7; 1 Chron. 17.13). Again nothing could make the clash of theological systems plainer.

> 1 Kgs 15.18 states that he 'took all the silver and gold that was left in the treasuries...', implying an earlier raid on these resources; C renders just, 'he brought out silver and gold from the treasuries'. He omits, 'and put them into the hand of his servants', and some further details on Ben-hadad's genealogy.

Despite thirty-five years of domestic reforming work, Asa's action amounts to a recognition of the superiority of Baal to the LORD and a denial of his own theological tradition (compare Rehoboam's departure from Jerusalem to Shechem in 2 Chron. 10.1 or Josiah's encounter with Pharaoh Neco at Megiddo in 2 Chron. 35.20). The consequences are disastrous: in the sacramental system, once the theology is set aside, the physical position becomes untenable.

Asa sinks deeper into the mire: having just sealed a covenant with God (2 Chron. 15.12) he now (v. 3) requests a covenant with Ben-hadad (the only time in C that 'covenant' is used in a secular context). He not only makes a covenant on his own behalf but also—somewhat strangely—on his father's behalf (or, perhaps, appeals to a long-standing agreement of which we otherwise know nothing). He implicates the earlier generations of the Davidic house in his action and therebycedes their right to rule on earth to be the LORD's vicegerents.

To conclude this covenant, Ben-hadad has to break the covenant he already has with Baasha. Asa is now deeming appropriate for his own kingdom the kind of relationship that political and military expediency requires for the breakaway state of the north.

Ben-hadad is only too happy to oblige (v. 4). It no doubt suits *his* pretensions at world dominion that two rival states should be at his mercy, Judah now as vassal, the north ravaged by his invasion. The area devastated by him is that in the far north of Israel, nearest to Damascus: Dan and Naphtali.

> For the location of Ijon see 2 Kgs 15.29. Abel-maim occurs only here but in the form of Abel-beth-maacah in the Kings parallel, which again is mentioned in 2 Kgs 15.29.

In the course of his invasion he plunders 'all the storehouses of the cities of Naphtali': for such store cities as part of the infrastructure of the rule of the Davidic house, see 2 Chron. 8.4, 6; 32.28.

The Aramaean intervention has the desired effect, militarily at any rate (v. 5). At the news of the invasion, Baasha desists from the work of fortifying Ramah.

> 1 Kgs 15.21 says he retires to Tirzah, again a piece of information not relevant for C.

With gleeful opportunism Asa seizes the building materials and instead strengthens his own frontier fortresses at Geba and Mizpah, implicating 'all Judah' in the process (v. 6). Asa appears to have gained considerable advantages by what he must now regard as his wise actions.

But precisely at this moment a prophetic voice interposes (vv. 7-9). Hanani ('my gracious one', or a contraction of Hananiah, 'the LORD has been gracious' [BDB]) appears only here (though it is presumably his son, Jehu, who provides the prophetic word and the prophetic commentary for Asa's successor, Jehoshaphat [2 Chron. 19.2; 20.34]). He delivers a two-part message: rebuke for the actions just taken (vv. 7b-9a); and prediction of war as a necessary consequence of these actions (v. 9b).

Hanani's message is based on the stark choice focused in C's key term, 'to rely' (*niš'an* [3×], vv. 7-8; cf. the two other occurrences of the root in C's work in 2 Chron. 13.18; 14.11): unconditional reliance on the LORD ensures the preservation of the peace that God's cosmic victory has already won; failure to rely inevitably brings forfeiture of that peace. In specific terms, Asa has relied on the Aramaeans. It is bad enough to rely on humans; but, even worse, the Aramaeans are in principle a nation that should acknowledge Israel's sovereignty, as in the time of David (e.g. 1 Chron. 18.6). Further, Asa has failed to appreciate the geographical extent in principle of his domain as covering the north: an Aramaean force has thus been allowed to invade the territory of Israel proper. Asa has failed to deal with an invader, when it is his task above all to rule from Israel on behalf of God. But even worse, it has been at his request that the Aramaeans have invaded. So far from being the protector of his realm, he has become the devastator of it. Wars from now on will be the inevitable consequence; had Asa relied on the LORD, there would have been no need of the Aramaean invasion and the peace would have remained intact. This stark choice matches the unconditional demand to look for help exclusively to the LORD (as in the words of Azariah in 2 Chron. 15.2-7), the opposite of which is *ma'al*.

Asa is without excuse (v. 8): he has himself already known what it is 'to rely' (same word again) on the LORD, and to have had his enemies at his mercy, on the occasion of the invasion of the Cushites (C adds 'Libyans', not so far mentioned since the invasion of Shishak in 2 Chron. 12.3, but equally credible as part of an invasion from Egypt). They were a far larger and, with their cavalry, a more formidable force than the Aramaeans.

Hanani's message contains a remarkable statement about the worldwide dominion of God, which Asa as his vicegerent should have known, trusted in, and sought to realize: 'God's eyes range over the whole earth so that every ruler whose heart is in tune with him is established' (v. 9). Two key words are used here: 'in tune' is related to the word for 'peace' (ironically, just used of Asa himself in 2 Chron. 15.17); 'is established' is the standard term for the confirmation of the Davidic king in his kingdom (e.g. Solomon in 2 Chron. 1.1). The establishment of the other kings of the nations in their proper places is no less a reflection of the universal rule of God: they too are his subjects, destined for peace. But they are ready also to be his agents against his own people for punishment, should that people fail in their task. Hanani speaks with all directness: Asa should have known better; he has been a fool; to denote his foolishness he uses the same word as David has used of himself in 1 Chron. 21.8 (the only other occurrence of the root in C).

Asa is enraged (v. 10; compare, using a different word, Hezekiah in

2 Chron. 26.19; cf. 2 Chron. 28.9; the reaction is the opposite of the necessary self-humiliation, 2 Chron. 7.14). The contrast between the prophet's judgment and his own self-congratulation at the brilliant diplomatic coup, the painless military intervention and the opportunist exploitation of raw materials for defence, could not be more extreme. In response to the denunciation that he has betrayed his whole theological inheritance, he seeks every means of self-justification. He claps Hanani in the stocks (cf. Jer. 20.2-3; 29.26), the first of the suffering prophets in C (as Zechariah is soon to be the first martyred prophet, in 2 Chron. 24.21). Hanani is not the only one to suffer: an unspecified number of his subjects Asa maltreats at the same time (quite in what way is not made clear).

Thus, a dark shadow falls across Asa's last five years. This is marked even in personal terms in some undefined illness (for the key term, cf. 1 Chron. 10.3) with which he is struck (in his feet, says the text, v. 12, which may be a euphemism for the genitals; compare Jehoram's fate, 2 Chron. 21.15).

> By omitting the phrase in 1 Kgs 15.23, 'Only in the time of his old age', C seems not to want to identify this affliction as part of a natural ageing process. It was punitive. The coincidence of the illness with the ending of the reign C makes clear by adding a date: this was in the thirty-ninth year—there were now but two years to go. C adds that his illness was 'severe' (*'ad lᵉma'lâ*, again perhaps a pun on *ma'al*, as in 1 Chron. 14.2). The remainder of v. 12 is added by C.

Once again (v. 12), Asa shows himself a failure theologically, now in his personal affliction. The approved reaction would no doubt be 'to humble himself' and acknowledge his guilt (compare 2 Chron. 12.6 of even Rehoboam in receipt of the oracle from Shemaiah). Instead of having recourse (key word, *drš*) to God, the source of his affliction, he consults the physicians ('healers' derived from a root that C uses elsewhere of restoration to the intended condition in constructing his theological pattern, see 2 Chron. 7.14; 21.18; 22.6; 30.20; 36.16). Asa ('he heals'?) should have known better the source of health. Indeed, one may assume that C's view is that, had Asa been faithful, he would not have fallen ill in the first place (cf. 1 Cor. 11.30), but would have died, like David, in ripe old age (1 Chron. 29.28).

C concludes his account of the reign of Asa with mostly his own data on the grandiose tomb and funeral arrangements Asa appointed for himself (vv. 13-14). He had had hewn for himself a new tomb (the plural is used perhaps to indicate imposing scale) and introduced the practice (at least it has not been mentioned earlier) of being laid out on a bier accompanied by the burning of spices (cf. 2 Chron. 21.19). These spices are mentioned in other contexts as luxury items brought to Solomon as tokens of homage by the monarchs of the earth, (2 Chron. 9.1, 9, 24; so also for Hezekiah, 2 Chron. 32.27). If that is the significance here, then it expresses the status that Asa enjoyed among the nations of the world and thus the claim that he has discharged successfully, at least for the most part, the responsibilities attached to the Davidic throne. But it is difficult not to detect a note of disapproval in C that this king, who had promised so well but had ended in such failure, should have arrogated to himself such tokens of significance. These spices are otherwise used in the cult (cf. 1 Chron. 9.29-30); it was surely scarcely appropriate for a compromised Davidic king so to infringe the sphere of the holy. It may be all part of the presumptuousness that precipitated illness in the last years of his reign (cf. Uzziah in 2 Chron. 26.16-23).

2 CHRONICLES 17.1–21.3: THE REIGN OF JEHOSHAPHAT

In the presentation of the reign of Jehoshaphat, the formal standard framework (see Introduction to 2 Chron. 10–36) is, for the most part, delayed until almost the end (2 Chron. 20.31–21.3). The narrative begins, rather, with simply a note on Jehoshaphat's succession (such a note is usually attached to the last element of the framework of the previous reign) and proceeds directly to an account of the measures he took to 'be established' in his kingdom. These notes lead into long narratives on the main events of his reign that are of most relevance for its evaluation (element [4] of the framework, of which a prelimi-nary formal statement is given in 2 Chron. 17.3-4, 6).

The chief paragraph-markers of MT provide, in the main, a clear structure for the presentation of the reign (there are further divisions and sub-divisions):

1. 2 Chron. 17.1-6: introduction; opening sketch of Jehosha-phat's measures to 'be established' in his kingdom;
2. 2 Chron. 17.7-11: the teaching of the Torah in Judah; the 'fear of the LORD' falls on the neighbouring kingdoms;
3. 2 Chron. 17.12-19: Jehoshaphat's military measures;
4. 2 Chron. 18.1–19.11: Jehoshaphat's disastrous alliance with the north in the battle at Ramoth-gilead, and its aftermath (divided after 2 Chron. 18.27);
5. 2 Chron. 20.1-30: the successful defence of the realm against Moab, Ammon and Edom (divided after 2 Chron. 20.13);
6. 2 Chronicles 20.31–21.3: the annalistic framework of the reign, with additional notes.

C has radically changed the presentation in Kings:

2 Chronicles	1 Kings
17.1a	15.24b
17.1b-18.1	no parallel
18.2-34	22.2b-35bα (close parallel)

2 Chronicles	1 Kings
19.1-20.30	no parallel
20.31-37	cf. 22.41-44, 46, 50, 49 (*sic*)
21.1	22.51
21.2-3	no parallel

In Kings, the presentation of the reign of Jehoshaphat has been heavily modified because of preoccupation with momentous events in the north, especially the emergence of the dynasty of Omri in Asa's thirty-second year, and the inclusion of the cycle of narratives concerning the prophet Elijah and his confrontations with Omri's son, Ahab.

1. 2 Chronicles 17.1-6 Introduction: Opening Sketch of Jehoshaphat's Measures to 'Be Established' in his Kingdom

In this introduction, dominant notes of C's theology are sounded. Jehoshaphat is 'established' on the throne (v. 1; 2 Chron. 1.1). His realm is called 'Israel': though, historically, ruling only the rump state of Judah [so in Kings], in principle as the next generation of the Davidic kings he reigns over the whole of Israel (the truth Asa had so catastrophically ignored in 2 Chron. 16.1-10).

> The NRSV rendering 'strengthened himself against Israel' can hardly be right: the verb and preposition are the same as those used of Solomon in 2 Chron. 1.1. Compare 2 Chron. 12.13.

Jehoshaphat took the appropriate military actions (v. 2): he stationed troops in garrison towns and fortresses throughout Judah, as Solomon, Rehoboam and Asa had done (2 Chron. 8.5; 11.5; 14.7). From 2 Chron. 21.3 it appears that these garrisons were under the command of his own sons: that is, other scions of the Davidic house were sub-contracted to exercise Davidic rule throughout the kingdom (cf. 2 Chron. 11.23). Not only so, the right of the Davidic house to rule over the north is affirmed by the appointment of garrisons 'in the cities of Ephraim which Asa had taken' (in fact it was Abijah, according to 2 Chron. 13.19, though 2 Chron. 16.6 may be what is being referred to).

In a word, 'the LORD was *with* [*'im*] Jehoshaphat' (v. 3). The innocuous wording hides a wealth of meaning: as in 2 Chron. 13.12 the whole tradition of Jerusalemite theology is implied by these words (1 Chron. 11.9). The true power behind the throne is not these physical measures the king took; they are but the sacramental expression of the peace established by the victory of God and of the divine power upholding the king's reign, often, as the sequel is to show, despite himself. 'With' is, in fact, one of the leading motifs of this chapter (2 Chron. 17). It expresses not only the support of God but the gathering support of the people to Jehoshaphat as once to David (vv. 8 [twice], 9, 10, 14, 15, 16, 17, 18; cf. 1 Chron. 12.18).

The reason for divine support is the standard one in C's presentation: Jehoshaphat's exclusive loyalty to God, as defined in archetypal terms ('the first ways') by David (only Hezekiah and Josiah are to match that standard, 2 Chron. 29.2; 34.2; for 'walk', see 2 Chron. 6.16). *drš* (1 Chron. 10.13-14) is again used, first negatively of *non*-resorting to the rival 'lords' (v. 3b).

> This is the first use in C of the title *ba'al*, 'lord', for the chief Canaanite rival (proper name, Hadad; cf. 2 Chron. 16.2) to the LORD. By contrast to the deuteronomic historian and the pre-exilic prophets, such as Hosea and Jeremiah, C's use is notably sparing: it occurs again only in 2 Chron. 23.17; 24.7; 28.2; 33.3; 34.4 (always in the plural, except 2 Chron. 23.17, suggesting either the various local cults of Baal or, more widely, the Canaanite pantheon).

drš is then used (v. 4a) positively of resorting to 'the God of his father [i.e. David]' (cf. 1 Chron. 5.25), defined precisely in terms of observance of the commandments (cf. Torah in v. 9). The sacramental correspondence between the cosmic King and the earthly king is intact. This loyalty is by definition lacking in the north (v. 4b).

> The text of 1 Kgs 22.43 evaluates Jehoshaphat's reign simply by reference to his father, Asa. C reproduces that text with negligible differences in 2 Chron. 20.32. Here in vv. 3b, 4 he offers an alternative evaluation based on the more fundamental, Davidic, theology.

The consequence is recognition, divine and human (v. 5): God confirms him in his position (the thematic term, *kûn*, 1 Chron. 14.2); his subjects bring him tokens of their loyalty (see 1 Chron. 16.29; *minḥâ* in this sense is otherwise used in C of the recognition of foreign kings). Thus he enjoys the same standing as David, the founder of his dynasty (1 Chron. 29.28, where again the fixed pair, 'wealth' and 'honour', are combined).

The phrase, 'his mind became inflated' (v. 6), is used for the only time in a positive sense in C. It expresses presumptuousness in the cases of Uzziah and Hezekiah (2 Chron. 26.16; 32.25-26; the latter defines it as the opposite of *kn'*, the necessary first acknowledgment of *ma'al*, 2 Chron. 7.14). While in the case of Jehoshaphat a potentially catastrophic wilfulness is evident (especially in 2 Chron. 18 and 2 Chron. 20.35-37), the point of the presentation is to be that the consequences of that very wilfulness are mitigated thanks to a proper enthusiasm in the 'ways of the LORD'.

That zeal is defined in terms of the removal of the high places and the symbols of the female deity. It is done 'again', despite Asa's reforming measures in 2 Chron. 14.3, 5: reformation is evidently not a once and for all achievement; it has to be continually redone and becomes an index of the commitment of the Davidic king of the day.

> This statement of Jehoshaphat's reforms stands in some tension with 2 Chron. 20.33 (and the underlying Kings text there). This provides a good example of how evaluative comments in framework elements are not to be taken absolutely at face value, but are modified by C's overall presentation (see comments on framework element [4] in Introduction to 2 Chron. 10–36). In Jehoshaphat's case, that presentation is more complicated than the two-part narrative of the reign in question that has broadly prevailed up till now in 2 Chronicles 10–16: the positive evaluation of 2 Chronicles 17 is continued in 2 Chron. 19.1–20.30; the negative in 2 Chronicles 18 is resumed in 2 Chron. 20.31-37.

2. 2 Chronicles 17.7-11: The Teaching of the Torah in Judah; the 'Fear of the LORD' Falls on the Neighbouring Kingdoms

The collocation by MT of these two elements in one section—Torah and fear of the LORD—admirably reflects C's fundamental purpose throughout his whole work: it is by the faithful discharge of its primary duty, the observance of the system of holiness as laid down in the Torah, that Israel fulfils its function among the nations of the world.

Jehoshaphat commissions five lay officials, nine Levites and two priests, to undertake the task of instruction throughout the cities of Judah (vv. 7-9; nothing further is known about any of these individuals). It is not absolutely clear that the lay officials are themselves instructors. If they are, their remit is presumably about such matters as the people's obligations to the king, such as are described in 1 Chronicles 27. But the Hebrew may mean no more than that the king 'sent to them to ensure the instruction'. At all events, the sole manual mentioned is 'the Book of the Law of the LORD'. Jehoshaphat enjoins nothing other than the system laid down in the Law of Moses as developed and applied by David (cf. 1 Chron. 22.12, 13). As the king 'walked in the commandments' of his father (v. 4), so must now his subjects.

The impact of the instruction is overwhelming—and not only at home (vv. 10-11). By these measures, the full system of obligations to God and to the king discharged, Jehoshaphat is perfectly equipped to fulfil his role among the nations of the world. The rendering by Israel of every duty to God as sovereign through his designated king prompts the recognition of that sovereignty among the nations round about; awe falls on 'all the kingdoms of the lands' (v. 10; cf. 1 Chron. 14.17 for David; 2 Chron. 14.14 for Asa); they, too, bring their tribute (same word as in v. 5). Peace between the nations and Israel is thus established. This is the ideal role of the Davidic monarch ruling in Jerusalem and that is the ideal which Jehoshaphat should have maintained (contrast 2 Chronicles 18).

> The emblematic foe, the Philistines (cf. 1 Chron. 1.12), bring an unspecified amount of silver (so, under David, 1 Chron. 18.11). The nomadic Arabs (contrast 2 Chron. 9.14) naturally bring rams and he-goats (for comparisons with the numbers here—7700 of each—cf. table at 1 Chron. 5.21).
>
> It is to be noted that the Philistines and Arabs act on behalf of Egypt/Cush (1 Chron. 1.8-10) in 2 Chron. 21.16, so that the pacification of still wider regions is perhaps implied, as in the parallel to 2 Chron. 17.10 in 2 Chron. 20.29.

3. 2 Chronicles 17.12-19: Jehoshaphat's Military Measures

This section records in detail the military measures Jehoshaphat took to confirm his position as king (vv. 1-2). The motif of the 'fortified cities' (v. 2) recurs in various guises in vv. 12, 13 and 19 and links the whole chapter together.

Jehoshaphat 'progressively grows exceedingly powerful' (v. 12).

> Again there may be a pun between 'exceedingly' (*l^ema'lâ*) and *ma'al* (1 Chron. 14.2).

This power is co-ordinate with the divine favour that rests upon him. It is expressed in mighty citadels (the word is the plural of that used for Solomon's building task in 1 Chron. 29.19) and storehouses (the fact that no names are specified for either may suggest an ideological factor in the writing; cf. 2 Chron. 14.5-6). The function of these storehouses for gathering the three staple products of the land, the corn, wine and oil, is explained in 2 Chron. 32.28. They are a standard feature of the reign of the loyal and, therefore, successful Davidic king (Solomon, 2 Chron. 8.4, 6; Asa, 2 Chron. 16.4; Hezekiah, 2 Chron. 32.28), for they represent not only the prosperity of stable times but the punctilious payment of all the tokens in kind by which the populace acknowledge the king's rule (cf. v. 5).

The citizen army, mustered for service by their households, is now organized (vv. 13-19). There is a slightly pyramidal structure in these verses (a device noted elsewhere in C to denote significance by centrality, e.g. 2 Chron. 11.19-20). The sequence in v. 13 (cities of Judah—Jerusalem) is reversed in v. 19 (Jerusalem—cities of Judah). In between, it is Jehoshaphat's army in Jerusalem, all battle-ready warriors, that is listed (MT ensures that due weight is given to each item in the list by putting a sub-paragraph marker in at the end of each of vv. 14-18). The play on words in v. 13 underlines the relative significance of these forces: the men in the outlying parts are for $m^e l\bar{a}'k\hat{a}$, all kinds of civil and defence work (1 Chron. 27); the warriors (1 Chron. 1.10; 11.10) in Jerusalem are for $milh\bar{a}m\hat{a}$, battle.

The key-term, $p^e qudd\hat{a}$, 'muster; mustering officers', is introduced in v. 14 (cf. 1 Chron. 21.4). Unlike David in 1 Chronicles 21, Jehoshaphat is punctilious in observing every requirement of the Law even in the mobilization of his troops: the LORD's host (the word appears in v. 17; cf. 1 Chron. 5.18) is to be mustered in accordance with the LORD's ordinance (Exod. 30.11-16).

The troops in Jerusalem are under a commander-in-chief and his two lieutenants from Judah, who lead between them 780,000 troops, and a warrior from Benjamin and his lieutenant, who lead 200,000 bowmen (Benjamin habitually provides the archers, 1 Chron. 8.40; 12.2; 2 Chron. 14.8) and a further 180,000 foot-soldiers (for the equipment, cf. 1 Chron. 5.18). Once again it is to be noted that Judah and Benjamin provide the outer framework of the ideal people (1 Chron. 2–8).

Again nothing further is known of these five commanders (though one, Jehohanan, the first Judaean lieutenant, is probably to be equated with the father of a commander at the time of the coup d'état against Athaliah [2 Chron. 23.1]—in which case, that is another indication of his loyal Yahwism).

For comparative statistics for these 1,160,000 troops, cf. table at 1 Chron. 5.18.

All these, and the others dispersed throughout the land, are Jehoshaphat's 'assistants' (v. 19): appropriately, C picks up the same word that he has used in 1 Chron. 27.1 and 28.1 of David's agents in the realization of the divine rule through the implementation of David's system.

4. *2 Chronicles 18.1–19.11 Jehoshaphat's Disastrous Alliance with the North in the Battle at Ramoth-gilead, and its Aftermath*

The section may be divided into two subsections (cf. MT):

(1)   2 Chron. 18.1–19.4a: Jehoshaphat joins Ahab, the king of the north, in a disastrous war of liberation against Ramoth-gilead (MT adds a major division after 2 Chron. 18.27, at the end of the final speech by the prophet, Micaiah son of Imlah);

(2)   2 Chron. 19.4b-11: Jehoshaphat's judicial reforms.

The section is laid out in a significant pattern. The first subsection provides a warning example of how not to set about the task of securing successful relations with neighbouring peoples (it contrasts with what has just been achieved in 2 Chron. 17.10-11). The second subsection resumes the task of implementation of Torah, begun in 2 Chron. 17.7-9.

2 Chronicles 18.1–19.4a: The Disastrous War of Liberation against Ramoth-gilead

The subsection opens with a restatement of Jehoshaphat's status: v. 1a repeats 2 Chron. 17.5b, using the fixed pair, he has 'wealth and honour in abundance'. What more could Jehoshaphat want? Thanks to the divine blessing on his faithfulness, he enjoys the recognition throughout the world of his neighbour states which that status deserved.

As if without a flicker of disapproval, C continues with the utmost terseness in these portentous words: 'and he allied himself by marriage to Ahab' (v. 1b). It is only by knowledge of the background presupposed—and of the sequel—that the implacable disapproval in tone can be detected. This alliance with Ahab is, in the next generation, to pose the deadliest internal threat to the continuation of the Davidic line, and thus to the discharge of God's rule on earth, in the whole history of the Judaean kings down to the exile itself. It is thus the extreme of folly and wickedness on the part of Jehoshaphat, as

2 Chron. 18.1–19.4a is about to expound, and is to result in the final disaster of his reign, as 2 Chron. 20.35-37 records.

> Ahab, the contemporary king of the northern kingdom, is mentioned here for the first time in C. The period leading up to his reign reflects the chronic instability of the throne in the north. Ahab was son of Omri, the army commander, who in Asa's twenty-seventh year had wrested the throne from the usurper of the preceding royal house that had itself in Asa's third year usurped the throne of Jeroboam's son (see 1 Kgs 15.25–16.28). The lack of any vestige of legitimacy to the throne on Ahab's part could hardly be more dramatically demonstrated: he was the son of one who by violence had seized at third hand the crown of a schismatic state.
>
> The alliance by marriage referred to is through the marriage of Jehoshaphat's son, Jehoram, to Athaliah, daughter of Ahab and his wife, Jezebel, the princess from Sidon in Lebanon. The lethal effects of that marriage are to be seen when Athaliah eventually becomes queen mother in Judah and uses that position to try to wipe out the Davidic dynasty, as 2 Chron. 22.10–23.15 is about to tell.

At the end of an unspecified period of time (1 Kgs 22.2 says it was in his third year), Jehoshaphat 'went down' (v. 2) to Samaria, the new capital of the north. As elsewhere in C (especially in the case of Rehoboam in 2 Chron. 10.1 and of Josiah in 2 Chron. 35.20), the departure of the sole accredited king of Israel from the sole recognized capital, Jerusalem, is the signal for a disastrous turn of events. C adds 'to Samaria' to the parent text to make the point unambiguous. The indiscretion is compounded: not only does he, the legitimate king of Israel, deem it appropriate to leave Jerusalem to go to parley with the son of a usurper of the throne of a country which by right belongs to himself, but he even treats it as an equal by allying himself to it by marriage. Even worse, he thereby introduces a foreign poison into the system of his own kingdom.

> The names affected by Ahab's three children, all compounded with 'the LORD' (cf. family tree at 2 Chron. 22.9: Ahaziah, 'The LORD has upheld'; Jehoram, 'The LORD is exalted'; Athaliah, 'The LORD has manifested his greatness' [KBS]), may be evidence that the north was seeking at least legitimacy, if not to usurp the place of the house of David.

The risks involved in penetrating so far into the northern state, when he has already encroached on its southernmost territory and has placed his garrisons there (2 Chron. 17.2), must be enormous: Jehoshaphat's journey must have been carefully and deliberately prepared by both, with diplomatic immunity ensured. Ahab clearly thinks he has much to gain from the alliance, as his sumptuous entertainment of Jehoshaphat and his retinue indicates; the prospect of immediate advantage overcomes long-standing antagonism. His designs soon become clear (v. 2b): he wishes to launch an attack on the Aramaeans of Damascus, who have encroached on his eastern frontier in Gilead, at Ramoth-gilead.

In Jehoshaphat's honour Ahab 'slaughtered sheep and cattle' (v. 2). The vocabulary is, however, sacral: this is a sacrificial feast. By sharing in it, Jehoshaphat gives recognition to the theological system underpinning Ahab's illicit regime that competes with his own. There is already a divine judgment written into the proceedings.

So Ahab 'enticed' Jehoshaphat to join his expedition. C again chooses his vocabulary with great precision. The verb is the same as that used for Satan's incitement of David to conduct the census of God's people in 1 Chron. 21.1. The previous section has shown Jehoshaphat as a new David in putting into effect the system of organization of the kingdom revealed to David (not least the muster of the LORD's host, 2 Chron. 17.14). No sooner has that been achieved than he falls away: in the present chapter he behaves like an innocent abroad, saved from ultimate disaster despite himself, thanks to the mercy of God.

> C's modification of the opening of v. 2 is studied. It reads, 'After some years he went down to Ahab, to Samaria' for the 'Jehoshaphat king of Judah went down to the king of Israel' of 1 Kgs 22.2. C's objection to that text is plain: Jehoshaphat alone is king of Israel in the global sense; he is not, then, merely 'king of Judah', nor can Ahab be dignified with the title 'king of Israel'. It is only after Jehoshaphat has compromised himself by the illicit shared feast that the illicit titles 'king of Judah' and 'king of Israel' are added by C at the beginning of v. 3.
>
> Verse 2aβb has been added by C to make the theological points and replaces 1 Kgs 22.3 in which Ahab reminds his forces that Ramoth-gilead belongs to them and urges them to go to reclaim it. From this point on to the end of chap.18, C is unusually close to the underlying text of Kings (1 Kgs 22.4-35).

In the brief dialogue (v. 3) Ahab cleverly commits Jehoshaphat: 'will you accompany me to Ramoth-gilead?', is all he asks. It is left to Jehoshaphat portentously to equate the forces of Judah and the forces of the north and to mention the word 'battle'. As the LORD's vicegerent on earth, any battles that Jehoshaphat fights should be the LORD's battles. Jehoshaphat's disloyalty to his heritage is indicated by his willingness to fight battles at the behest of a 'king' without legitimacy rather than at the direction of God. Tragic consequences are already inevitable.

In Kings Ahab invites Jehoshaphat to war. C transposes 'war' to the end of Jehoshaphat's speech, where '[my people] are with you in war' replaces the third phrase of the identification in Kings of Jehoshaphat's forces with Ahab's: 'my horses are as your horses'. The identification of the forces of Judah and of the north is heightened in C by the chiastic arrangement of the personal pronouns and pronominal adjectives: Kings reads, 'I am like you; my people are like your people'; C reads, 'I am like you; your people are like my people'.

Nonetheless, Jehoshaphat is not without his hesitations. As a loyal follower of the LORD, he requires that they 'consult' the LORD (v. 4). The key term, *drš*, is used (borrowed from Kings, but exactly suiting C's purpose): it was precisely for Saul's failure so to 'consult' the LORD that he was eliminated as king (1 Chron. 10.13-14).

Ahab, anxious to allay his scruples (v. 5), collects four hundred prophets (C ignores the nicety in Kings '*about* four hundred...'), and enquires of them, 'Shall we launch the attack on Ramoth-gilead?'

C may be emending the 'Shall *I* attack...' of Kings to the plural in order to implicate Jehoshaphat fully. If so, the change is not carried through consistently (cf. v. 14).

The prophets' reply is enthusiastically positive, yet theologically guarded, '*may* God'—the general term for deity (Kings, 'the Lord')—'hand it over to the power of the king'.

Jehoshaphat is quick to detect the uncertainty and asks (v. 6) if there is not yet another prophet of the LORD to consult (*drš* again).

Ahab has to admit that there is: Micaiah ben Imlah (v. 7; his name is full of portent: Micaiah—'who is like the LORD?'; Imlah—'may it be accomplished'). But he is loth to consult him, because he habitually prophecies disaster for him ('evil', the opposite of 'good', already defined as the intended quality of life for the LORD's people, 2 Chron. 10.7). How can it be otherwise? Ahab is king of a schismatic and apostate state that is devoid of theological legitimacy; a prophet of the LORD has no option but to adopt a stance of consistent opposition.

As so often, there are tiny but telling differences between C and Kings. Kings renders in the future tense, indicating a statement about one event: 'he will not prophesy about me success but failure'; C renders in the present tense, expressing a consistent attitude, 'he never prophesies welfare for me but, all his days, disaster'. C has not made this adjustment in the subsequent occurrence in v. 17.

Micaiah is duly sent for (v. 8). Meanwhile, the prophets rant before the two 'kings' enthroned at the gateway of Samaria in their most impressive finery (v. 9). Their antics include the acted symbolism of Zedekiah son of Chenaanah (v. 10). By his name Zedekiah ('the LORD is my victory') is a would-be prophet of the LORD and he does not scruple to use the name of the LORD as authority for his word; but he is in the mould of the traditional prophets of Canaan (ben Chenaanah, 'son of Canaan'). He sports a pair of iron horns to represent invincible might, as of the bull, the traditional symbol of the supreme deity of the Canaanites: that is, the cosmic power through which Ahab should 'gore' his enemies into annihilation. The prophets have convinced themselves of their message; it is now expressed unambiguously (v. 11): 'If you attack Ramoth-gilead, you will succeed. The LORD will hand it over…' 'Succeed' is, of course, yet another of C's key terms (1 Chron. 22.13), but for its realization it depends on unconditional obedience to the LORD's revelation. The messenger sent to fetch Micaiah reports to him their unanimity; the overwhelming majority of four hundred to one in the king's favour is added as the final touch to make him conform his word to theirs (v. 12).

But Micaiah has no choice but to convey the word of 'his God' (v. 13).

Kings at this point reads 'the LORD'; C changes that to indicate the total isolation of Micaiah and his sole access to the word of 'his God'—who is the LORD.

At first (v. 14), Micaiah replies with an ambiguity similar to the original oracle of the rival prophets: 'advance…that they [the Aramaeans] *may* be handed over to your power'.

The Kings form of words, 'and the LORD will hand it over into the power of the king', is ironical.

Only when he is rallied by Ahab (v. 15), does Micaiah communicate his word directly: Ahab does not have to be lured to his fate by misleading promises; he advances towards it open-eyed, driven by his predetermined will.

Micaiah's oracle (v. 16) uses the figure familiar in the ancient Near East of the king as shepherd of his people: Israel will become a flock of sheep scattered over the mountains without a shepherd to direct and

protect. It is a prophecy of the death of the king and of the endanger-
ment of Israel. The miscalculation of the kings has exposed already
their incapacity to lead; it would be better that the war camp should be
demobilized now and that every Israelite should return forthwith to
his house while there is still peace of a kind (see the ideas already
expounded at 2 Chron. 11.4 in connection with Rehoboam). Under the
present regime, Israel is powerless to regain lost territory and to take
its appointed place among the nations of the world.

The basis of Micaiah's word is then expounded in v. 18, 'I have seen
the LORD reigning on his throne, with all the host of the heavens
standing in attendance at his right and at his left'. This must count as
one of the central theological statements of the whole work.

> The wording is virtually unchanged from Kings and must be assumed to
> have been adopted by C as entirely serviceable for his purposes. There are
> only a few minor adjustments, such as the use of the plural imperative in
> the opening phrase, 'Hear the word of the LORD', so that Jehoshaphat is
> also included in the audience and judged by the implication of the words.

The full tradition of the theology of the cosmic reign of the LORD,
with all the elemental powers at his disposal, sacramentally expressed
through the royal house of David and the hosts of Israel, centred in
Zion and focused on the ark, is brought into play (compare many
Psalms, for example, 46, 132, and Isaiah, for example, ch. 6: the
parallels between Isaiah's account of his vision in the Temple and
Micaiah's experience here are very striking). What happens on the
plane of history is but the counterpart to the decisions of the divine
court in the unseen realm. The truths and values of the eternal purposes of God cannot be thwarted by the misguided and self-conceived
actions of human beings, try though they may.

Only Micaiah possesses that steady perception that enables him to be
privy to the decisions in the cosmic realm and thus to interpret aright
the course of events on earth. Thus, in the present situation, given that
nothing happens on earth that is not the counterpart of the cosmic
realm, the mass hysteria of the nationalist prophets of the north can
only be interpreted in terms of 'a lying spirit' sent from the divine
court. Because of the illegitimacy of the reign of Ahab, there is no
fitting counterpart in the north to the reign of God and his cosmic
hosts that will enable the recovery of lost territories. The plan is
fruitless; the campaign is foredoomed to failure.

Micaiah's words are frank and direct (vv. 18-22; MT places them in a separate sub-paragraph for full effect). Not only has a 'lying spirit' possessed Ahab's prophets, but it is the LORD's doing that it should be so, and the sole purpose of that possession is to lure Ahab to his death. Ahab may think he is in control but in fact he is being duped by God. In the phrase, 'who will delude Ahab?' (v. 19), Micaiah uses the violent language of rape (Exod. 22.16): the related adjective 'simpleton' describes the inexperienced and impressionable youth, open to being taken advantage of because he is susceptible to any influence or suggestion (e.g. Prov. 1.32).

Zedekiah ben Chenaanah—he of the iron horns and no doubt leader of the prophetic opposition to Micaiah—is cut to the quick (vv. 23-24). The question is, which of the rival sides possesses the word of God? Zedekiah takes the direct line and punches Micaiah on the face: 'See now how I have delivered the word inspired by God to you!' The gesture well expresses the bullying arrogance of the regime, which tries to silence the uncomfortable dissident by humiliation and brute force. But the word is not so easily neutralized, nor the truth suppressed: Micaiah rests his case on the outcome: 'You will see!' The turn of events will show that Zedekiah is a charlatan, who will pay for his false claims to have access to the word of God with an equally humiliating flight (whether because of an invading enemy or because he has become totally discredited and fears for his life is not made clear).

But meantime Micaiah too has to vouch for the truth of his word by risking his own life (vv. 25-27; there are again here parallels in ancient Near Eastern prophecy). Ahab orders his arrest and his detention by the prefect of Samaria and by one of his own sons, in order to await the outcome of events.

> Neither of these figures, Amon the city commandant (a royal appointment according to Judg. 9.30 and 2 Kgs 23.8) and Joash the king's son, into whose joint custody Micaiah is consigned, figures again in the Hebrew Bible. But both, holding influential positions, would be among the first to learn of the death of Ahab and thus, ironically, of the fulfilment of Micaiah's prophecy. No further information is given about the fate of either Micaiah or Zedekiah.

With a deft touch, C highlights the competing claims of the regime and of the LORD through his prophet: Ahab's boast that Micaiah is to be held in custody 'until I *return in peace*' (v. 26; [Kings reads merely, 'come']), exactly matches Micaiah's word, 'let each one *return* to his house *in peace*' (v. 16). The critical matter is peace and how to attain it: for Micaiah it can only be by the way of truly 'seeking the LORD' in all things, not by the charade of Ahab and Jehoshaphat, who are attempting to elevate the human desires of an illegitimate regime into God's will.

Micaiah's last word is a defiant, 'Hear, O peoples—all of them' (v. 27). Perhaps these words are, as *BHS* suggests, a gloss from the later canonical prophet Micah (Mic.1.2). Yet they suit C's purpose: all that is done within Israel is for the attention of the nations of the world.

The battle at Ramoth-gilead and its outcome are recorded in vv. 28-34. Ahab seeks to thwart any possibility of the fulfilment of Micaiah's word by going disguised into battle (v. 29). As though the declared warning of God could be nullified by such an act of childish defiance! The same ruse is attempted by Josiah in 2 Chron. 35.22: the king, who is wilfully set on pursuing his own goals despite a specific word from God to desist, seeks to evade the prohibition and to escape the consequences. In both cases, the king plunges inevitably to destruction.

A further safeguard occurs to Ahab: with callous calculation he commands Jehoshaphat to don *his* royal garb, so that any Aramaean marksman on the lookout for a royal figure would automatically aim at him. Ahab, with great cynicism, is happy to sacrifice his new covenant partner to save his own skin.

> For the last phrase of v. 29 1 Kgs 22.30 reads, 'The king of Israel disguised himself and went into battle'. C, reading, '...and *they* went into battle', appropriately underlines the high risk in the joint venture to *both* kings.

Ahab has correctly anticipated the Aramaean tactics (v. 30): the Aramaean king had indeed ordered his cavalry commanders to engage with none but the king of Israel.

> C omits the detail that the commanders were thirty-two in number.
> The Aramaean king is not named. One may recall that, in 2 Chron. 16.2, Jehoshaphat's father, Asa, had called in the help of the Aramaean king, Ben-hadad, against the threat of Israelite blockade only five years before Jehoshaphat's accession to the throne. From the Aramaean point of view, the Judaeans have changed sides and might be regarded as meriting punitive action. But the Aramaeans obviously regard the northern kingdom as the ringleaders.

They immediately assume (v. 31) that Jehoshaphat, the only recogniz-ably royal figure on the battlefield, must be Ahab. They surround him [C is more graphic than Kings's 'they turned upon him'] and are only prevented from slaughtering him by Jehoshaphat's cry for help (cf. 1 Chron. 5.20).

C adds the crucial theological factor to the Kings account (v. 31): it is no human agency—his self-identification or even his distinguishing southern accent(?)—but God, who saves him. C uses both terms for God, the distinctively Israelite and the international. 'The LORD helped him': the divine patron of the Davidic throne remains the pro-tector of his anointed. The verbs 'cry' and 'help', expressing uncondi-tional reliance on the LORD, belong to C's key vocabulary (they are already linked in 1 Chron. 5.20; cf. 2 Chron. 14.11). Furthermore, 'God diverted them from him'—the LORD as universal deity has power even over foreign nations to control affairs at the mundane level. 'Divert' is also a key term: it is none other than the verb used of the Satan's 'inciting' of David to hold the census in 1 Chron. 21.1 and of Ahab's incitement of Jehoshaphat in this very chapter (v. 2). This time, human initiative is overruled by divine.

So it was also in the fate of Ahab; he is handed over to human power for destruction (v. 33, which begins emphatically, 'But a man...'). His disguise avails him nothing. An archer drawing his bow to full stretch looses an arrow that strikes Ahab at precisely the joint in his body armour (v. 33). Ahab, mortally wounded, is conveyed out of the Israelite battle lines (literally, 'war camp'). The word has again theological overtones: the war camp of Israel ought in principle to be the LORD's (1 Chron. 12.22). But here the self-styled 'king of Israel' has no divine warrant and perishes in his own self-conceived schemes.

Even human fortitude counts for nothing (v. 34). With immense bravery, Ahab props himself (more resolutely than 'is propped' as in Kings) in his chariot facing the Aramaeans all day long (a point C stresses beyond Kings) in order to give his troops the motivation of a visible presence on the field of battle. But, theologically, the fate of Ahab, misguided through his own folly as he is (cf. vv. 19-20), how-ever brave he be, is inescapable. With great pathos C records the death of 'the king of Israel' (Kings has just 'the king') at sunset. The day of battle ends with the end of the reign of the impotent king: the chaotic powers of the world of the nations have destroyed the leader of the illegitimate Israelite regime.

The whole incident closes, by contrast (2 Chron. 19.1), with the return of Jehoshaphat unscathed to Jerusalem. ('Returned to his house in peace' picks up Micaiah's prophecy in 2 Chron. 18.16, which was the very point of dispute between Micaiah and Ahab in 2 Chron. 18.26-27. The material from 2 Chron. 19.1–20.30 is now C's own.) This is no thanks to his naivety but due solely to the sovereign protection of God.

The seer, however, Jehu ben Hanani ('the LORD is he, son of my gracious one'), confronts Jehoshaphat with the truth.

> This is Jehu's first appearance; he is mentioned again in 2 Chron. 20.34 as the prophetic commentator on the life of Jehoshaphat. His father, Hanani, is presumably the prophetic figure recorded in 2 Chron. 16.7, who functioned in the time of Jehoshaphat's father, Asa.

His speech is divided into three parts: accusation (v. 2a); explanation (v. 2b); and message (v. 3a) with reason (v. 3b).

In two terse sentences, 'Should the wicked be helped? You love those who hate the LORD', Jehu launches a comprehensive accusation that Jehoshaphat has been false to the fundamental truths of his own and of his people's status.

- The root 'wicked' occurs in C in two connections. In Solomon's prayer in 2 Chron. 6.23, 37, it is defined as the opposite of 'righteous', that is, it describes activity which is not in conformity with the norms laid down by God. There, it specifically denotes the behaviour that will lead Israel into exile. Concrete examples of that behaviour all concern Jehoshaphat's alliance by marriage with the house of Ahab and its outcome. First, it is used in this passage of Jehoshaphat's own alliance with Ahab himself. In its verbal form, it is used again of Jehoshaphat in 2 Chron. 20.35, when he joins the ill-fated maritime ventures of Ahab's son, Ahaziah. Then it describes the malign influence of Ahab's daughter, Athaliah, which results in damage to the Temple and the handing over to the Baalim of all the holy offerings of the LORD, the very symbols of Israel's dedication to its vocation (2 Chron. 24.7; cf.2 Chron. 22.3). No root could express more radically activity that is antagonistic to the central role of Israel.
- 'Be helped' picks up 2 Chron. 18.31: help is the fruit of reliance on the LORD. Instead, Jehoshaphat has faithlessly relied on a power that rejects the LORD.

- 'Love' is used predominantly in C of God's care for his people, and through them for his rule on earth, shown in instituting the Davidic monarchy (2 Chron. 2.11 and 9.8— both times confessed by non-Israelite rulers). The paragon of human love for God is Abraham (as Jehoshaphat himself is about to recognize, 2 Chron. 20.7).
- 'Those who hate the LORD' is exemplified in the present context by Ahab, who 'hates' Micaiah ben Imlah and, thus, the word of the LORD that he bears (2 Chron. 18.7). C uses the expression elsewhere to describe specifically those who are the enemies of the LORD's anointed, and, thus, of his divinely ordained task (2 Chron. 1.11). The phrase expresses in the tersest possible way the utter inappropriateness of Jehoshaphat's association with Ahab who both rejects the word of God and refuses to recognize the exclusive status of the Davidic king.

No wonder the LORD is angry with his king (v. 2)—just as he had been with David in the archetypal sin of the census (1 Chron. 27.24). It is precisely to make amends for these failings that Jehoshaphat sets his reform in train (v. 10).

Nonetheless, the penalty has been mitigated (v. 3). Jehoshaphat has been the recipient of 'good things' (as was Rehoboam, 2 Chron. 12.12), because of his reforming acts at the beginning of his reign and because of his commitment to 'seek the LORD' (2 Chron. 17.1-6). These 'good things' should be understood not as a reward but, in accordance with sacramental theology, as a concomitant of devoted behaviour: the divine and human kings are but the two sides of the one reality. The 'good things' in the human are mediated through the life of commitment to the divine (contrast Rehoboam, 2 Chron. 12.14, where the same vocabulary is used).

> NRSV (as do other English versions) takes the 'good things' to be Jehoshaphat's own achievements, perhaps influenced by such a passage as 1 Kgs 14.13 (where, however, the preposition is different: 'in' not 'with'). In that case, the prophetic oracle merely becomes descriptive of Jehoshaphat's qualities and lacks any statement—except by implication— about the outcome, for example, 'therefore, you will not be destroyed'. But in 2 Chron. 12.12 'good things' are what *God* does, despite his anger, to the repentant king (here, to the king who has been faithful, at least up to a point). They are a statement of modified grace.

In the light of the complex of ideas of Jerusalemite royal theology, v. 4a means 'So Jehoshaphat reigned in Jerusalem' (cf. 1 Chron. 29.23; 2 Chron. 11.5).

> The paragraph marker at the end of v. 4a in the MT shows that this is the final statement of the subsection, again *contra* NRSV ('Jehoshaphat resided at Jerusalem; then he went out...') and other English versions, which are dominated by thoughts of historical sequence.

2 Chronicles 19.4b-11: Jehoshaphat's Judicial Reforms

The debacle of the campaign against Ramoth-gilead, and the stinging rebuke by the prophet that follows it, induce Jehoshaphat to repeat the reforming acts undertaken in his third year (2 Chron. 17.7-11). The geographical area covered, 'from Beer-sheba to the hill country of Ephraim' (for the sequence, cf. 1 Chron. 21.2), includes not only his territory of Judah but the southern frontier zone of the Northern kingdom annexed by Asa (cf. 2 Chron. 17.2). The impression is that the earlier teaching reform needs to be reinforced ('he brought [the people] back to the LORD', v. 4; for 'the God of their fathers', cf. 1 Chron. 5.25). He now backs up the teaching by the appointment of permanent judges throughout all the towns in Judah which he had fortified (v. 5; cf. 2 Chron. 17.2).

> It is notable, in view of C's proclivity to provide names, that both the cities and the judges are unnamed. What is important is not the historicity of the undertaking—which would have been enhanced by named locations and figures—but the theological pattern which is being woven: the life of holiness requires constant reinforcement, not least after the naive blunderings of the previous chapter.

Jehoshaphat imparts a two-fold exhortation to his new judges. Their task is to administer justice with the utmost circumspection, for they judge, 'not on behalf of humankind but on the LORD's behalf and under his authority' (v. 6). Their judgment must, therefore, be conducted with total reverence for God ('fear', as in 2 Chron. 17.10) and share the quality of the divine judgment: just, impartial, and incorruptible (v. 7).

Equally, in the capital, Jehoshaphat appoints a tribunal of priests, Levites and lay heads of families (v. 8) as a high court. They too are exhorted with the utmost gravity to discharge the justice of the LORD. They must act in fear of the LORD, in truth (1 Chron. 9.26) and in integrity (v. 9; the distinguishing characteristic of Solomon, 1 Chron.

29.19). The portfolio of cases referred to them is defined in v. 10: disputes involving blood-guilt, rulings on points of the Law, whether sacral, criminal or civil (v. 10).

The point of these reforms is made unambiguous in central terms of C's theology. It is to enable Israel to avoid incurring guilt (cf. 1 Chron. 21.3) of any kind with regard to the LORD, so that no anger from the LORD (cf. 1 Chron. 27.24) befalls them. Jehoshaphat speaks from experience (v. 2)! What is true of the people, must also be true of the judges.

At the apex of the system stand two figures in whom is vested the final ruling: one, the chief priest to pronounce on any matter concerning the rights of the LORD, the other, the head of the senior family of Judah (cf. the use of the same title in 1 Chron. 27.16 and, perhaps, 2 Chron. 28.7), from whom the royal house is sprung, to adjudicate on any matter concerning the rights of the king.

> Neither of these named figures recurs elsewhere in the Hebrew Bible—a particularly remarkable fact considering that the first was the 'chief priest' (but see the comments on the defective list of high priests in 1 Chron. 6.1-15).

The co-ordination of God and king again emphasizes the sacramental nature of Jerusalemite theology. The system for ensuring the joint interest of God and king is equally emphatic: only so can Israel be pleasing to God. As elsewhere (1 Chron. 9.17-34), the Levites stand in climactic position, ever in readiness 'in front' of the Jerusalemite tribunal (v. 11) as monitors of the whole practice of holiness.

Jehoshaphat concludes with an exhortation and a prayer. 'Be strong' matches the calling of the king as successor to David (1 Chron. 22.13), as originally the community had rallied to David (1 Chron. 11.10); 'May the LORD be with the good' reflects the Jerusalem theology of Immanuel, 'God with us' (1 Chron. 11.9). 'Good' forms a fitting climax to the reform. It equally echoes sacramental theology: it is in the practice of the revealed goodness of God that the community realizes its own nature and destiny as good (cf. v. 3).

5. 2 Chronicles 20.1-30: The Successful Defence of the Realm Against Moab, Ammon and Edom

The incident provides a model example of Israel's relations with the world of the nations. This is what happens to the nations if they withhold their tokens of recognition (2 Chron. 17.10) and launch unprovoked attacks. Israel's response can only be unconditional reliance on God. The passage is replete with C's standard vocabulary, as will be indicated below.

MT divides the material into two sections at the end of v. 13: the prophetic word of the Levite, Jahaziel, is thus bought into greater prominence in response to the powerlessness of Judah.

'After that', Israel's neighbours to the east, Moab, Ammon and Edom, make war on Jehoshaphat (v. 1).

The text of v. 1 must be in some disorder—Ammonites are mentioned twice after Moabites. The Edomites, termed 'Mount Seir', figure in the subsequent narrative (vv. 10, 22-23), so that it is probable that they should be read in v. 1. 'Edom' should probably be read for the orthographically similar 'Aram' in v. 2. The route they choose for their invasion, via En-gedi on the western shore of the Dead Sea, would confirm strong Edomite participation. Hazazon-tamar occurs again in the narrative of a conflict in the Dead Sea area in Gen. 14.7.

C is not concerned with any possible motive these nations may have had (2 Kgs 3.4-5 gives some reasons for economic and political grievances Moab may have harboured). The question is simply: how does Israel respond in this typical example of the mindless assaults of the nations of the world among whom she is set?

The invaders are termed 'a mighty horde' (v. 2): the overtone is an unruly and unpredictable mob that will spread havoc throughout the land (2 Chron. 13.8). The threatened disorder is the opposite of the peace, security and harmony that God has intended for his people, and to extend from his people to the world of the nations.

Jehoshaphat's response is exemplary (v. 3). In this emergency ('he was afraid'), he has no recourse to human assistance, but immediately refers the matter directly to God (the standard term, *drš*, 1 Chron. 10.13-14). To reinforce the statement of human impotence, of self-abasement and of absolute dependence upon God, Jehoshaphat proclaims a fast. The only other time a fast is observed in C is, suggestively enough, on the occasion of the death of Saul (1 Chron. 10.12): the present observance of humiliation before God by the submissive king *before* the encounter with the enemy contrasts directly with the lament for the death of the defiant king, who would not refer matters to God, *after* the disastrous defeat into which he has led his people.

The response of Judah is equally exemplary (v. 4). With one accord they 'gather' (*qbṣ*, the key term used of the unitary action of Israel under David, 1 Chron. 11.1). They too 'seek' (*biqqēš*, a synonym of *drš*, 1 Chron. 16.11) the LORD

Within this sacral assembly (*qāhāl*, v. 5; cf. 1 Chron. 13.2) Jehoshaphat, as sacramental representative of God and humanity, functions as spokesman. He stands, thus, in the Temple 'before the new court', presumably at the very point of transition from the concourse of the laity to the inner court of the priests (2 Chron. 4.9; cf. 2 Chron. 7.7 and sketch-plan at 2 Chron. 23.5. In Jer. 26.10; 36.10, the gate between the court of the priests and the outer court is called the 'New Gate'). The verb 'to stand before' is used of approved officials taking up the position appropriate to their office (cf. the Levites as musicians in 1 Chron. 6.32).

Jehoshaphat's prayer (vv. 6-12) is a well crafted composition. It is divided into two major sections, the affirmation (vv. 6-9) and the petition (vv. 10-12), introduced by 'so now' (cf. 1 Chron. 17.7).

> Verses 6 and 12 match one another with the motif of 'strength', under-
> lined by means of the vocative and the emphatic rhetorical question, 'O
> LORD, God of our fathers, are you not...?'/'O our God, will you
> not...?'. Verses 7 and 11 equally match with the motif of 'inheritance':
> 'You dispossessed'/'your possession which you made us possess' (the
> same root throughout in Hebrew).

The affirmation (vv. 6-9) gives the grounds on which the petition is made. It is expressed in the language of the hymn celebrating the nature and the acts of God. It begins (v. 6) with the invocation, 'O LORD, the God of our fathers', which encapsulates in his name all that God is in himself to his people Israel and the promises he has made and fulfilled to them throughout the generations (cf. 1 Chron. 5.25; Abraham and David will be the 'fathers' particularly in mind). It continues with a general affirmation about God's universal rule, opening with a rhetorical question, 'Are you not God in the heavens?, which amounts to the very strong statement, 'You are indeed...' God's rule in the cosmic realm, 'the heavens', is matched by his dominion 'throughout all the kingdoms of the nations' of the earth (for the fundamental link in the Jerusalemite theological tradition between the cosmic and the earthly, cf. the Psalm in 1 Chron. 16.26). The fundamental point of C's work, Israel's role among the families of humankind, is thus reaffirmed by Jehoshaphat at the outset of his prayer. 'Power and might', as God's to bestow, echo the language of David's prayer in 1 Chron. 29.11. None can, then, withstand his power.

The LORD's particular act for his people is affirmed with a similar emphatic opening question: 'Was it not you yourself, our God, who…?' (v. 7). The act affirmed is the exclusive gift of the land. It has been given 'in perpetuity to the seed of Abraham who loves you' (the title is used again in Isa. 41.8; compare 2 Chron. 19.2). The authority of the original founding father and, through him, genetic intimacy with God are invoked: in the spatial metaphor of holiness (cf. 1 Chron. 6.49), the land promised to Abraham is the essential theatre for the realization of Israel's destiny, the sphere for all time where love for God has to be realized by Abraham's descendants and whence its influence must spread.

The affirmation continues in vv. 8, 9: 'They [the seed of Abraham] have taken up residence there and have built a holy place for your name'. This is not just a claim to merit on the part of the 'fathers', especially David and Solomon. The deeper factor is that by their actions the sacramental system has been instituted and maintained intact. They 'have taken up residence', because God has at once dispossessed the pre-Israelite population and granted possession to Israel in *his* inheritance (the point is to be made by the play on words in v. 11; cf. on 1 Chron. 11.4). To 'take up residence' is the same word as is used of Jehoshaphat's 'taking up rule' in Jerusalem in 2 Chron. 19.4a and is used for the same sacramental reason: as the king can only 'take up rule' because he occupies the LORD's throne (1 Chron. 28.5), so Israel can only take up their inheritance because it is the LORD's inheritance. The Temple—termed here 'holy place' in restatement of Israel's vocation—is the focal point of this symbolism, the meeting point of symbol and reality as C has expounded in 1 Chronicles 17–2 Chronicles 7. Specifically, it is built in honour of the LORD's name (cf. 1 Chron. 13.6): to articulate to all the world the significance of who the LORD is in himself and for his people, and to provide the place where all that God is and does can be invoked.

The occasions when that revealed character of God might be invoked are listed in v. 9: disasters of many varieties—'sword, judgment, plague, famine'. These are included precisely among the emergencies envisaged by Solomon in his great prayer of petition at the dedication of the Temple in 2 Chron. 6.22-39 ('enemies' in the second clause, 2 Chron. 6.24; famine and plague in the fourth, 2 Chron. 6.28). They are, furthermore, listed in the response of God in

2 Chron. 7.13-14 in which he acknowledges that he has indeed chosen the Temple as the place where he may be called upon (1 Chron. 5.20) to provide assistance. That prayer and God's response to it provide Jehoshaphat with his warrant.

There is, however, a difference in the present emergency. In Solomon's prayer in 2 Chronicles 6, and in the LORD's response in 2 Chronicles 7, the crises are, in the main, provoked by Israel's unfaithfulness. They do not arise by accident but are punitive (2 Chron. 6.23). They are indeed 'judgments', designed to bring Israel to her senses and to make her invoke the Name in acknowledgment of guilt (2 Chron. 6.24). Here the situation is entirely different: Jehoshaphat has just re-established the whole system whereby there is rendered to God all that is due to him. The crisis has happened despite Jehoshaphat's reforming zeal.

It is thus with a still profounder sense of staking all upon the dependability of his theological tradition, that Jehoshaphat rehearses the appropriate action to take when such crises happen: 'we should stand before this house and before you—for your name is in this house—and cry to you out of our distress so that you may hear and deliver' (v. 9). Jehoshaphat has learned the truth of these statements from his own experience: for 'stand before' as the posture of the dutiful officiant, see v. 5; for 'cry out' as the reaction of the submissive servant, see 2 Chron. 18.31. The request for God to hear is part of the recurrent refrain in Solomon's prayer (2 Chron. 6.23, etc.; for 'save'. cf. 1 Chron. 11.14).

There is thus an impassioned element in Jehoshaphat's words as he turns to the plea proper (vv. 10-12). The whole affirmation has adduced grounds for divine outrage at the disturbance of the divinely imposed order. So far from this crisis being understood as an act of punishment by God for Israel's failures, it has happened despite its faithfulness (passages from the Psalms of Innocence from Jerusalem theological tradition, like 'For your sake we are slain all the day long' [Ps. 44.22], come to mind). Jehoshaphat, however, confines to the human level his outrage at the injustice. Israel, at God's own instructions, respected the territorial integrity of these very neighbours at the time of the exodus (cf. Deut. 2.2-22): they made no encroachment on their lands and certainly did not destroy them (v. 10; *hišmîd* is the technical term for the destruction of the pre-Israelite population, 1 Chron. 5.25; 2 Chron. 33.9). At the level of common humanity these neighbours should then respond with equal consideration; instead, they are paying Israel back with threats of destruction (v. 11a). There is the added poignancy that these neighbouring peoples are recognized in the Hebrew Bible as blood relatives, whether as descendants or collaterals of Abraham (Edom claimed descent from Abraham, Gen. 25.19-26; Moab and Ammon were descended from Abraham's nephew, Lot, Gen. 19.30-38).

Jehoshaphat (his name, after all, means 'The LORD has judged'!), therefore, puts all the onus on God, not in blame but for action. It is not Israel's inheritance that is under threat, but God's own inheritance which he has bestowed upon Israel (v. 11b). He turns, therefore, in direct appeal in v. 12: 'O God will you not judge them?' The impartial judgment of God envisaged in Solomon's prayer, echoed in v. 9, but now unjustly falling on Israel, should be turned on their enemies. But the matter is entirely in God's disposal; it is for him to note the violation and redress the wrong. Israel has no strength of its own and, in any case, this onslaught from the nations (the chaotic horde, as in v. 2) is not so much on itself as fundamentally on God himself. 'We do not know what to do; we look entirely to you'.

Both to add pathos and to express the unreserved dependency upon God, C adds (v. 13) that the whole community, including the toddlers, the women and the children, 'were standing before God' in obedience to the requirement of v. 9.

The divine response (vv. 14-17) is mediated through a Levite.

> This response follows immediately in reply to Jehoshaphat's prayer, as in the Jerusalem tradition of Psalms of Lamentation (cf. Ps. 60.6).
>
> This Levite is otherwise unknown in the Hebrew Bible. But he is introduced with unusual emphasis on his credentials. The section opens with the emphatic construction, 'As for Jahaziel...' (cf. 2 Chron. 15.1), and he is given a pedigree of four generations. His grandfather, Benaiah, is related by Mandelkern to the levitical musician of that name in 1 Chron. 15.18, 20; 16.5; his great-grandfather, Jeiel, by BDB to the musician of that name in the same lists (1 Chron. 15.18, 21; 16.5); his great-great-grandfather may be related to the Mattaniah of 1 Chron. 25.16; cf. 1 Chron. 9.15. In particular, his connection through a long family pedigree to the family of Asaph (1 Chron. 6.31-47) demonstrates that Jahaziel was thoroughly steeped in the Jerusalem theological tradition, especially the hope for the vindication of the LORD's sovereignty associated with the ark (1 Chron. 16.1-7, 37).

The revelation is by the standard means of 'inspiration' (1 Chron. 5.26). It takes place in the midst of the receptive audience of the sacral assembly (v. 5).

Jahaziel's speech is also carefully constructed. It opens with a summons to hear, typical of prophet (2 Chron. 33.10; cf., with a different verb, 2 Chron. 13.4) and wisdom teacher (e.g. Prov. 4.1) It is solemnly addressed to 'all Judah, the inhabitants of Jerusalem and the king, Jehoshaphat' (v. 15). Although not an 'official' prophet, Jahaziel ('God has caused to see/to be a seer') uses the standard 'messenger formula' of the prophetic oracle, 'This is what the LORD has said' (e.g. 1 Chron. 17.4).

Thereafter, there is a certain symmetry in the construction—a three-fold pattern thrice repeated, with some freedom in the elements and their sequence:

A1   the reassurance (v. 15bα)
A2   the reason for confidence (v. 15bβ)
A3   an instruction (v. 16)
[B1   no equivalent]
B2   the reason for confidence (v. 17a)
B3   an instruction (v. 17bα)
C1   the reassurance (v. 17bβi)
C3   an instruction (v. 17bβii)
C2   the reason for confidence (v. 17bβiii)

The reassurance (A1, C1) is standard at the beginning of an oracle of salvation: 'Do not fear; do not be terror stricken' (1 Chron. 22.13). It is developed in A to refer to the cause of the community's present perturbation: 'because of this great horde' (vv. 2, 12).

The reasons for confidence (A2, B2, C2) are precisely what Jehoshaphat needs to hear in terms of Jerusalemite theology: 'the battle is not yours but God's' (cf. 1 Chron. 14.15); 'it is not for you to fight in such a battle'; 'the LORD is with you' (cf. the Immanuel sign, 'God with us', Isa. 7.14; 1 Chron. 11.9).

The instructions in A3 tell the time of the action: 'tomorrow descend upon them' (so C3, 'take the field against them') and the place of the action (in an otherwise unknown location somewhere in the Arabah: 'the ascent of Ziz ['the blossom'] east of the wilderness of Jeruel ['shot by God'?]')

The heart of the speech is the series of instructions in B3 that

develop Jerusalemite theology in terms of the exodus: 'Present yourselves [as at a sacral event, v. 6; 2 Chron. 11.13]; take up your
appointed position ['*md*, cf. 1 Chron. 6.31; 2 Chron. 7.6] and see the
deliverance of the LORD [Exod. 14.13; cf. 1 Chron. 11.14] with you
[again Immanuel theology]'.

This instruction by Jahaziel is not quietism (any more than
Jehoshaphat's prayer was fatalism). It is pure sacramentalism: Israel's
role is totally participatory—it goes fully armed into the battle (v. 21,
below); but the battle is the LORD's. Israel, as the LORD's host under
the LORD's anointed, is caught up unreservedly and with no volition
on its own part into the action of God against the invading hordes of
the nations. With total openness to God and entire dependence upon
him, it is borne irresistibly to victory (compare such sacral battles as
Josh. 6 and 1 Sam. 7).

The response of Jehoshaphat, and of Judah and Jerusalem with him,
is, appropriately, the same as the response of Israel in the context of
the exodus (v. 18): bowing and prostrating in expression of adoration
and of total reliance and self-giving (Exod. 4.31; 12.27; cf. 1 Chron.
29.20).

The Levites of the Kohathite and Korahite families articulate the
response to the LORD in praise (v. 19) 'with exceedingly loud voice'.
'Exceedingly' (*l^ema'lâ*) may be another of the puns on the key word
ma'al, 'unfaithfulness' (1 Chron. 14.2), in order to highlight by contrast the piety of Jehoshaphat. Significantly, for this occasion of sacral
war, the LORD is given his full Israelite title, 'God of Israel' ('the God
of Judah' does not exist as a divine title).

> It is at first sight surprising to find the family of Korah co-ordinated with
> the family of Kohath since, according to 1 Chron. 6.22, 37-38 (and pas-
> sages outside C, like Exod. 6.18-24), the Korahites are but one family
> within the much wider branch of the Kohathites, from whom, for
> example, the Aaronic priesthood is descended (for the interrelationships,
> cf. Table of Descent at 1 Chron. 26.1-3).
>
> The key issue here is the leadership of praise in the Temple; thus it is
> no doubt the musicians of the family of Kohath who are intended here,
> that is, the family of Heman (cf. 1 Chron. 6.33).
>
> Since this act of worship takes place in the Temple, the question of
> monitoring access to the courts of the Temple must be also prominent. It
> is the Korahites who provide the 'guardians of the thresholds' at two of
> the gates of the Temple, the north and the east (1 Chron. 26.14; cf.
> 1 Chron. 9.19, and the place at the east gate where Jehoshaphat stands to
> deliver his prayer, 2 Chron. 20.5). The 'sons of Korah' have a dozen

> psalms in the Psalter attributed to them (cf. at 1 Chron. 6.22), so that
> they, too, may be involved in song.

What the Kohathites and Korahites sing is not disclosed. It is to be
noted that the refrain, 'Give thanks to the LORD, for his faithful love
lasts for ever', which is about to be sung on the battlefield (v. 21) is
precisely the epitome of the music of the family of Kohath (and of
Merari) at the Tabernacle in 1 Chron. 16.41 (and also of Gershon at
the ark in 1 Chron. 16.34). It was also the refrain with which all three
families of musicians hailed the dedication of the Temple in 2 Chron.
5.13.

> The first phrase occurs in Pss. 33.2; 105.1; 106.1; 107.1; 118.1, 29;
> 136.1 (the closest parallels insert 'for he is good' after the first phrase, as
> in 1 Chron. 16.34 = Ps. 106.1); the last phrase appears in Pss. 106.1;
> 107.1; 118.1-4, 29; 136.1-26.

The next day (v. 20) the host sallies out to the wilderness of Tekoa,
some 20 km to the south of Jerusalem, overlooking the arduous ascent
from the Arabah that the invaders have set themselves. As they 'go
forth' (the technical term of sallying forth as the Lord's host; cf.
1 Chron. 1.12), Jehoshaphat addresses 'Judah and the inhabitants of
Jerusalem': the customary summons to hear in the prophetic mould
(cf. Abijah in 2 Chron. 13.4), and an exhortation. His exhortation is
based directly on the Jerusalem tradition: it is modelled on the words
of Isaiah precisely to Judah and Jerusalem in Isa. 7.9, 'If you will not
believe, you will not be established'. It adds piquancy to C's sense of
the unity of history that he uses words recorded in the time of Ahaz,
six reigns later than Jehoshaphat! In Jehoshaphat's address co-ordinated imperatives and jussives amount to conditional statements: 'If
you place your security in the LORD your God, you will be secured; if
you rely on his prophets [in this case a Levite and a king!], you will
succeed [another of C's key terms, 1 Chron. 22.11]'. There is also an
echo in these words of the narrative of the exodus, significant in the
light of the other references to the exodus narrative in this story:
there, too, belief in God and in his human spokesman and agent are
co-ordinated (Exod. 14.31)

The preparations for the engagement (v. 21) involve consultation
with the people (exactly as in David's preparations regarding the ark
in 1 Chron. 13.1): it is with perfect unanimity that the expedition is
undertaken in God's name. Jehoshaphat 'sets' (cf. 1 Chron. 6.31) the
levitical musicians in first position at the head of the armed host. They

hymn on lute and lyre his awesome majesty, clad in holy array (an allusion, surely, to the summons to the nations to submit to the LORD in 'holy array' in the Psalm in 1 Chron. 16.29). No doubt, the people answer with a shout of acclamation (cf. v. 22). 'The trumpets' in v. 28 also imply the presence of the priests announcing with ear-shattering clarion the arrival of God on the field of battle (cf. 2 Chron. 5.13a, where the refrain is also associated with the priests; does 2 Chron. 35.3 even imply the presence of the ark on the field of battle, despite 2 Chron. 5.9?)

Verse 22 proclaims the realized sacramentalism: precisely at the moment of the acclamation of the LORD's arrival on the field of battle, the LORD himself intervenes. 'The LORD sets ambushes' against the invading horde (compare the deliverance of Abijah in 2 Chron. 13.15). They turn on each other in self-destruction: first Ammon and Moab against Mount Seir (v. 23)—those who had planned 'to destroy' Israel (v. 10) are themselves laid under ban (1 Chron. 2.7); then those that are left 'assist' (a grisly play on the key term, 1 Chron. 5.20) one another's destruction. C again uses the language of the exodus (cf. 2 Chron. 5.10): they 'are smitten' and consign one another to 'the destroyer' (Exod. 12.13, 23; cf. 1 Chron. 21.12). Deliverance, as of the passover, is re-enacted.

When Judah looks down from a vantage point towards the Arabah, they can see that the whole 'horde' (2 Chron. 13.8) lies slaughtered (v. 24). All Judah has to do (v. 25) is to help themselves to the spoils of war (cf. Asa, 2 Chron. 14.12). Here, too, there is a cross-reference to the exodus narrative: 'Jehoshaphat and his people...get spoils for themselves', just as the Israelites departing from Egypt 'spoiled the Egyptians'. It is only in this passage and in Exod. 3.22 and 12.36 that this word is found in this form with this meaning. The 'three days' it took them to strip the corpses is a conventional expression for completeness (cf. 1 Chron. 12.39; 21.12).

The victory is celebrated with a commemorative name-giving ceremony at a sacral assembly at the site of the battle (v. 26): it is for ever thereafter known as 'Beracah', 'blessing' (a place name not, in fact, found elsewhere in the Hebrew Bible). Whereas in the 'curse narrative' of the original settlement in Judg. 2.1-5 rebellious Israel entered the land at a similar location, which they named 'Bochim', 'weepers', here, Israel, having conducted themselves in an entirely obedient manner, enjoy the full blessing of God.

As Jehoshaphat had led his people out in trust, so he leads their return in triumph to Jerusalem (v. 27; for 'joy' , cf. 1 Chron. 12.40). As they went out with the Levites at the head, sounding the battle alarm of the arrival of the invincible God in the midst of his host, so they return with again the priests and Levites in the van, with the same musical instruments, leading the praise and announcing the return of the victorious God of Israel to the Temple (v. 28).

> A surprising omission is any mention of dedication of spoils to the LORD as giver of victory. Given the ambivalence of Jehoshaphat, evident in 2 Chronicles 18 and about to be manifested in 2 Chron. 20.35-37, this lack of full scrupulousness may be part of C's deliberate presentation.

The whole episode ends with a note of the pacification of the whole world of the nations of the earth, 'all the kingdoms of the lands' (v. 29): 'the fear of God' rests upon them, the awe arising from the recognition that it is the LORD himself who fights with the enemies of his people. The whole of v. 29a repeats 2 Chron. 17.10: what Jehoshaphat had been installed to do he has indeed accomplished; Israel's vocation among the nations of the earth has been fulfilled in exemplary fashion.

The truth is further expounded in v. 30: Jehoshaphat's own realm is at peace (1 Chron. 22.9). Even more fundamentally, 'the LORD has given him rest on all sides': here, at the climax of the entire narrative the vocabulary of the Temple as the place of rest for the ark (1 Chron. 22.9; 28.2), the symbol of the LORD's prevailing power on earth, is deliberately resumed.

6. 2 Chronicles 20.31–21.3: The Annalistic Framework of Jehoshaphat's Reign, with Additional Notes

2 Chron. 20.31 resumes the very opening phrase of the presentation of Jehoshaphat's reign in 2 Chron. 17.1a.

> In 1 Kgs 22.41-51 (on which this section is based, but with many changes) the order is inverted: 'Now Jehoshaphat, son of Asa, had become king over Judah'.

The information about the age of Jehoshaphat at his succession (framework element 1) and the length of his reign (element 2) is purely annalistic: in contrast to 2 Chron. 17.1b where, theologically speaking, he is 'established over Israel', here, in strict historical terms, he 'reigns' only over 'Judah'. The names of his mother and maternal grandfather are recorded (element 3); nothing further is known about them).

In the theological evaluation (element 4) in v. 32, C sticks closely to Kings: Jehoshaphat is compared in his righteousness to his father, Asa, not, as in 2 Chron. 17.3, to David, the founder of the dynasty and setter of the absolute standard (for the standard term for faithfulness, 'not turn aside', see 2 Chron. 8.15; 34.33).

In contrast to Jehoshaphat's own righteousness in 'abolishing the high-places and the symbols of the female deities from Judah' (2 Chron. 17.6), it is noted (v. 33) that the high places were not, in fact, removed, and still the people at large 'did not fix their hearts on the God of their fathers' (unlike Jehoshaphat himself, 2 Chron. 19.3). This, again, is the likelier scenario, historically.

> Kings reads even more explicitly, 'Still the people were sacrificing and burning incense on the high places'. Kings adds that Jehoshaphat finally abolished the male cult prostitutes, which his father Asa had not completely accomplished. It does not belong to C's patterning of events to include this negative comment on Asa.

The prophetic commentary for this reign (framework element 5) is contributed by Jehu ben Hanani, the prophet who had confronted Jehoshaphat after the failed campaign against Ramoth-gilead (2 Chron. 19.2-3).

But to continue the ambivalent portrayal of Jehoshaphat, C adapts from Kings the account of a final, disastrous, incident in his reign (vv. 35-37). Just as Jehoshaphat had 'allied himself by marriage to Ahab' (2 Chron. 18.1), with calamitous consequences, so he now 'allies himself' (same intensive reflexive stem, though of a different verb) to Ahab's son, Ahaziah, with similarly calamitous consequences. C notes tersely, 'He acted wickedly in doing so', using the stem for 'wicked' that he has reserved explicitly for the house of Ahab (2 Chron. 19.2).

The nature of the joint enterprise is the construction of a fleet at Ezion-geber to go to 'Tarshish'. The location of the shipyards at Ezion-geber at the head of the gulf of Aqaba makes a destination in the Red Sea or Indian Ocean more likely, as the comparable co-operation between the sailors of Solomon and Huram of Tyre in 2 Chron. 8.17-18; 9.10, 21 suggests.

It is striking that, whereas Solomon's joint activities with Huram are noted with appreciation as further evidence of his international status, here Jehoshaphat is condemned for apparently precisely the same kind of action. The difference must be that the association with the gentile king, Huram, who is given a consistently favourable assessment in C (cf. his confession in 2 Chron. 2.10-11), is approved because it is further evidence of worldwide recognition of the house of David and the benefits of its rule, whereas the alliance with the schismatic northern kingdom of Israel raises Ahaziah, son of Ahab, inappropriately to equal status with the Davidic monarch. The problem lies not in collaboration as such, but in the specific alliance.

This is made explicit in the prophetic commentary that C provides: 'It is because of your allying yourself with Ahaziah that the LORD has shattered your undertakings: the ships have been wrecked and have never been able to reach Tarshish' ('been able' is a key term, in abbreviated form, deliberately used in the negative to contrast with David's success, 1 Chron. 29.14). The final word of evaluation on Jehoshaphat's reign is 'failure'.

> The prophet Eliezer is otherwise unknown in the Hebrew Bible, as is his father, Dodavahu. His home town, Mareshah, in the Shephelah of Judah (not to be confused with the nearby Moresheth, the place of origin of the prophet Micah, with whom Micaiah, another prophetic commentator on Jehoshaphat's reign, is associated [2 Chron. 18.27]), was one of Rehoboam's garrison towns overrun by Pharaoh Shishak (2 Chron. 11.8), and the place of encounter between Asa and the Egyptian, Zerah the Cushite, in 2 Chron. 14.9-10. Its inhabitants thus knew only too well how strategically vulnerable the spot was and the potential cost of political miscalculations by the Davidic house.
>
> The presentation in Kings of the joint maritime venture is markedly more friendly towards Jehoshaphat. It is simply noted, without theological evaluation, that 'he made peace with the king of Israel' (1 Kgs 22.45). The initiative for ship-building was his, taken at a time of Edomite weakness, and only subsequently did Ahaziah wish to participate with him, a request that Jehoshaphat declined.
>
> C has not made use of Jehoshaphat's further joint campaign with the house of Ahab (against Moab, 2 Kgs 3).

The final framework elements—(6), Jehoshaphat's death and burial, and (7), the name of his successor, Jehoram, follow in conventional manner in 2 Chron. 21.1 (virtually = 1 Kgs 22.51; cf. 2 Kgs 8.16). But the cold-blooded atrocity with which Jehoram's reign begins (2 Chron. 21.4), the murder of all six of his brothers, is prepared for by the note on the careful policy that Jehoshaphat had pursued with regard to his sons (vv. 2-3), which should have made such an outrage impossible. Jehoshaphat had designated Jehoram, his first-born, as his successor. His remaining six sons he had distributed round Judah in fortified cities and had provided for them, just as Rehoboam had done with his sons (2 Chron. 11.23).

'Six sons' assumes that the two Azariahs (v. 2; spelt slightly differently in Hebrew) are separate individuals. None of these brothers figures elsewhere in the Hebrew Bible.

There is an appropriateness in this final note on Jehoshaphat's reign. With the best of intentions, he has sought to secure an orderly succession; but those intentions are about to be thwarted by circumstances beyond his control, but which he has been responsible for creating. Jehoram, the son concerned, is none other than the one whom Jehoshaphat had married to Ahab's daughter, Athaliah. That alliance by marriage has already precipitated major crises (2 Chron. 18; 20.35-37), including a threat to Jehoshaphat's own life (2 Chron. 18.29-31). It is about to threaten the very existence of the house of David: when Jehoram's son, Ahaziah, is killed (2 Chron. 22.9; see family tree appended there), Athaliah herself, as queen mother, seizes power in another blood-purge of the Davidic house and almost succeeds in wiping it out. C's major task in these chapters (2 Chron. 18–23) is to trace the near fatal influence of the 'wickedness' (cf. 2 Chron. 20.35) of the house of Ahab through four generations of the house of David, from the marriage of Athaliah alluded to in 2 Chron. 18.1 until her death in 2 Chron. 23.15, 21. It is thus appropriate that MT prepares for these troubles to come by linking the circumstances of the succession of Jehoram to the provisions that his father Jehoshaphat has made in 2 Chron. 21.2-3.

MT divides the presentation into two sections:

1. Jehoram's atrocities and their consequences (2 Chron. 21.4-11);
3. Elijah's prophecy and its fulfilment (2 Chron. 21.12–22.1).

C has taken the conventional annalistic account of Jehoram's reign found in Kings, with its by now standard theological commentary, as the framework for his presentation. But he has considerably modified that framework. On the one hand, there are two significant additions, v. 4 (following on from vv. 2-3 which are also his own material) and vv. 10b-19. On the other hand, he has drastically reduced the length of the Kings presentation by omitting 1 Kgs 22.52–2 Kgs 8.15 (212 verses), which is largely concerned with narratives about the prophets Elijah and Elisha and their relations with the kings of the north. Elijah remains in C's presentation, but in a quite different way from that in Kings.

The details of the layout in C in comparison with Kings are as follows:

2 Chronicles	*2 Kings*
21.4: Jehoram's murder of his brothers	no parallel
21.5-10a: framework elements (1), (2) and (4); revolt of Edom	cf. 8.17-22
21.10b-19: reason for the revolt of Edom; the letter of Elijah; the invasion of the Philistines and the Arabs; the illness and death of Jehoram	no parallel
21.20–22.1: resumption of framework from v. 5: elements (1), (2), (4), (6) and (7)	cf. 8.24

The omission of C's framework element (5), the written prophetic commentary on Jehoram's reign, is notable. The letter of Elijah must be held to be its replacement.

C's purpose is to show how the poison introduced into the system by Jehoshaphat's alliance with the royal house of the north, sealed by

Jehoram's own marriage to Ahab's daughter, Athaliah, continues its deadly influence. C has just recounted how the two disasters of Jehoshaphat's reign—the campaign to liberate Ramoth-gilead and the merchant-venture in the Red Sea—were caused by his association with Ahab and with Ahab's son, Athaliah's brother Ahaziah, respectively. The poison now spreads into the heart of the life of Judah itself. The next two paragraphs expound this developing crisis:

- 2 Chron. 21.4-11: the atrocity of the murder by Jehoram of his brothers and the general posture of his life as influenced for evil by the house of Ahab, C's parade example of wickedness (2 Chron. 6.23); the ruinous consequences of that influence;
- 2 Chron. 21.12–22.1: the letter of Elijah, announcing comprehensive disasters that will strike people, royal house and the king's own person, and the fulfilment of these announcements.

1. Jehoram's Atrocities and their Consequences
(2 Chronicles 21.4-11)

The section begins apparently innocuously, but with deep irony, by stating that Jehoram 'took charge [the verb is from the same root, *qûm*, that is used in the promise to David in 1 Chron. 17.11; cf. 2 Chron. 6.10; 7.18 of Solomon] of the kingdom of his father and became established [the thematic term, *ḥzq*, of 2 Chron. 1.1]'. Jehoram's way of 'becoming established' has nothing to do with reliance on the promise of God. It is to eliminate all possible rivals: 'he slaughtered all his brothers with the sword and also some of the leaders of Israel' (v. 4). The reign that thus begins in terror and repression is soon to end in disaster.

In vv. 5-10a C adheres closely to the underlying Kings text: Jehoram's age at accession, the relative brevity of his eight years' reign (v. 5) and the baneful influence of the house of Ahab (v. 6) are all present in Kings.

The text of C heightens, if anything, the influence of the house of Ahab on Jehoram by stressing the permanency of his marriage to Athaliah: whereas 2 Kgs 8.18 reads, 'because Ahab's daughter *had become* wife to him', C reads, 'because Ahab's daughter *was* wife to him'.

Highly serviceable to C's purpose is the echo of the language of the Passover narrative in Exodus in v. 7: 'The LORD was unwilling *to destroy* the house of David'. 'To destroy' in C's usage cross-refers to 'the destroyer' in Exod. 12.13, 23, the agent of the LORD who slew the first-born of Egypt, and from whom Israel was protected by the blood of the Passover. Repeatedly C makes use of the motifs of the Passover, both positively and negatively (cf. 1 Chron. 21.12). Here it is the very first-born of the current generation of the house of David who threatens to bring the destruction of a 'negative Passover' down on his own house and people (compare the further reference to the exodus in 'plague' in v. 14).

> C makes two adjustments to 2 Kgs 8.19 in v. 7a: 'The LORD was unwill-
> ing to destroy *the house of David* [Kings: 'Judah'] for the sake of *the
> covenant which he had made with* [italicised phrase added] David'. The
> play on the first-born of the house of David in this context requires the
> introduction of the house of David itself in the first adjustment. The
> promise to preserve a 'lamp' for David (v. 7b), the guttering light of one
> tribe, was made in the prophecy of Ahijah of Shiloh in 1 Kgs 11.36,
> which C has not reproduced (cf. 2 Chron. 10). C complements that figure
> (the only time it appears in C) with 'the covenant with David' (2 Chron.
> 13.5) and explains it as a promise to give David and his sons an unbroken
> succession.

The revolt of Edom to the south and of Libnah in the lowlands to the west (vv. 8-10a) is also reproduced almost word for word from Kings.

> For v. 9, 'with his captains' (those left whom he could trust; cf.v. 4b),
> 2 Kgs 8.21 reads 'to Zair' (an otherwise unknown location, presumably
> in Edom; the text in Kings may not be sound). Kings also adds at the end
> of v. 9, 'and the people fled to their tents', i.e., Israel's flight before the
> Edomites.

For C these revolts are unfailing evidence of Israel's loss of status and function among the nations of the world, among even her nearest neighbours. The point is driven home by the preservation of the phrase from 2 Kgs 18.20: 'they [the Edomites] appointed for them-selves a king' (v. 8b). For the exercise of the LORD's rule on earth there can be but one king in the region, the current descendant of the house of David in Jerusalem. When there is a king in Israel, there can, in terms of the theology of the Davidic house, be no king in Edom (1 Chron. 1.43). The revolt of Edom also has economic consequences, with still further implications for Israel's loss of status. The connection of Judah with the Red Sea is now severed. The lucrative expeditions initiated by Solomon (2 Chron. 9.10), which no doubt Jehoshaphat was trying to revive (2 Chron. 20.36-37), are no longer possible. The standing which that influx of wealth represented has been forfeited.

The revolt of Libnah is significant because it lies precisely between Israelite territory and the territory of the Philistines, who are to figure in the next episode (v. 16).

C spells out the theological reason for this forfeiture in his own material in vv. 10b, 11: it was because Jehoram had 'abandoned [cf. 1 Chron. 28.9] the LORD, the God of his fathers' (v. 10b; cf. 1 Chron. 5.25). The 'fathers' here will be specifically David and Solomon: it is only through the maintenance of their institutions that Jehoram can retain his role as the LORD's representative on earth (the verb 'abandon' brings Jehoram's failings close to those of Saul, the first rejected king).

This abandonment is made specific in v. 11 in terms of the reconstruction of the high places that his immediately preceding 'father', Jehoshaphat, had taken the lead in destroying (2 Chron. 17.6). Throughout even his own territory, 'the hill country of Judah', the powers of rival deities, each on its own hilltop shrine, are being reaffirmed in competition to the God of Israel. Jehoram by that action has invalidated the basis of his rule.

C uses the stock biblical figure of fornication to express participation in the cult on the high places (the archetypal sin of the settlers on the East Bank, which had led to their forfeiture of their status, 1 Chron. 5.25; so in v. 13 [twice] below). Jehoram has implicated his people in failure to accord God his exclusive rights to Israel's allegiance, as of one spouse to the other; he has 'driven his people away' from practising their role (2 Chron. 13.9; the verb may be continuing the metaphor of fornication—it is used of seduction by a prostitute in Prov. 7.21).

2. Elijah's Prophecy and its Fulfilment (2 Chronicles 21.12–22.1)

The prophetic intervention—and, for this reign, written commentary combined—is provided by Elijah.

> This is the sole occasion on which Elijah makes an appearance in C. Elijah
> in Kings is a northern prophet; it thus adds to the realism of the presenta-
> tion that his communication to the king of Judah should be by letter rather
> than in person. Despite the extensive materials on Elijah in Kings (1 Kgs
> 17–19; 21; 2 Kgs 1–2), there is no parallel there to this document.

Elijah's message opens (v. 12) with the standard 'messenger formula',
'This is what the LORD has said' (cf. 1 Chron. 17.4), in order to
authenticate the prophet as spokesman for God. Additional force is
given to the formula by the continuation: 'the God of David, your
father'. The significance of the whole theological tradition of the
house of David is brought to bear in evaluation of Jehoram's conduct.

The message is in two parts:

  – the reason for the LORD's impending act of punishment
    (vv. 12-13): a description of Jehoram's actions in the past
    tense, introduced by 'because';
  – the announcement of that impending act (vv. 14-15), intro-
    duced, this time (contrast 1 Chron. 17.7) by 'behold, the
    LORD is about to…' (the 'inceptive participle').

The reason for the impending punishment is given twice: Jehoram's
sins both of omission and of commission. The standard against which
he is measured is now scaled down from the whole Davidic tradition
within which he stands to the example of his immediate predecessors
as kings of Judah: he has *not* (v. 12) 'walked' (cf. 2 Chron. 6.16) in
the ways of his father, Jehoshaphat, nor in those of his grandfather,
Asa (whose negative features in 2 Chronicles 18; 20.35-37 and
2 Chronicles 16, respectively, are ignored for this purpose); he *has*
(v. 13) capitulated to the practice of the Northern kingdom.

> The alternation between the plural 'ways' of the righteous Judaean kings
> and the singular 'way' of the north is probably without significance.
> Compare 2 Chron. 22.3, where the plural is used of the house of Ahab.

In particular, it is the involving of 'Judah and the inhabitants of
Jerusalem' in the religious 'fornication' perpetrated by the house of
Ahab. The fundamental nature of this violation of the LORD's rights
on C's scale of values is made clear by the fact that even the murder
by Jehoram of his six brothers, all better men than himself (at least
they had not married into the house of Ahab!), a murder tantamount
to wiping out the whole dynasty of his father, is subordinated to it. As
he had eliminated his brothers, so he is now to lose his sons.

The impending act of God (v. 14) is another 'negative exodus'. God's great acts of deliverance are now thrown into reverse: 'massive blows' ('plagues', cf. 2 Chron. 13.15), such as had once struck Egypt (Exod. 8.2; 9.14), but from which Israel itself had been protected (Exod. 12.13, 23, 27), are now turned upon Israel, 'upon your people, your sons [probably not 'children', NRSV, in the light of v. 17], your wives, all your property, even you yourself' (v. 15). The list of persons and things threatened is highly significant: the threat to the king is a threat to the people whose representative he is; the threat to his sons and to his wives is a threat to the royal dynasty, and the means of perpetuating that dynasty; the threat to property is to those physical emblems of prosperity and recognition that lie at the heart of the Davidic regime (1 Chron. 27). Jehoram himself has become like Pharaoh, the object of God's own punitive actions, and thus the cause of the ruin of his people (2 Chron. 12.2-12). His own fate is to die the slow, agonizing and degrading death of a progressive disease of the bowels, a stricken king like Saul (1 Chron. 10.3; *ḥlh*, 'be sick', the antonym of *rp'*, 'heal', 2 Chron. 7.14, occurs three times in v. 15).

Verses 16-18 record the fulfilment of Elijah's prophecy. The agents of retribution are the Philistines (1 Chron. 1.12) and the Arabs, the very peoples who had brought their tribute to Jehoram's father, Jehoshaphat (2 Chron. 17.11). This time it is stated explicitly that they are invading Judah 'at the direction of the Cushites' (1 Chron. 1.10).

> Others take the phrase to mean, 'who are beside the Nubians' (cf. NRSV), but a mere geographical sense seems too weak. For the meaning, 'at the direction of', see, for example, 2 Chron. 26.18.

This is the last reference in C to the Cushites, the ultimate terrifying menace from the furthest extremity of Egypt, both geographically and psychologically speaking, who had already intervened in the reigns of Rehoboam and Asa (cf. 2 Chron. 12.3; 14.9-13; 16.8). The disruptive powers of the nations to break in and reduce God's people to chaos is represented above all by the primordial enemy, Egypt. The verb used of their invasion, to 'split open and annexe' (v. 17), though in a different conjugation, occurs in Isa. 7.6, again of foreign military action against Judah and Jerusalem. Here, the negation of the exodus and the reversal of the Jerusalem tradition of theology are rolled into one.

But it is all willed by the LORD: it is he who has 'aroused their spirit' (v. 16), an expression used by C only of foreigners prompted to action by God, here for woe (as of Pul, 1 Chron. 5.26, as punishment for *ma'al*), but also for weal at the denouement of the whole presentation (Cyrus, 2 Chron. 36.22). It is on that inspiration by God that Israel's hope ultimately depends.

The goal of their invasion (v. 17) is first 'all the wealth found in the king's palace', that is, all the symbols of the supremacy of the house of David among the nations of the world, acquired through tribute, plunder and trade, and in its own kingdom. In a reversal of roles, it is now these very nations who carry off the spoils of war (contrast 2 Chron. 14.13-15; 20.25). But even more deadly is the assault on Jehoram's 'sons and his wives': this attack on the royal family and the royal harem is nothing less than an attack on the dynasty itself and its power to reproduce itself. The Davidic house is indeed all but wiped out: it has but one 'guttering lamp' in the reigning line left to it, Jehoram's youngest son, Jehoahaz (contrast v. 3b).

Finally, the king's own death ensues (v. 18). Elijah's prediction is fulfilled in all its gruesome detail. This is no chance ailment: it is the LORD himself who strikes him with incurable disease of the bowel. As before, there is a correlation between health and uprightness of life, sickness and wickedness (2 Chron. 16.12; the antithesis of sickness and health is well brought out in this verse). The loathsome manner of his death reflects the abhorrent manner of his life. The continuing apostasy of the king and his murderous barbarity find expression in the excruciating pain of his long, drawn out terminal illness and his final death in agony.

His people recognize the dissonance between life and status. They deny him the customary funerary rights of the burning of fragrant spices (v. 19b) that even Asa had been allowed (2 Chron. 16.14).

The account of the reign is rounded off with a resumption of the annalistic material from v. 5 (v. 20a). Verse 20b opens with the same word as the theological evaluation in v. 6a: 'he behaved'. But, instead of repeating how and why Jehoram adopted the ways of the house of Ahab, it contents itself with the all-purpose condemnation, 'disgracefully'.

> NRSV does not take the opening of v. 20b as a resumption of v. 6 and renders, 'he departed with no one's regret'.

His unfitness to be regarded as a true Davidic king is expressed by the way in which the populace take the initiative in his burial. While they bury him 'in the city of David', they refuse him a place in the royal graves of the house of David. His unworthiness to be recognized as a genuine ruler of the Davidic House is marked even in the formulation of framework element (6): the standard element, 'he lay with his ancestors' is omitted.

> There seems to be no difference in significance between the active, used here, 'they buried him' (so already for Solomon, 2 Chron. 9.31), and the passive 'he was buried' (so already for Rehoboam, 2 Chron. 12.16).
>
> The disapproval is much stronger in C than in 2 Kgs 8.24, which has no such resumption of the evaluation, and merely notes that he 'lay with his fathers and was buried with his fathers in the city of David'.

In 2 Chron. 22.1 C adds to his Kings source the reason why it is Ahaziah, Jehoram's youngest and sole surviving son, who succeeds to the throne by referring back to the invasion of the Arabs described in 2 Chron. 21.16-17.

In the wake of the crisis of the almost total extinction of the royal house, the populace take the lead in the appointment of the king (cf. 1 Chron. 11.10). In truth, they have no choice. Once again the forfeiture by Israel of its divinely ordained status is underlined by the vocabulary used. It was a 'raiding party' among the Arabs who inflicted these losses on the royal house; it had been precisely as a 'raiding party' that David's followers had first established themselves (1 Chron. 12.18, 21). That raiding party of Arabs had penetrated the 'camp' of Israel, that traditional term for the host of Israel on the field of battle (1 Chron. 12.22). Such were Israel's reduced circumstances that the LORD's sacramental host had themselves now been worsted by a mere band of raiders; as they had gained power, so now they have almost lost it.

2 CHRONICLES 22.2–23.15: THE REIGN OF AHAZIAH AND THE USURPATION OF ATHALIAH

The account of the reign of Ahaziah ends with his death in 2 Chron. 22.9, but MT takes it as part of a single unit (2 Chron. 22.2-12), which also encompasses the beginning of the usurpation by Athaliah. Nothing could more graphically display how entirely Ahaziah's reign is enmeshed in the fateful alliance with the north, sealed by his father Jehoram's marriage to Athaliah and reinforced by his own actions. Ahaziah's reign was ill-fated from the start.

> C follows the parallel material in Kings (2 Kgs 8.26-29; 11.1-3) relatively closely in 2 Chron. 22.2-6, 10-12 (but with many alterations and additions). Verses 7-9 are largely his own.

2 Chronicles 22.2-9: The Reign of Ahaziah

Ahaziah bears a name of high Yahwistic orthodoxy: 'The LORD has upheld'. But the annalistic framework elements in vv. 2-4 (especially elements [2]–[4], the length of his reign, his mother's name, and theological evaluation) already indicate how far Ahaziah has sunk from the truths of that affirmation.

> Framework element (1), Ahaziah's age at accession, can hardly be correct in C. The text reads 'forty-two', an impossibility since his father was already dead at the age of forty (as has just been said in 2 Chron. 21.20). 2 Kgs 8.26 reads, 'twenty-two'.

His reign lasts for one year (v. 2): he comes to an untimely end because of the surrender of his principles through alliance with the north, as vv. 5-9 are about to recount.

His mother is, of course, Athaliah, daughter of Ahab (Omri, Ahab's father, the founder of the northern dynasty, is given here for the only time in C; see on 2 Chron. 18.1).

> The title in Kings for Omri, 'king of Israel', is omitted by C: none from the north should claim that status. With some inconsistency C adds the

title, however, after 'Jehoram, son of Ahab' in v. 5, but that may be to ensure differentiation between Jehoram, current king of the north, and Ahaziah's father, Jehoram, the late king of Judah (cf. family tree at v. 9). The confusing identity of names between the royal houses of north and south at this time may be part of their rival claims to legitimacy (cf. on 2 Chron. 18.1).

That C is indeed tracing the baneful effect of the house of Ahab on the house of David through several generations is made clear by his emphatic reading at the beginning of v. 3: '*he* [Ahaziah] *too* walked in the ways [for the figure, cf. 2 Chron. 6.16] of the house of Ahab'.

2 Kgs 8.27 reads simply the narrative tense, 'and he walked...'. In contrast to 2 Chron. 21.13 the plural 'ways' is used of the northern kingdom (Kings reads the singular).

C adds to the Kings text the reason for Ahaziah's following of the ways of the house of Ahab: it is 'because his mother was his counsellor to make him act wickedly' (for the official status of the counsellor, see 1 Chron. 27.32-33). He reserves his key term, 'wicked' (2 Chron. 6.23), for the special influence for evil of the house of Ahab: 'wickedness' is not just the failing of individuals; it becomes systemic, genetic and contagious, militating against the 'righteous' regime of the house of David. It is thus that it manifests itself in the behaviour of individuals of both houses.

C thus accounts in his own terms for how 'what he did was just as evil in the sight of the LORD as what the house of Ahab did' (v. 4a). The point is developed in C's emphatic revised reading in vv. 4b, 5aα: 'because they [the house of Ahab] were counsellors of his after the death of his father so that they became his destroyer. Follow their advice he did.' 'Destroyer' again picks up the vocabulary of Exod. 12.13, 23. Here once more the motif of the 'negative Passover' (1 Chron. 21.12) is being employed: the king of the house of David is called to realize in his day the Mosaic tradition of deliverance and duty; but this king permits the house of Ahab to continue to be the agent of destruction against his own people more effectively than any Pharaoh.

Kings simply reads, 'because he was related by marriage to the house of Ahab'.

Ahaziah's specific act of folly is, like his grandfather Jehoshaphat before him (2 Chron. 18), to join the northern kingdom in a campaign against the Aramaeans to liberate Ramoth-gilead, a campaign that is necessarily foredoomed to failure (v. 5). As there, his fundamental error is to sally forth from Jerusalem, the sole centre of the power of God on earth, to give credence to the illegitimate regime of the north and, by so doing, to deny his own status.

> Hazael ('God has seen'), king of the Aramaeans, is mentioned only in this context in C but exercizes considerable influence on the course of the history of Israel and Judah in Kings down to the time of Ahaziah's son, Joash (1 Kgs 19.15-17; 2 Kgs 8–13; C entirely omits, except for some echoes, the material in 2 Kgs 9–10).

The king of the north, Athaliah's brother J(eh)oram (2 Kgs 1.17; 3.1), is wounded in the engagement and has to withdraw to Jezreel to recuperate (v. 6). Although this is material inherited by C from Kings, it is highly significant for C's purpose. In the one verse, two of C's contrasting key terms are used: the verbs 'to be healed' (2 Chron. 7.14) and 'to be sick' (1 Chron. 10.3). Reasons for human infirmity and the divine sources of health are part of C's fundamental concerns in his whole work. Ahaziah, having joined Jehoram on the battlefield, now goes to visit his sick uncle in Jezreel.

> C reads 'Azariah' for the 'Ahaziah' in Kings, a clear textual error that NRSV tacitly corrects.
>
> Again, this is the only time that the important site of Jezreel is mentioned in C. The location of the winter palace of the kings of the north, it played an important part in the fate of Athaliah's parents, Ahab and Jezebel (1 Kgs 21; 2 Kgs 8.29–10.11).

In vv. 7-9 C provides his own theological commentary. The 'downfall' [BDB; a unique word in the Hebrew Bible] of Ahaziah is at the hands of Jehu ['The LORD is he']. Again C refers to Jehu only in this context (apart from the line of descent in 2 Chron. 25.17 borrowed from Kings), introducing him without further background information.

> Jehu is the northern army commander at the battle at Ramoth-gilead. He is anointed king of the north under the inspiration of Elijah and Elisha to avenge the atrocities committed by the house of Omri and is acclaimed as king by his troops in the aftermath of the wounding of Jehoram (1 Kgs 19.16-17; 2 Kgs 9–10).
>
> These isolated references to Hazael, Jezreel and Jehu in this chapter (not to mention Elijah in 2 Chron. 21.12) are good examples of how C

can, by the mere mention of a name, conjure up a whole realm of association (cf., e.g., on 1 Chron. 1).

Considerable figure though Jehu is in the light of his wider role in
Kings, the point that C wants to make is that he is merely the agent of
the LORD in the removal of the house of Ahab. Thus, 'Now it was
God's doing' stands at the opening of v. 7. It is God's doing that
Ahaziah should come to Jehoram (cf. 2 Kgs 9.16); that he should
encounter (an ironical use of the technical term *yṣ'*, cf. 1 Chron. 1.12)
Jehu with Jehoram (cf. 2 Kgs 9.21); and that Jehu should have been
anointed for this task (cf. 2 Kgs 9.6-10; but C is careful to avoid
saying that he is anointed to be 'king' of the north).

Jehu performs his task in a thoroughgoing way. First, he metes out
justice on the royal house of the north. Then he encounters Ahaziah's
entourage, his courtiers and nephews, the sons of his brothers killed in
the Philistine–Arab invasion, and thus grandsons of Athaliah. Finally,
Ahaziah himself is tracked down in hiding in Samaria (the Davidic
king skulking in the capital of the non-kingdom of the north!); he is
brought to Jehu and executed. In contrast to 2 Kgs 9.27-28, Ahaziah is
not transported to Jerusalem for burial 'with his fathers in the city of
David'. In this respect he is like the 'kings' after Josiah in 2 Chronicles 36: he has brought the house of David so low that he has surrendered his right even to be buried in their sepulchre. That any respect
is shown to his corpse by burial is thanks only to the merits of his
grandfather, Jehoshaphat, who, despite his naivety, had at least set his
heart 'to seek the LORD' (*drš*). At the climax of the narrative, C's key
word for behaviour that is acceptable to the LORD in the ultimate
degree is introduced: *dāraš* is to accord to the LORD all that is due to
him by giving him priority in all things (1 Chron. 10.13-14). By
contrast with the competence of Jehoshaphat for rule, the 'house of
Ahaziah' is reduced to total impotence (the key term of 2 Chron.
13.20).

It may be helpful at this moment of deep crisis precipitated by the
influence of the house of Ahab on the house of David to draw up a family
tree showing once again the interconnections between the chief personages mentioned in 2 Chron. 18–24:

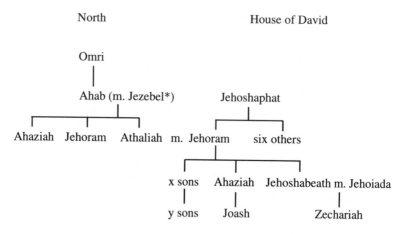

*not mentioned in C

2 Chronicles 22.10-12: Athaliah's Purge of the House of David and Seizure of Power

MT proceeds without break into Athaliah's seizure of power. The eclipse of the reigning king of the house of David in death and burial in the north has as its counterpart the usurpation of the throne of Judah by the queen mother, herself (after Jehu's purge) the sole survivor of the house of Ahab. This is the darkest hour of the house of David—before, that is, the final night of the exile (already anticipated in Ahaziah's death and burial in the north).

The north, to judge by the names of the family of Ahab (see under 2 Chron. 18.1), are claiming to be true followers of the LORD; they have made a systematic attempt to align Judah with northern policy since the first joint expedition of Jehoshaphat and Ahab and to ally it ever more closely with them (2 Chron. 18–22). Now this movement has reached its climax with the attempt to destroy the house of David and to install a purely northern regime.

At the end of v. 10, 'she destroyed [a variant verb to that used in 2 Kgs 11.1] all the descendants of the kingdom', C adds 'of the house of Judah'. Athaliah is seeking reunification of Israel on northern terms by the elimination of the royal house of Judah.

Yet a puzzle remains about her motives. With the bloody coup d'état of Jehu just recorded (2 Chron. 22.7-8), nothing of her native house of Ahab is left in the north for her to represent, only a new hostile regime. Athaliah, the ageing queen mother, with father, brothers, husband, sons and grandsons now dead (apart from the infant Joash, about to be introduced, v. 11) is left stranded without royal house. To judge from 2 Chron. 24.17, it may be that she has a power-base among certain of the nobility, who are intent on drawing Judah into the mainstream of traditional Canaanite culture. At any rate, with her son out of the way (whether he was willingly or, as his sister's behaviour in v. 11 might suggest, unwillingly compliant), she can pursue her ultimate ambition: she is no longer merely counsellor, the power behind the throne; she is herself the ruler.

But there is another factor in the situation (v. 11). As the poison had been introduced by a woman, so it is neutralized by a woman. Athaliah's own daughter, Jehoshabeath ('The LORD is abundance' [KBS]), sister of the dead king, Ahaziah, who is also the wife of the high priest Jehoiada ('The LORD knows'), frustrates her mother's ultimate design by rescuing her infant nephew, Joash ('the LORD has provided' [KBS]), son of Ahaziah, and hides him with his nurse in a bedchamber in the Temple complex. Thanks to her position as high priest's wife, she is able to keep Joash concealed in an area inaccessible to the laity for six years (v. 12; for the labyrinth of chambers associated with the Temple, see Ezekiel's account in Ezek. 42).

The form of Jehoshabeath's name in C is merely a variant of the Jehosheba of 2 Kgs 11.2.

If Jehoiada was high priest (as 2 Chron. 24.6, 11 suggests), his marrying even a royal princess would be at variance with the law in Lev. 21.14, unless it is still recognized that, in principle, the king remains priest among his people (compare the possibility of keeping the king-in-waiting, Joash, within the precincts of the Temple).

C emphasizes Jehoshabeath's status by drawing together in one sentence, and in part repeating, all her connections, as daughter, wife and sister, with royal house and Temple; the last phrase, 'for she was the sister of Ahaziah', may imply that she regards herself as responsible as Joash's guardian. C heightens her instrumentality by adding, '*she put* [him and his nurse] in the bedchamber' and by stating that '*she hid him*' for '*they*' as in 2 Kgs 11.2. C also heightens Athaliah's culpability: '*she did not put him to death*' (though she would have if Jehoshabeath had not forestalled her), as opposed to '*he was not put to death*' as in Kings.

In v. 12, C reads, 'he was concealed with *them* in the house of God', rather than 'with *her*' as in Kings. It would be inappropriate in any case for a woman to be resident in the Temple, but the wider significance of the plot against Athaliah is thus indicated: it was not just the act of an individual, but of the central representatives of the Jerusalem tradition.

> The universal term for deity is used instead of 'the LORD' as in Kings:
> this event affects nothing less than the expression of the cosmic rule of
> God. It is striking that the same verb 'to be concealed' is used of both
> father and son in vv. 9 and 12.

The parallels in this narrative with the rescue of the infant Moses are
striking and highly apposite. It is part of C's intention in his whole
work to explore the potentiality of the Davidic house to bring the
Mosaic revelation to fruition within the life of Israel. That is explicitly said in this section of C's work in 2 Chron. 23.18: 'in accordance
with what is written in the Law of Moses…through the instrumentality of David'. It is, accordingly, highly appropriate that there should
be parallels between the tale of the infancy of Moses in Exodus 1–2
and the infancy of Joash, the new Davidic king. In both cases there is a
systematic attempt to slaughter all the relevant male children; in both
there is a royal princess, the ruler's own daughter, who frustrates the
designs of the royal parent; in both there is the hiding of the child and
the procuring of a wet-nurse. C preserves here from Kings a further
example of the typology that he has been developing between David
and Moses (1 Chron. 22.13).

2 Chronicles 23.1-15: The Counter-revolution Led by Jehoiada, the High Priest

The counter-coup engineered by the high priest, Jehoiada, against
Athaliah's usurpation is presented in three sub-sections:

1.   the counter-revolution planned and executed (vv. 1-11);
2.   Athaliah's discovery of the counter-revolution (vv. 12-13);
3.   Athaliah's fate (vv. 14-15).

> 2 Chronicles 23.1-15 is parallel to 2 Kgs 11.4-16 (with, again, many
> variations in detail).

The Counter-revolution Planned and Executed (verses 1-11)
It is in Athaliah's 'seventh year' (v. 1) that Jehoiada engineers the
counter-coup against the queen mother. The seven years' delay may
have more to do with waiting for Joash to reach sufficient years of
maturity than with the strength of Athaliah and the weakness of the
opposition to her. C begins the narrative of the counter-revolution by
saying that Jehoiada 'gathered his strength' [Kings reads merely
'sent']: this is the same word that is used to describe a new king 'being
established' on the throne (2 Chron. 1.1). On Joash's behalf, Jehoiada

invokes the inherent rights of the legitimate Davidic successor with the sanction of theological justification that that implies.

The first step is to gather support from the traditional leaders within the community. Accordingly, Jehoiada binds five 'captains of hundreds' by a covenant oath, presumably to commitment to the plan to restore the Davidic monarchy and to secrecy about it, and dispatches them round Judah to gather (the key word of 1 Chron. 11.1) the Levites and the lay heads of households (1 Chron. 27.1) to a sacral assembly (*qāhāl*, 1 Chron. 13.2) in Jerusalem (vv. 2-3).

> The Levites come from 'all the cities of Judah' (cf. 1 Chron. 13.2). According to 1 Chron. 6.64-65, the levitical cities assigned in Judah were all to the priests. There had been an admixture of non-priestly Levites with the influx from the north in the time of Rehoboam (2 Chron. 11.14). The lay heads of households are described as 'of Israel', not 'of Judah': it is the theological ideal of the representation of the whole people of God that stands in the forefront here.
>
> The complexion of events in 2 Kgs 11.4 is quite different (in the second part of v. 1 and in vv. 2-3 C has radically recast the material). The coup there is much more 'realistic'—initially a military operation, involving 'the captains of the hundreds' of the mercenary troops, 'the Carians' (2 Sam. 20.23 [*kethib*]), and the king's personal emissaries, 'the runners' (2 Chron. 12.10). Here it is communal sacral power that is being invoked: five 'captains of hundreds' are named from the intermediate echelon of command of the citizen army and they act only as messengers. None of them is known outside the confines of this narrative, except possibly Ishmael's father, Jehohanan [so BDB], who, if is he the same figure as that mentioned in 2 Chron. 17.15 (cf. a Zichri in 2 Chron. 17.16), had been part of Jehoshaphat's reorganization of the citizen army.

Without hesitation (v. 3), the whole *qāhāl* enters into a covenant with the young king in 'the house of God' (again the universal significance of the act is indicated by the term used for deity). Jehoiada proclaims that the prince will become king, in accordance with the promise of the LORD concerning the princes of the house of David (1 Chron. 17.12-14).

> Again, in Kings the record is more measured. Jehoiada makes a covenant with the leading conspirators in 'the house of the LORD', puts them under oath, shows them the child king and then confides in them his plan of action. C's adjustment makes the link back towards the Kings text rather rough: the subject of 'and he said to them' at the beginning of v. 3b must be Jehoiada, though the two nearest masculine singular nouns are 'the king' and 'all the assembly'.

The plan is right. The necessary actions follow.

Some of the details of the procedure are obscure, but the main outline is clear. The young prince is to be escorted through the Temple for his coronation and acclamation as king (vv. 4-8). He is then to stand beside 'his pillar' (v. 13), one may assume at the junction of the inner and the outer courts (cf. Jehoshaphat in 2 Chron. 20.5), where he is to be crowned.

The forces are divided into three. One third of them are the priests, Levites and keepers of the thresholds; as 'entrants of the Sabbath', they have access to the Temple proper (v. 4). The reference to 'entrants of the Sabbath' is to the fact that the keepers of the threshold change weekly (1 Chron. 9.25), as do the Levites in charge of arranging the showbread in the nave of the Temple (1 Chron. 9.32; cf. Ezek. 46.1). Another third of them will be in the royal palace, and the remaining third in 'the Gate of the Foundation', while all the people (the representative heads of families of v. 2, presumably) will occupy the '[outer] courts of the house of the LORD' (v. 5; 'courts' is used here in the 'plural of local extension' to indicate the different parts of the 'outer court' disposed around the inner court).

> At this point some kind of sketch-plan of the layout of the Temple and Palace as envisaged by C must be attempted. The attempt is difficult for a number of reasons. Nowhere does C give a complete list of dimensions, or of the precise disposition of structures. C is writing in the period of the Second Temple, probably at least two hundred years later than the destruction of the Temple he is portraying—and five hundred years later than the reign of Joash. It must remain uncertain, therefore, how far he is working with historical, and how far with ideal, ideological or anachronistic features. It is thus also uncertain how far it is appropriate to supplement C's data with information drawn from elsewhere in the Hebrew Bible; even if one does draw on that information, it must be realized that it too may have its own ideology, for example, Ezekiel's visionary temple in Ezekiel 40–47, which has many interpretative problems of its own. Nonetheless, for the sake of clarity a sketch of the relative positions of structures as apparently envisaged by C is appended (needless to say, because of lack of information, this cannot be to scale).
>
> The name, 'Gate of the Foundation' (v. 5), is not otherwise used of a gate in the Temple–Palace precinct. From the context it lies between the inner court of the Temple and the palace. In all probability it is the same as the 'Gate of the King to the east' (1 Chron. 9.18; cf. the 'Eastern Gate' of Neh. 3.29).

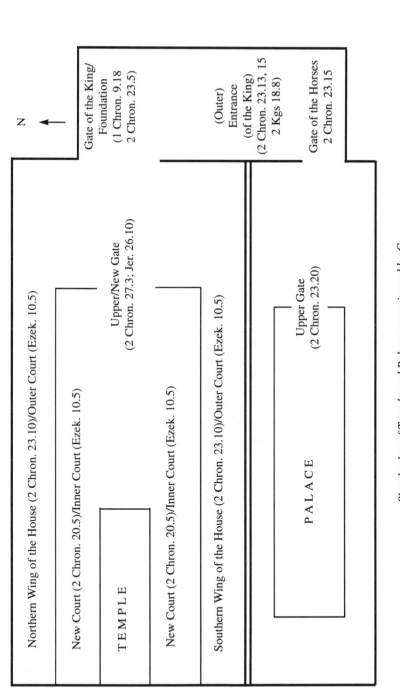

N ←

Northern Wing of the House (2 Chron. 23.10)/Outer Court (Ezek. 10.5)

New Court (2 Chron. 20.5)/Inner Court (Ezek. 10.5)

T E M P L E

Gate of the King/
Foundation
(1 Chron. 9.18
2 Chron. 23.5)

Upper/New Gate
(2 Chron. 27.3; Jer. 26.10)

New Court (2 Chron. 20.5)/Inner Court (Ezek. 10.5)

Southern Wing of the House (2 Chron. 23.10)/Outer Court (Ezek. 10.5)

(Outer)
Entrance
(of the King)
(2 Chron. 23.13, 15
2 Kgs 18.8)

P A L A C E

Upper Gate
(2 Chron. 23.20)

Gate of the Horses
2 Chron. 23.15

Sketch-plan of Temple and Palace as envisaged by C

The significance of 'Foundation' is not explained from the context. It is striking that the verb 'to found', to which it is related, occurs in 1 Chron. 9.22 of David's 'appointment' of the gatekeepers: is the reference to this institution? Alternatively—and more probably, perhaps—one may note that it is in this area that so many of the actions portrayed in C take place. In particular, it is the area where the king addressed the people (Solomon, 2 Chron. 6.13; Jehoshaphat, 2 Chron. 20.5). It is here, then, that the 'king's pillar' (v. 13), beside or on which the king stood for coronation to the acclamation of the people, is to be sought (hence, indeed, the name, the 'Gate of the King'). The common meaning 'foundation' (as commonly of the altar, e.g. Exod. 29.12) may thus rather in context mean 'base, plinth', on which the king's pillar stood, and on or at which the king stood to address his people.

It is further striking that the word usually translated 'pillar' is related to the verb 'to stand', and occurs with it in v. 13 and in both 2 Chron. 6.12-13 and 2 Chron. 20.5. The context suggests that it means here, therefore, not 'pillar', but 'platform' (this suggestion has been anticipated—see BDB for references; but it cannot, as preferred in BDB, refer to the pillars, in any case plural, of Jachin and Boaz, which were located immediately in front of the Temple porch, 2 Chron. 3.15-17). Compare 2 Chron. 34.31, where, in parallel to 2 Kgs 23.3, 'pillar', C has 'standing'.

2 Kgs 11.5-6 has a rather different (and even more problematical) text. It remains the professional troops and runners who are involved. The first third come on duty on the sabbath and guard the palace; the second are in the 'Gate of Sur', while the third are 'in the gate behind the runners'. The 'Gate of Sur' may be the equivalent of C's 'Foundation' (though it is in second place, not third), but is equally otherwise unparalleled (the verb related to it means 'to remove'; oddly enough, that verb is used of appointed personnel, including gatekeepers, not removing from duty, 2 Chron. 35.15; thus, the name may refer to the 'changing of the guard'). The suggestion in *BHK* and *BHS* that it should be read *sûs* (= 'horse') would relate it to the palace (cf. 2 Chron. 23.15).

Verse 6 underlines the sacral nature of C's presentation. Because the whole community, clergy and laity alike, is involved, it is essential that every part of the community respects its proper place, and that every requirement of the system of holiness in the Temple be thus observed: only those participants with the requisite degree of sanctification may have access to the appropriate parts of the Temple precinct. None must enter the sanctuary but the priests and their duly consecrated levitical assistants, for they alone possess the necessary sanctification. Israel must not undo the restoration of the Davidic monarchy by any slovenly breach of the LORD's requirements for holiness.

The sacral nature of C's presentation is made plain by comparison with 2 Kgs 11.7: there, the professionals are to guard the security, not the holiness, of the Temple.

From start to finish, those escorting the king into and out of the Temple must, then, be Levites (v. 7): just as the ark, the symbol of the victory of God on earth, is thus conveyed (1 Chron. 15.2), so the king of the house of David, the representative on earth of that victorious God, must be thus accompanied. The Levites will go with their 'instruments'. In the light of the use of the word in 1 Chron. 9.28-29, it would be natural to take 'instruments' in the sense of cultic utensils and implements (or musical instruments, cf. 1 Chron. 15.16). But, in the immediate context, it is more likely that 'weapons' are intended (cf. bloody reprisals of the Levites with their swords in Exod. 32.27-29), so that any profane person presuming to enter the Temple may be ejected by force.

Once again, in 2 Kgs 11.8 it is the professional soldiers who form the protective bodyguard round the king. It is they who bear arms lest anyone 'break through the ranks' (not 'into the Temple'). It is possible that C in his desire to turn the occasion into a sacral one did not consider the inappropriateness of the Levites bearing arms in the Temple.

At the end of v. 7, C inverts the verbs to produce the order: 'as he went in and as he came out'. This is the definitive departure of Joash from the Temple to take up his reign.

The account of the carrying out of the plan in v. 8 adds another detail to the procedure. The conveying of the king in and out of the Temple is enabled by the fact that both sets of priests, Levites and doorkeepers, those responsible for the new week of arranging the showbread and those whose week of duty has now expired, are kept on duty. This is a quite exceptional procedure for a quite exceptional moment (compare the other exceptional occasion of the dedication of the Temple in 2 Chron. 5.11). The organization of the replacement sets of Levites in connection with the showbread is prescribed in 1 Chron. 9.32. The same verb is used in 1 Chron. 9.33 for the normal succession of sets of Levites as in v. 8 here of Jehoiada's exceptional suspension of that practice. This procedure enables the king to be properly escorted without leaving the Temple unattended. For the unanimity of the action leading to the coup, it is essential to have all present: thus the text stresses that each leader brings his men with him, in fulfilment of the stipulations of 1 Chron. 9.25.

In 2 Kgs 11.9 the mustering of all the professional troops is connected
with the military success of the coup: it is the captains of hundreds who
gather their troops, not C's 'Levites and all Judah'. They then report
directly to Jehoiada for arming; C has replaced that note with the note on
Jehoiada's suspension of the normal roster of duties.

The commanders of the hundreds now cease to be mere messengers
and marshalls and assume their military role—but as the leaders of the
LORD's sacramental host (cf. the battle in 2 Chron. 20.21). Jehoiada
distributes the arms (v. 9), the spears, the shields and bucklers laid up
in the Temple, the house of the universal God, by David (1 Chron.
18.7) as tokens of the pacification of the kings of the earth. How more
appropriately could the LORD's host be armed than with the tokens of
the victory of his own purposes?

C has added 'the shields' (for completeness?) to the text of 2 Kgs 11.10
(cf. 2 Chron. 9.15-16; 12.9-10) and has changed the domestic name 'the
LORD' into the universal 'God'.

Jehoiada frames the action by drawing up (cf. 1 Chron. 6.31) the
common people around the outer court from the southern to the
northern wing (v. 10). They, too, are armed, each man with his lance,
as members of the LORD's host, ready for action.

In 2 Kgs 11.11 it is yet again the runners who are drawn up, 'each man
with his weapons'.

When all has been prepared, the escorts as representatives of the
whole community bring forth 'the son of the king' (v. 11 echoes
Jehoiada's words in v. 3) to be invested with the regalia proper to his
office. Four elements in the coronation ceremony are specified: the
crown, the testimony, the anointing and the acclamation. Each
expresses an aspect of the conferring of power or of the acknowledgment of authority.

–   The word for 'crown' is related to 'Nazirite', the individual
     who is separated from ordinary life by an oath of abstinence
     and dedication (Num. 6.1-21). The crown is thus the symbol
     of exclusive dedication to the one to whose service he is set
     apart (thus it is also used of the high priest's consecration and
     of the diadem, which is the symbol of that consecration,
     Exod. 29.6; Lev. 8.9; 21.12).
–   'Testimony' no doubt refers in the first instance to a state-
     ment of the rights and duties of the king. 1 Samuel 10.25

suggests that such a formal statement existed. The representatives of the people would be appropriate figures to present
such a list to the new king. The strongest association of the
word 'testimony' in the Hebrew Bible is, however, with the
Decalogue (Exod. 31.18; Deut. 4.13), as attestation of the
nature of God's relation with Israel, and with 'the ark of the
testimony', so called because the ark contained the tablets on
which the Decalogue was inscribed (Exod. 40.20). Such an
association is unlikely to be foreign to C for whom the
Davidic house is the means of realizing the significance of the
relationship between God and his people as once revealed to
Moses (cf. in near proximity to this passage 2 Chron. 24.6).
Quite what regalia, analogous to the crown, represented this
'attestation' is nowhere stated in the Hebrew Bible, unless it is
the *'eṣ'ādâ*, seemingly an armband, mentioned in association
with the crown in 2 Sam. 1.10, a word which also looks and
sounds quite like the word for 'testimony', *'ēdût* [cf. BDB].

– Anointing confers the authority of the one in whose name the
anointing is being carried out (cf. 1 Chron. 11.3). It is performed by those who are themselves anointed, Jehoiada the
high priest and his priestly sons. By authority of the duly
consecrated priest, God's authority is vested in the king.

– The shout, 'Long live the king!', is the traditional acclamation of the new monarch by the populace, as in 1 Sam. 10.24;
2 Sam. 16.16; 1 Kgs 1.25, 34, 39. Strikingly enough, all
these cases concern disputed succession, just as here the rights
of Joash to succeed have to be claimed against the usurping
queen mother. Popular acclamation has not figured in C's
presentation up until now: there has been no dispute about the
succession of the Davidic king within Judah until this crisis.

C has stressed the communal nature of the coronation: the verbs refer to
the people as a whole throughout, except for the anointing. In 2 Kgs
11.12 the bringing out of the king and the crowning are performed by
Jehoiada; the making king, the anointing and—Kings reads for 'Jehoiada
and his sons'—the clapping of the hands and acclamation are all performed by the people.

Athaliah's Discovery of the Counter-revolution (verses 12-13)
At the sound of the commotion, Athaliah emerges from the Palace. As
self-styled monarch, she makes her way along the kings' private

entrance (2 Kgs 16.18) to the Temple: the verb 'makes her way' (v. 12) comes from the same root as 'entrance' (v. 13).

It is likely that a still closer date may be put on the event. Ezekiel tells us that the inner eastern gate is open only on Sabbath and first of the month for the sacrifice of the 'prince' (Ezek. 46.1-2). The most significant first day of a month is New Year's Day (cf. Num. 29.1), the day of the celebration of the kingship of God (Lev. 23.24; Ps. 47) and, by extension, of his representative on earth, the Davidic king (e.g. Ps. 2). Thus, the chronological note at the beginning of the chapter, 2 Chron. 23.1, may be still more significant: this is the first day of the seventh year, New Year's Day, when the whole tradition of Jerusalem theology is celebrated. On such a day, then, popular expectation and religious excitement are at their peak. On such a day, furthermore, it would be possible for a great assembly to gather in Jerusalem without exciting suspicion.

> The phrase 'people of the land' occurs for the first time in C as a distinct technical term (cf. 1 Chron. 17.21). It recurs in 2 Chron. 23.20, 21; 26.21; 33.25; 36.1.

All Athaliah's self-proclaimed pretensions to rule in Jerusalem would on this day thus be under the scrutiny of the most intense religious expectation. How much more on the day when the High Priest, the authorized deputy of the Davidic house in the religious sphere, has contrived to arrange the coronation of the new Davidic king, the very day of the traditional coronation and renewal of vows!

No wonder that on this day Athaliah advances to claim her rights and to have her credentials endorsed. No wonder that, when she sees Joash enthroned at the same 'entrance' (v. 13, C's deliberate change from the 'according to custom' of 2 Kgs 11.14), on which she is advancing to claim her rights as the divine representative on earth in the Temple on this day of national renewal, she senses that the situation is irretrievable, and can only acknowledge (C has, merely, 'say', for the 'cry out' of Kings), 'Conspiracy! conspiracy!' Here is insurrection of the most basic sort: her pretensions, national and international, to rule in the name of God, are being challenged on the day of the highest religious claims and expectations possible. In a gesture of impotent rage and utter desolation (traditionally of mourning, as in 2 Sam. 1.2), that was at the same time the symbol of the passing of her power (cf. 1 Kgs 11.30?), she 'rent her garments'.

There are several features in the narrative with intense sacral significance and associations which make this interpretation about the occasion likely. These chiefly echo the tradition of the Jerusalemite cult, with its acclamation of the LORD as divine king and David as his agent and representative on earth. 'Praising the king' (v. 12, C's added phrase) echoes the major division of the Psalms, the hymns and thanksgivings sung by the levitical musicians, celebrating the triumphs of the LORD (cf., e.g., 1 Chron. 16.4); the 'blaring trumpets' around the king sounded by the priests, are associated with the announcement of the arrival of God in irresistible power and ineffable glory on the field of battle and in the ritualization of these cosmic conflicts within the liturgy of the cult (cf., e.g., 2 Chron. 7.6).

> C makes other notable adjustments to the underlying Kings text. The 2 Kgs 11.13 text of v. 12 begins with a difficult apposition: 'When Athaliah heard the voice of the runners [or: 'the pleasure?'], the people, she came...' C has transposed the difficult words, and eliminated any possible reference to the professional military, by reading, 'the people running...'
> In v. 13, after 'all the people of the land rejoicing and sounding on the trumpets', C adds, 'and the singers with the instruments of song and proclaiming to praise'.

Athaliah's Fate (Verses 14-15)
Jehoiada has a further commission for the 'captains of hundreds' (the 'appointed ones of the army' picks up the technical term, *pqd*, 1 Chron. 21.5): the removal of Athaliah from the Temple and her execution (v. 14). In the context of the time, there would be no hesitation about the execution of those who set themselves up in opposition to God and king (the action of Athaliah's parents against Naboth would provide a grim and ironical precedent for her fate, 1 Kgs 21.10). But that execution could not take place in the Temple; after all, it was because David had shed blood that he was debarred from building the Temple in the first place (1 Chron. 22.8). The death penalty must be exacted by those duly commissioned for the task, not by any unauthorized hand. As soon as she had crossed back over the threshold of the royal Palace out of the realm of the sacred, she was executed (v. 15).

> For the opening word of the section C has substituted 'and Jehoiada *brought out* the captains...' for the orthographically rather similar 'commanded' of 2 Kgs 11.15. It may be a case of a textual variant rather than a deliberate change, though 'bring out' matches the opening of v. 11. It also matches the form of the word, 'the appointed ones of the army',

which some wish to read as 'those in charge of the army' [*BHK*]. On the other hand, the repeated use of the same word in the same verse, 'and they brought her out', is inelegant.

C has retained 'ranks' in v. 14, although the word was replaced in v. 7. The voice and mood of 'be put to death' are changed: for Kings 'him who goes after her slay with the sword...let her not be put to death in the house of the LORD', C reads, 'he who goes after her shall be put to death...do not kill her...' The judicial death penalty falling on Athaliah is thus strengthened. Similarly at the end of v. 15, C reads, 'they put her to death', instead of 'she was put to death' as in 2 Kgs 11.16.

The phrase, 'they laid hands on her', may be idiomatically translated, 'they opened a passage for her' (cf. JPSV).

C makes it absolutely unambiguous that she is clear of the Temple area before she is put to death, by reading, 'she went to the entrance of the Gate of the Horses in the royal palace', for 'she went towards the Entrance of the Horses...' as in Kings.

For the Gate or Entrance of the Horses as one of the city gates, see Jer. 31.40 and Neh. 3.28.

2 CHRONICLES 23.16–24.27: THE REIGN OF JOASH

The reign of Joash is presented by MT in three main sections:

1. 2 Chron. 23.16–24.14: the restoration of the house of David under Jehoiada;
2. 2 Chron. 24.15-22: Joash's apostasy after the death of Jehoiada;
3. 2 Chron. 24.23-27: the Aramaean invasion of Judah and the assassination of Joash.

The material in 2 Chron. 23.16–24.27 is broadly based on 2 Kgs 11.17–12.21 but with many significant variations. The main independent section in C is 2 Chron. 24.15-22.

1. 2 Chronicles 23.16–24.14: The Restoration of the House of David under Jehoiada

The material is presented in two subsections which are in sacramental correspondence with one another: the restoration of the house of David (2 Chron. 23.16-21) and the restoration of the Temple (2 Chron. 24.1-14). For the interrelation of royal house and Temple, see 1 Chronicles 17. In this section the relationship between 'Levi' and 'David' is being explored (cf. 1 Chron. 2–8): between Jehoiada, the priest, who wields royal authority (2 Chron. 23.1; 24.16); and Joash, the king, who exercises initiative in the sphere of the cult (2 Chron. 24.4-14).

The Restoration of the House of David (2 Chronicles 23.16-21)
The king has been invested with crown and armband, anointed and acclaimed, but there still remain a number of formal aspects to the restoration of legitimate monarchy within Israel:

– the covenant with priest and people (v. 16);
– the destruction of the Baal cult (v. 17);

- arrangements for the protection of the Temple (vv. 18-19);
- the installation of Joash as king in the palace (v. 20).

A summary rounds off the account (v. 21), recording the joy of the community and the peace of the city. Finally, a line is drawn under the whole series of episodes of the disastrous links with the north, which had begun in 2 Chron. 18.1, by noting, once again, the execution of Athaliah.

Jehoiada's strong role in leadership is evident throughout this paragraph. Before the whole mighty *qāhāl* is dismissed from the Temple, he makes a covenant with them (v. 16). What the precise terms of the covenant are is not stated, merely, 'in order that they may become a people to the LORD'. What that means is indicated by the covenant partners. The covenant is not between God and people. It is three-way, between priest, people and king; it is through the due balance between these three parties, that the people will become the people of God. Jehoiada is, thus, no mere covenant mediator: he is himself an interested party, whose status is secured by the terms. As priest, he represents the vital role that the Temple has to play as the means of the sanctification of the people. The king has the essential function to discharge: to express and realize in the mould of David and Solomon what it means for Israel to be God's people in terms both of their own life and of their relations with the kingdoms of the earth. The people, for their part, must renew their commitment to render all that is due to Temple and Crown, in acknowledgment that it is only through these mechanisms that Israel's destiny can be realized.

> The distinctiveness of C's concept of the covenant is made clear by comparison with the Kings text. 2 Kgs 11.17 runs (chief differences italicized): 'Jehoiada made *the* covenant *between the* LORD, the king and the people to become a people to the LORD, *and between the king and the people*'. The LORD is covenant partner; Jehoiada is covenant mediator; the relation between king and people is subordinate to the covenant between God and people.

The destruction of the Baal cult (v. 17; cf. 2 Chron. 17.4) is an immediate corollary of the covenant. The sacramental bond between God and people is totally exclusive; no relationships with alternative deities are possible. It is all or nothing (e.g., 2 Chron. 15.2). The Baal sanctuary, with its altars and images, is, accordingly, razed to the ground; its priest becomes victim, defiling his own altars by his death. C has given no precise information about the setting up of such a cult in Jerusalem, only rather generalized references to the 'high places' (most recently in 2 Chron. 21.11) or the ways of the house of Ahab (2 Chron. 22.4); the plurals, 'altars' and 'images', indicate the worship of a multiplicity of deities from the Canaanite pantheon. The fundamental outrage for which that cult stands is the diversion of recognition that is due to God alone (as is expressed in 2 Chron. 24.7): the priest's name, Mattan ('gifts', given only in this context), expresses the benefits the people hope to receive from the cult, but which come from God alone, to whom alone the corresponding credit and thanks are to be given.

> The verse is reproduced almost unchanged from 2 Kgs 11.18. C abbreviates, omitting 'of the land' after 'all the people', and the adverb 'well' after 'they shattered its images'.

The positive side of the covenant is the safeguarding of the sole legitimate rights of the Jerusalem Temple (v. 18). Jehoiada installs those charged (root, *pqd*, cf. 1 Chron. 21.5) with responsibility for the Temple. By itself the word used might imply a military force (2 Chron. 17.14; that may be what is meant in the parallel in 2 Kgs 11.18, 'The priest set detachments [of troops] over the house of the LORD'). But in material now peculiar to himself, C proceeds to define the nature of those responsible (compare 1 Chron. 24.3, where the word is used of the priests). Within the inner court of the Temple these can be none other than 'the levitical priests whom David has assigned over the house of the LORD'. The double authority of Moses, the primary recipient of revelation (2 Chron. 17.9), and David, the executor, is invoked. With the system of the dedication of the people in place, the response of the worshipper can only be one of 'rejoicing [1 Chron. 12.40] and song'. Likewise, at the gates, Jehoiada positions (1 Chron. 6.31) the guardians to prevent the entry of anyone or anything unclean (v. 19; cf. 2 Chron. 29.16; 36.14 and the legislation in, for example, Lev. 10–15): again, these can be no secular armed force but only the levitical gatekeepers (1 Chron. 9.17-32).

The final act is the installation of Joash as king on the throne in his palace (v. 20). Once again, Jehoida marshalls the escort, the 'captains of the hundreds', as all through 2 Chronicles 23, the nobility (only here in C), the governors (the expression used otherwise in C only of God as ruler of the nations or of the kings) and the 'people of the land' (v. 13). The contrast is stark. They convey the new king in triumph through the upper gate (only here in the Hebrew Bible) of the courtyard of the Palace to sit on the throne of the kingdom (cf. 1 Kgs.7.7) past the very place in the Horse Gate where Athaliah is executed.

The whole populace is enraptured with joy (cf. 1 Chron. 12.40); the city is at peace (the condition of absence of strife, when the whole system is in equilibrium, 1 Chron. 22.9); the usurper is dead (v. 21). None of these elaborate installations is an end in itself, but the means whereby the quality of life intended by God for his people can be realized.

> C has again made subtle changes in vv. 20-21. The fundamentally military character of the incident is sustained in 2 Kgs 11.19-20: after, 'he took the captains of hundreds', it reads again 'the Carians and the runners' (cf. v. 1) for C's 'nobility and governors'. It is that armed escort that brings the king down from the Temple to the palace. They enter the palace by way of the 'Gate of the Runners' (cf. 2 Chron. 12.11). Thereafter, Joash is not made king, but simply 'sits/rules on the throne of the kings'. The contrast with Athaliah is made vivid in Kings by a final note that they slew her 'in the palace'.

The Restoration of the Temple (2 Chronicles 24.1-14)
The first phase of the presentation of Joash's forty-year reign (vv. 1-14) accounts for the major proportion of his life: he matures from childhood to youth, is married to two wives and has several children (v. 3); he 'later' busies himself about the maintenance of the Temple and this is done in two stages, the gathering of funds over a number of years (vv. 4-11) and the actual reconstruction (vv. 12-14). The major preoccupation of the reign, then, as befits a worthy descendant of David and Solomon, is the renovation of the Temple.

> 2 Kings.12.6 dates the situation which Joash confronts at the end of 2 Chron. 24.5 to his twenty-third year.
>   The note on Joash's mother, Zibiah ('gazelle', v. 1), who is otherwise unknown in the Hebrew Bible, may confirm the traditional values at least latent in his background: she comes from Beer-sheba, the southernmost outpost of Judah and thus the region furthest from the influences of the north. It is to be observed—however it is to be explained—that it was not she who sheltered the young prince during Athaliah's usurpation of the throne.

The assessment of the reign, 'he did what was right in the eyes of the LORD', is, however, ominously tempered: only 'as long as Jehoiada the priest was alive' (v. 2).

C emphasizes that that positive influence lasted all through Jehoiada's life. For the last phrase of v. 2, 2 Kgs 12.3 reads, 'during all his years in which Jehoiada the priest taught him', which suggests that the departure may have been during Jehoiada's last years.

At this point, C omits the qualification on Joash found in 2 Kgs 12.4: 'only the high places were not removed; the people were still sacrificing and burning offerings on the high places'. That negative element comes in later in vv. 17-27 (there is specific reference to the worship associated with the high-places in v. 18). C has thus taken the Kings evaluation, both positive and negative, split it and expounded each half separately with specific reference to attitudes towards the Temple (cf. discussion of framework element [4] in introduction to 2 Chron. 10–36).

The dependence of Joash on Jehoiada has to be total. It extends even to the arrangement of Joash's marriages by the chief priest (a detail peculiar to C, v. 3). The chaste limitation to two wives (enough, however, to enable the royal house 'to be fruitful and multiply', considering the parlous condition to which it had been reduced by the influence of the house of Ahab, 2 Chron. 21.4, 17; 22.8, 10) contrasts with the excesses of Rehoboam in 2 Chron. 11.23 and Abijah in 2 Chron. 13.21.

The dependence of king on priest is seen again in the matter of the restoration of the Temple (vv. 4-5). At first sight, it seems wholly laudable that Joash should 'conceive the notion' of 'renovating' the Temple (v. 4). It seems equally unexceptionable that he should have 'gathered' (v. 5, C's key term for securing the unanimity of Israel, 1 Chron. 11.1) the priests and the Levites to enlist their support for the project (the same verb is repeated later in the verse about the 'gathering' of the money). All the more puzzling, then, that, initially, the Levites did not expedite the matter.

C chooses his language deliberately in v. 4, 'it was in Joash's mind to renovate the Temple', in order to signal the problem of tension between king and Levites. This is precisely the expression used for David's plan to build the Temple in the first place (1 Chron. 22.7; 28.2; contrast 2 Chron. 29.10), the plan which was immediately modified by the word of the LORD through the prophet Nathan. Joash in his impulsiveness is a new David, and Jehoiada is to Joash as Nathan was to David.

A certain lack of theological harmony between king and Levites may be also indicated by his reference to the Temple as the 'house of *your* God' (v. 5), perhaps a portent of Joash's apostasy in vv. 17-18—unless the use

of the pronominal adjective is simply an attempt to give added urgency to
Joash's appeal to the Levites.

What was wrong with Joash's plan? His instructions are that the priests
and Levites should go round the cities of Judah on an annual basis to
collect contributions for the purpose from 'all Israel', and to do so as
a matter of urgency (v. 5a). It is only when Joash, in hurt and sur-
prise, summons Jehoiada as 'head', that is, as responsible for the
oversight of all the priests and Levites, in order to confront him with
the inaction of the Levites and with his own failure as their leader to
impress upon them the necessity for action (v. 6), that the truth of the
matter begins to dawn on Joash. He now states for the first time that it
is not simply a matter of eliciting voluntary contributions; what is
required is the enforcement of the levy stipulated by Moses and the
whole sacral assembly of Israel for the upkeep of the sanctuary.

It is not explicit which law in the Pentateuch C has in mind. But
Exod. 30.11-16, concerning the payment for the upkeep of the Tent of
Meeting of a ransom of a half-shekel per head when the people are
enlisted (for military or civil service, as in 1 Chron. 26.30; 2 Chron.
17.14; 26.11), provides the likely authority (cf. Num. 31.48-54). It is
striking that the words for 'duties' and 'enlistment' in Exod. 30.12
come from the same root (pqd) as the words for the king's
'supervision' and the 'official' of the chief priest, which are used in
the immediate context in 2 Chron. 24.11. The payment is to avert any
'plague', any possible punitive action against the people because they
are being numbered (cf. the presumptuousness of an improperly conducted census now familiar from 1 Chron. 21, where the root pqd
occurs in v. 5, and the staying of the 'plague' of the 'negative
Passover' at Ornan's threshing-floor in vv. 9-17).

C thus uses here vocabulary and ideas that are fundamental to his
purpose. The upkeep of the Temple is not a matter of the Levites
going about like itinerant tax-gatherers exacting from Israel whatever
Israel is disposed to pay: it is, as Joash now realizes, a matter of the
required rendering to God of the ransom price of the entire community (cf. 2 Chron. 34.9). The Temple thus maintained becomes the
visible expression of the petition by the people for the sparing of their
lives and of the acceptance by God of that petition. This annual payment, by which Israel acknowledge their vulnerability before God and
dependence upon him, is one of the 'holy things' that symbolize the
dedication of the whole of life to God. In this case, it is the stark

symbol of the fact that humanity depends on God and of total commitment to realizing what that dependence means. It is thus the absolute responsibility of Israel to bring these offerings to the Temple *themselves.* This again is but the rendering to God of what is his due and is to be done not *by* the Levites but *under* their supervision and monitoring.

Joash's lack of fundamental understanding may be indicated by the fact that he uses the key verb, *drš* (1 Chron. 10.13-14), in the sense of impressing a sense of duty upon the Levites rather than of rendering fundamental duty by the community as a whole. In Exod. 30.16 the term for the sanctuary is the 'Tent of Meeting'; here it is modified to the 'Tent of the Testimony', echoing the term used for the investiture of the king with the armband in 2 Chron. 23.11. In the Pentateuch the term 'Tent of the Testimony' is used only four times (Num. 9.15; 17.7-8; 18.2) as a shortened form of the 'Tent of Meeting in which is the ark of the testimony', or some such phrase (cf., e.g., Num. 7.89).

The above reading is based on the assumption that Joash is not entirely in the right nor is he enjoying a period of brief, if justifiable, ascendancy over Jehoiada; on the contrary, Jehoiada and the Levites are acting with total propriety—as the Levites are consistently throughout C's work, and as Jehoiada is in this section—and Joash is unjustified in his complaint against them. But it must be acknowledged that, on this assumption, the flow of ideas is somewhat difficult: 'The king summoned Jehoiada the chief; he said to him, "Why have you not required the priests to bring from Judah and Jerusalem the imposition of Moses the servant of the LORD and the sacral assembly of Israel to the Tent of the Testimony"'. The reading above takes the text of v. 6 as it stands, assuming that Joash is the speaker and that he undergoes a change of perspective as he begins to upbraid the priest.

This reading may be too influenced by the Kings text, where the opening, 'King Joash summoned Jehoiada the priest *and the priests* and said *to them...*', makes it unambiguous that Joash is, indeed, the speaker. But the text in C after 'why' is quite different in 2 Kgs 12.8 ('why are you not repairing the breaches in the Temple...?'). In C it is possible that Jehoiada is the subject of the verb 'he said' and that it is Joash that is the indirect object, 'to him' (for such an abrupt change of subject see, for example, v. 22). That is, it is Jehoiada who instructs Joash on the rights of Temple maintenance, basing himself on the Law of Moses.

Another possibility is that the text has suffered some elision in the adaptation from Kings or even some damage (it is difficult to see how the phrase, 'the sacral assembly of Israel' fits into the whole: in v. 9, the closely parallel text runs: 'the imposition of Moses the servant of God upon Israel in the wilderness'; v. 7 may well be displaced from following v. 4). The sequence of thought expected is that, when Joash summons Jehoiada, he asks him why, as the person in charge, he has not set the Levites to work. It is then Jehoiada who replies, pointing out the requirements already stipulated in the Law and the consequences for the collection of that money which that Law implies. In the light of that explanation, Joash then installs a chest for the collection of the payments.

In vv. 4-6, while there are many verbal echoes, C has very radically recast the underlying text in 2 Kgs 12.4-8. The reference there seems to be to a quite different law in the Pentateuch, that concerning vows in Leviticus 27 (compare the notion of 'assessment' of ability to pay linking the two passages, which contrasts absolutely with Exod. 30.15, where the insistence is on the need for all, rich and poor alike, to pay the same amount). In C's view, it is not such casual payments, which ordinarily belong to the emoluments of the priests (which even in Kings they are now to surrender), that are appropriate for the upkeep of the Temple. Only the stated obligation of the community as a whole, as it is enrolled for specific service to God, suffices for the maintenance of the sanctuary.

It is striking that the idea of 'assessment' also appears in connection with guilt and atonement in Lev. 5.15, 18; 6.6. This might seem to tie in well with C's overall use of these ideas throughout his work. But the concept of atonement is different between Exod. 30.11-16 and Lev. 5.14–6.7: in Exodus it is concerned with protecting existing oneness ('prospective, prophylactic atonement'), whereas in Leviticus it is about the restoration of a relationship that has been broken ('retrospective, reactive atonement'; cf. on 1 Chron. 21.5). Monies from this tainted source are inappropriate for repair work in the Temple (as already Kings points out, 2 Kgs 12.16).

The need for the renovation of the Temple is given in v. 7, which provides new details about the outrages of the regime of Athaliah. In its present context, v. 7 may be intended to be part Joash's speech to Jehoiada, rather than a free-standing explanation (which it could have been, had it followed v. 4). The reason for holding the explanation back until this point is the last phrase of v. 7. The sons of Athaliah, the embodiment of wickedness (2 Chron. 6.23), presumably before the Philistine–Arab invasion recorded in 2 Chron. 21.16-17; 22.1, had not just neglected the Temple, but had actively 'broken it down' and had left it in a ruinous condition. Worse, they had taken the 'holy things', the tokens of the people's loyalty to the LORD (1 Chron. 6.49; 26.26), paid year by year, and had applied them to the worship of the Baalim. In context, this taking of the 'holy things' may be not just the looting of the Temple; it may be the intercepting of the regular payments for the upkeep of the Temple and the diversion of them to a pan-Canaanite religious purpose. Athaliah's regime had meant not simply carelessness of Israel's tradition; it had posed a direct threat to the continuation of the house of David and the house of God, and had intended their replacement with a rival system.

Joash, as divinely delegated leader of the community, then gives command for the construction of a great chest for the collection of the 'levy for the upkeep of the sanctuary' (vv. 8-9). This is set 'outside the gate of the house of the LORD': for security, but also for freedom of access for the laity, one may assume that this chest is located at the east gate in the outer court of the Temple, near where other major transactions (cf. 2 Chron. 23.5) take place.

> Again, C has radically altered the text of 2 Kgs 12.10. There, it was Jehoiada who 'took a chest, bored a hole in its lid and placed it beside the altar on the right as one enters the house of God. The priests, the guardians of the threshold, put there all the silver...' Because C knows no intervention of the priests (let alone their duty as 'guardians of the threshold'; cf. 1 Chron. 9.17-29), he has to place the chest outside the inner court at a point where the laity, who make their contributions directly, are permitted entry.

The whole population, leader and ordinary person alike (cf. Exod. 30.15), respond with joy (C's key term for the ideal, united response of the community, 1 Chron. 12.40) to the proclamation of the levy (v. 10).

As the silver accumulates (vv. 10-11), the chest is emptied periodically (the expression may mean, precisely, 'daily'). Full formal procedures are followed: the Levites as keepers of the threshold bring the chest for the supervision of the king, the leader, in principle, of the people. But both anointed figures, the king and the chief priest, as the king's now necessary representative in cultic matters, have the shared responsibility of supervising the storing of the levy: the king through his secretary (a Levite?; cf. 1 Chron. 18.16) and the priest through an unnamed delegate.

> C in his desire to follow procedures of access to the Temple courts punctiliously has added the phrase, 'when the time came to bring the chest for the supervision of the king by the hand of the Levites', which links rather poorly with the underlying 2 Kgs 12.11 text, 'when they saw that the silver had accumulated'. The chest being ceremoniously presented to the royal official, there is now no need for him to 'come up' (Kings) to the Temple; C reads only 'come'. In Kings it was the 'High Priest' himself,

no deputy, who, along with the king's secretary, put the silver in bags
and dispensed it to the craftsmen. C adds a phrase about the return of the
chest to its position.

It is then king and priest directly who hand on the money to the foreman (perhaps read 'foremen', as implied by 2 Chron. 34.10) of the
works. The necessary craftsmen, stone-masons and metal-workers, are
hired (v. 12). There is a strong correspondence between the works
necessary for restoration and the works originally required for construction under David and Solomon (for example, for the phrase, 'the
work of the service of the house of the LORD', cf. 1 Chron. 28.20).
The work of restoration proceeds apace; they put the Temple to rights
in accordance with its original plan (v. 13). When all has been accomplished, there are still funds left over and the balance is applied—
again conjointly by king and priest—to make implements for use in
the Temple cultus, as in Solomon's original execution (v. 14; cf.
2 Chron. 4.22). Thus is made possible the restoration of the rites in
the Temple, symbolized by the resumed daily burnt offerings morning
and evening, the *tāmîd*, 'all the days of Jehoiada'. The life's work of
the aged priest has been accomplished.

Again the material in C, though it contains echoes of 2 Kgs 12.12-17
(besides obvious ones like, 'workmen', 'reinforce', 'the house of the
LORD', there is a more subtle one: the word 'original plan', *matkōnet*,
v. 13, is strikingly similar to the silver *mᵉtukkān* ['allocated'] in 2 Kgs
12.11 [12, MT]), is markedly different in a number of respects. Kings
adds craftsmen in wood to the number of tradesmen employed. The information about cultic implements contradicts Kings, where it is explicitly
stated that the surplus silver was *not* applied for the making of utensils.
Kings adds a note that no accounts were kept: the craftsmen were implic-
itly trusted to get on with the job in total honesty.

2. 2 Chronicles 24.15-22: Joash's Apostasy
after the Death of Jehoiada

It would appear that the period of Joash's apostasy occurs only in the
very last years of his life. The prophecy of Jehoiada's son, Zechariah
(vv. 20-22), is followed the next year by the murder of Joash (vv. 23-
27). It is not stated what length of time intervened between the death
of Jehoiada, the falling away of Joash and the prophecy of Zechariah
(vv. 15-19), but the impression is that it all took place in a relatively
short period.

This section is divided into three sub-sections: vv. 15-16, the death of Jehoiada; vv. 17-19, the apostasy of Joash and vv. 20-22, the murder of the prophet Zechariah, son of Jehoiada.

This section has no counterpart in Kings.

Verses 15-16: The Death of Jehoiada
Jehoiada is a paragon figure. The prodigious length of his life, surpassing even the one hundred and twenty years of Moses (Deut. 34.7), is testimony to a superabundance of blessing. The unique blessing is matched by the unique regard in which he is held. Alone of commoners in C, he receives burial in the royal tombs in Jerusalem. It is not simply that he had married into the royal house (2 Chron. 22.11); he is himself virtually a royal figure (2 Chron. 23.1). His honorific burial is richly deserved through his actions in his own right. It was he who kept the faint flicker of the Davidic house and of the LORD's worship alive through the dark days of Athaliah's usurpation. It was he who organized the successful coup against Athaliah that brought about the restoration of the Davidic house and of the Temple. After the restoration, he remained the power behind the throne; Joash could do nothing without his sanction, not even such an apparently laudable act as the renovation of the Temple. (There is also a contrast being prepared here with the ultimate fate of Joash himself who was *not* buried in the royal graves, v. 25. Jehoiada was the truly royal figure, in all but name.) The outcome of Jehoiada's life and work is summed up in one of C's key terms: 'good' (2 Chron. 7.10; 10.7; 12.12; 19.3), defined here as a three-way harmony between people, God and priestly house.

This is a moment in which much of the argument of C is summed up: a priest can attain to royal dignity, but only in so far as he has succeeded, through commitment to God, to deliver welfare for his people. This is, of course, a reflection of the realities of the post-exilic period in which C was writing, when the royal house is in abeyance and the High Priest has taken over the status of the anointed one (cf. Zech. 6.11). But C's view is no mere reflection of historical realities or of political expediencies. God's fundamental aim is to realize through Israel his purpose of welfare for the human race. It is the instrumentality of Israel in that task that remains in the forefront. The means whereby Israel is enabled to attain that role may be through monarchy; but its status is conditional. If it fails, it is replaced. What will endure is the Law of Moses and it is that law which Jehoiada has been instrumental in maintaining and vindicating.

Verses 17-19: The Apostasy of Joash
As soon as the strong influence of Jehoiada is removed, Joash falls away. Dependency turns into impressionability. A wilfulness has already been seen in him in vv. 4-6; now that wilfulness is compounded with megalomania as the leaders in the country come and prostrate themselves to him (v. 17). Here is a perversion of the Davidic tradition. The king is the representative and agent of God on earth; the human king sits on the divine throne; prostration is an acknowledgment of this status (1 Chron. 29.20). But, if the divine element is misconstrued, the honour to the king becomes a blasphemy.

These nobles must represent a survival of the faction that had supported Athaliah. They follow a policy of a return to the old gods, of the integration of Judah into the internationalism of the older Canaanite religion.

Verse 18 expresses in compressed form the overall case that C is arguing against his people in his work; almost every term is loaded with theological significance. Together, king and nobility 'reject the house of the LORD, the God of their fathers'. 'Reject' is C's key term for the depriving of God of what is due to him (1 Chron. 28.9, where it is coupled, as here, with 'serve'). What has been rejected is succinctly but comprehensively stated: the Temple with all its symbolism of the cosmic reign of God, the personal relationship with God under the name, 'the LORD', by which he is known to Israel, and the tradition handed down from the fathers, David and Moses (cf. 1 Chron. 5.25). In immediate terms, all that Jehoiada had risked his life for, all that Joash himself had been preserved for, and all that Joash has hitherto accomplished, is forfeited. Those in leadership in the community revert not just to the ways of the house of Ahab, but to the condition of the time of Saul: to the worship of the *asherim*, the wooden posts symbolical of Canaanite female deity (2 Chron. 14.3), and the 'idols' (the only other occurrence of the word in C is in 1 Chron. 10.9 in relation to Saul's defeat by the Philistines, that ever-present lurking alien force, 1 Chron. 1.12). Little wonder that the 'fury' of God (1 Chron. 27.24) is unleashed against a king who at one stroke has undone his own and his mentor's life's work and has taken his people back to a state of primordial alienation and guilt (1 Chron. 21.3).

Equally, in v. 19, C focuses on the unwavering purpose of God. He 'sends' prophets: they are unnamed but a succession is implied (cf. 2 Chron. 25.15; 36.15). They are sent to 'bring them back' to God (2 Chron. 19.4) and 'to warn' (the verb from the root of 'testimony', v. 6) of dire consequences, but to no avail.

Verses 20-22: The Murder of the Prophet Zechariah, Son of Jehoiada
The prophet singled out for mention is Zechariah, son of the lately deceased chief priest, Jehoiada—and so, through his mother, Joash's protector, first cousin to Joash (see family tree at 2 Chron. 22.9). None could be more aware of the turmoil of the momentous days through which Temple and dynasty had recently passed. None could be more painfully conscious of the cost of the forfeiture of all the gains made by Jehoiada.

His words are prompted by the Deity in his cosmic form: 'the spirit of God clothed him' (v. 20). This is one of the standard expressions for enrapture by inspiration (already in 1 Chron. 12.18, where, again, it is no professional prophet who is involved, but a lay person who has been actively engaged in events; compare an alternative form of the metaphor in 1 Chron. 5.26).

Zechariah takes his stand on some eminence (the vocabulary recalls the location of Abijah's address as of a prophet to the north in 2 Chron. 13.4, or of Jehoshaphat to his army in 2 Chron. 20.20); might it, with great irony, be the very spot where Joash himself had once stood in full view of the people to be acknowledged as king (2 Chron. 23.13; compare the place where he is stoned in v. 21)?

Zechariah's prophetic word, concise though it is, is in four parts and compasses essentials of C's theology (v. 20):

- the opening 'messenger formula', 'Thus says the LORD', to authenticate the word (cf. 1 Chron. 17.4);
- a rhetorical question that functions as an accusation, 'Why are you transgressing the commandments of God?'—the basic fault of Israel is the denial of God of his rights;
- the verdict: 'you will not prosper'; 'prosper' is C's key term for the blessings that flow from commitment to God's rights (1 Chron. 22.11);
- the reason: 'if you forsake the LORD, he will forsake you', the use of the key verb as in v. 18, expressed now in terms of sacramental theology. If the duly appointed agents of God

forsake him, they by that act invalidate themselves for their role (2 Chron. 15.2).

Joash will have none of continued dependence on the tradition of Jehoiada and of continuing influence from his family. It is he himself who gives the order for conspiracy against Zechariah. This is yet another irony—as he had come to the throne by conspiracy against Athaliah (2 Chron. 23.13), so he now rids himself by conspiracy of the support that had brought him to the throne (he is himself to be the target of conspiracy in v. 25). The ironies mount with the outrages. Though on his accession care was taken not to pollute the Temple with the blood of the 'wicked' Athaliah, now, by Joash's order, Zechariah is murdered in the Temple where he officiates as priest. The fate that had been meted out to Mattan, priest of Baal (2 Chron. 23.17), is now meted out to the son of the chief priest of the LORD in his own sanctuary. The act was no doubt intentional: Joash, having abandoned the Temple of the LORD, now wished to pollute it and thus make it unfit for worship. The means of the murder—by stoning—implies that it was a judicial act undertaken by the whole community—an act of judicial murder (cf. 2 Chron. 10.18).

So Joash repays the debt he owes to Jehoiada's steadfastness. What Joash wants to pass off as a judicial sentence, carried out by due process of law (as did his great-grandfather, Ahab, in the case of Naboth, 1 Kgs 21.13), C calls by its proper name, 'murder' (v. 22).

The incident closes with a grim inclusio. 'Joash did not remember' (v. 22) picks up Zechariah's own name, 'the LORD has remembered' (v. 20). What man conveniently forgets, the LORD notes. Zechariah dies with such an appeal on his lips, in words of ominous import: 'May the LORD see and may he exact!' 'May the LORD see' picks up the association of the sacrifice of Isaac at the sanctuary on Mount Moriah, where the Temple now stands (2 Chron. 3.1), which Abraham had called, 'The LORD will see' (the 'Jehovah-jireh' of AV, Gen. 22.14). The phrase, 'May the LORD exact', picks up precisely the key word, *drš* (1 Chron. 10.13-14), now used in an awesome sacramental sense: those who do not seek are by that act themselves sought out.

3. 2 Chronicles 24.23-27: The Aramaean Invasion of Judah and the Assassination of Joash

Verses 23-25: The Aramaean Invasion

When disorder is rife in the people whom God intends to be for the nations what the nations themselves cannot be, that people forfeits its status and becomes absorbed by those very nations from among which it took its origins (so, e.g., 2 Chron. 12.2-12). This time the Aramaeans are the agents. Those enemies, because of whom Joash's great-grandfather, Jehoshaphat, had become so inextricably enmeshed with the house of Ahab (2 Chron. 18), and against whom his own father, Ahaziah, had campaigned in alliance with the house of Ahab with such disastrous consequences (2 Chron. 22.5-9), are now the instruments of condign punishment against Joash.

It is no doubt with such memories of Judah's earlier complicity in attacks on Aramaean-held territory, that the Aramaeans launch their attack on Judah (v. 23). It is time for such a recurrent menace to be dealt with once and for all. But of such military considerations C takes no note (except to record that the campaign takes place at the regular season for war, see 1 Chron. 20.1). C is concerned with the theological factors: in sacramental theology where punishment is the counterpart of failure, as reward is of faithfulness, punishment has to fit the crime exactly.

- Judah and Jerusalem, precisely the realm of Joash, are the goal of the Aramaean invasion.
- The invaders 'destroy': this is again the 'negative Passover', as in 1 Chron. 21.12.
- It is the 'nobles' who are singled out. They are the ones who had 'prostrated themselves' to Joash in v. 17 and had been instrumental in leading him astray. But the common people have to suffer the loss of status as a people with them. As in the case of Saul, no man dies to himself, let alone a misguided aristocracy.
- The booty is sent to the king of Damascus. The spoils of war that Israel had expected as a matter of course to take for themselves (e.g. 2 Chron. 14.12), indeed to offer to God in the Temple as testimony to his universal sovereignty—the very point at issue in 1 Chron. 2.7—are now dispatched to

Damascus. The gods of the Aramaeans are seemingly the cosmic victors.

- The outcome of the battle is determined by the righteousness of the cause, not by the size of the opposing armies: that point had been argued in Israel's favour in, e.g., 1 Chron. 14.15; 2 Chron. 14.11; now it is turned against them (v. 24).

- The 'negative Passover' motif is again employed in the 'judgments' that are enacted against Joash (v. 24): 'judgments' picks up the LORD's demonstrations of power against Egypt and the gods of Egypt in Exod. 6.6; 7.4; 12.12.

- Joash's end matches the fate of his own victims (v. 25): when the Aramaeans withdraw leaving him totally incapacitated with wounds (yet another key root, cf. 1 Chron. 10.3), his own followers conspire against him, as Athaliah's had against her to bring him to the throne (2 Chron. 23.13). As he had arranged the murder of Jehoiada's son (v. 25 now reads, 'sons' to compound the felony) at his own altar to pollute his own sanctuary, so he, as murder victim, is denied a resting place in the royal sepulchre (cf. Ahaziah, 2 Chron. 22.9).

C's account corresponds to 2 Kgs 12.17-18, but with marked differences. The campaign of Hazael, king of the Aramaeans of Damascus, is primarily against the Philistine town of Gath. Only then did he turn his attention to Jerusalem. Joash by raiding the treasuries of palace and Temple buys Hazael off. The conspiracy against Joash and his murder are mentioned (2 Kgs 12.20-21), but in rather different terms: C links Joash's death with the deaths of Jehoiada's sons and has changed the verb 'to murder' to make it correspond to the death of Zechariah in v. 22. Kings further states that Joash *was* 'buried with his fathers in the city of David'.

Verses 26-27: The Assassins of Joash

The names of the two conspirators (which otherwise do not occur in the Hebrew Bible) are given as in 2 Kgs 12.22 (with modifications), with the addition that their mothers were respectively Ammonite and Moabite. The half-foreign origin of the two assassins may serve two purposes for C: they remove blood-guilt from Israel; they show the constant readiness of destructive powers to invade Israel from the world of the nations, if Israel in any way falls short of the destiny envisaged for her.

A further note alludes to the running prophetic commentary on the reigns of the kings: in Joash's case, it deals with his sons, the pronouncements concerning him and the refounding of the Temple. C has provided material on each of these except the first (apart from the note in 2 Chron. 24.3). C is interested only in his son and successor, Amaziah, to the account of whose reign he now turns.

2 CHRONICLES 25.1–26.2: THE REIGN OF AMAZIAH

The presentation of the reign of Amaziah is dominated by his tangled relations with Judah's immediate neighbours to south and north: his campaigns against Edom, and the impact these campaigns have on his relations with the Israel of the north. The point at issue is how far Amaziah is true to the tradition of David and whether he can exercise effective rule in the name of the LORD over these unruly neighbours and rivals. The answer turns out to be largely negative.

Though the reign lasts for twenty-nine years (v. 1), it is the first fourteen of these (v. 25) that preoccupy C, the period of his particular rivalry with Joash, king of the north. The reign is divided into five main sections:

1. 2 Chron. 25.1-4: standard annalistic framework elements (1)–(4); Amaziah's consolidation on the throne;
2. 2 Chron. 25.5-10: the mustering of Judah and the abandoned hiring of assistance from the north;
3. 2 Chron. 25.11-16: the campaign against Edom and its consequences;
4. 2 Chron. 25.17-24: Amaziah's disastrous campaign against the north;
5. 2 Chron. 25.25–26.2: the assassination of Amaziah.

2 Chronicles 25.1–26.2 is broadly based on 2 Kgs 14.2-22, but with much freedom and independent material, especially vv. 5-11a, 12-16.

The cross-references between Judah and the north in this reign require a preliminary review of the family trees of the respective royal houses (the source is 2 Kgs 10–14, taken at face value). To avoid confusion, C provides pedigrees in vv. 17, 23, 25.

Amaziah bears a name of high orthodoxy, 'The LORD has been strong'; the verb is the same as in 'be courageous', in the standard exhortation to the successor to the Davidic king (1 Chron. 22.13). As always at the accession of a new Davidic king, hopes are high that in this generation Israel will attain its true destiny.

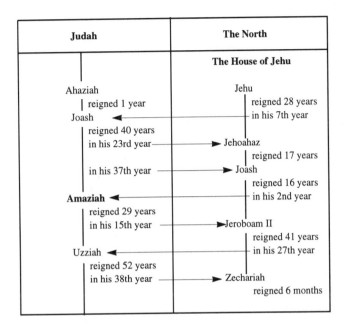

1. 2 Chronicles 25.1-4: Standard Annalistic Framework Elements; Amaziah's Consolidation on the Throne

Amaziah's mother, who is otherwise unknown in the Hebrew Bible, bears a name equally programmatic to that of her son: 'The LORD is delight' (KBS); her origin in the capital, Jerusalem, places her in a good position to appreciate the yearnings associated with the Davidic house and the practical ambiguities involved in trying to realize them.

In the light of the subsequent narrative, the positive theological evaluation, 'he did what was right in the eyes of the LORD' (v. 2), retained in part from 2 Kgs 14.3, is surprising. Only in the first recorded episode of his reign (vv. 5-10) does Amaziah heed prophetic warning—and that during an incident in which he should never have become embroiled. Well might, then, C add the qualification, 'but not with a whole heart' ('whole', *šālēm*, may be an ironical play on the name of 'Solomon' [1 Chron. 29.19], the original recipient of the encouragement, 'Be courageous').

> Kings relates rather to David, 'yet not as his ancestor David', and adds, 'as all his father Joash had done'.

Once again, as in the case of Joash (2 Chron. 24.2), C has delayed the exposition of the negative element in the evaluation of 2 Kgs 14.4, 'only, the high places were not removed...' (see discussion of framework element [4] in the Introduction to 2 Chron. 10–36). C will deal with a specific example of this refusal to give the LORD his due in worship in vv. 14-16.

The first step is the confirmation of the new king in his position (rather than 'in his possession' as in 2 Kgs 14.5; the same root is used at the beginning of v. 3 as of Solomon in 2 Chron. 1.1; so again in the resumption in v. 11, after C's explanation of how he was confirmed). To purge the guilt of his father's murder, and, no doubt, to clear himself of any suspicion of complicity in the act, he has the assassins put to death (cf. 2 Sam. 1.1-16).

C changes the verb from Kings to make it correspond with his description of the action of the culprits in 2 Chron. 24.25.

As in 2 Kgs 14.6, the families of the murderers do not suffer for the crimes of their fathers (v. 4). The law restricting liability appealed to is in Deut. 24.16.

For the, 'in the book of the Law of Moses' of Kings, C reads, 'in the Law, the book of Moses', thus seeming to draw a distinction between the Law and the work in which it is codified.

The formulation of the law is slightly different from the version in Kings and Deuteronomy: C reads three times, 'shall die', for the 'shall be put to death' of Kings (*qere* in last case). C has broadened out the legislation into a general principle.

This law, dealing with inter-human crimes and the limitation of penalties between the families of wronged parties, is quite distinct from crimes committed by the individual Israelite, or by the nation of Israel as a whole, against God (the theme of C's work). In that case, collective, cumulative guilt has been incurred, the effects of which it takes generations to efface (cf. the Decalogue, Exod. 20.5). Thus, foreign nations guilty of atrocity against God's people must also bear collective guilt, as in the case of the Edomites, whose penalty is about to be recorded in v. 12.

Out of the record of Amaziah's single campaign against the Edomites, which immediately follows in 2 Kgs 14.7 (picked up momentarily by C in v. 11), C has developed a number of incidents to expound the evaluation, both positive and negative, of Amaziah's reign.

2. *2 Chronicles 25.5-10: The Mustering of Judah and the Abandoned Hiring of Assistance from the North*

Amaziah 'gathers' (the key word for the unified action of God's people, 1 Chron. 11.1) Judah (v. 5). So eager is C to raise the theological issues that he does not even delay to inform the reader in this section about Amaziah's objective in raising this 'host' (presumably, it is in connection with the campaign against the Edomites, v. 11). He draws up (1 Chron. 6.31) Judah ('and Benjamin' is now added) in traditional order as the citizen army 'by fathers' houses', under their military leaders, 'the captains of thousands and captains of hundreds'. Then he 'musters' them: here again a technical term (*pqd*) is introduced, which leads deep into theological matters.

The reference is once more to the legislation on the national muster in Exod. 30.11-16 (referred to already in 2 Chron. 24.6; see 1 Chron. 21.5). As there, the age group concerned are 'the twenty-year-olds and upwards', that is, all those old enough to bear arms (Num. 1.3, 20-45; 26.2). The troops at Amaziah's disposal (those who 'sally forth [1 Chron. 1.12] as the host [1 Chron. 5.18]') from Judah and Benjamin, infantrymen armed with 'lance and shield' turn out to be 300,000 (for comparative statistics see 1 Chron. 5.18; no 'bowmen' from Benjamin this time, contrast 2 Chron. 17.17).

Now comes Amaziah's astonishing action (v. 6). When the people are numbered for war, each, according to the legislation in Exod. 30.13, should pay a half-shekel 'redemption', a prospective indemnity for the life of Israel in anticipation of killing in battle. A force of 300,000 would thus pay 150,000 shekels, or 50 talents of silver.

> For the calculation of the number of shekels to the talent, see Exod. 38.25-26. There those mustered amount to 603,550. At a half-shekel redemption per head they should contribute 301,775 shekels. What they contributed is defined as 100 talents, 1775 shekels. Therefore, 100 talents = 300,000 shekels; 1 talent = 3,000 shekels.

This sum, again according to the legislation in Exod. 30.13, should be devoted to the maintenance of the sanctuary. It is precisely double this payment that Amaziah proposes to misapply in order to hire 100,000 troops from the north.

No wonder the unnamed 'man of God' is outraged (v. 7). His message is a straightforward prohibition and imperative: 'do not let the northern host go with you; you go alone'. The reason why the north must not go with Amaziah is that the LORD is not 'with' them. The 'messianic' significance of the apparently commonplace preposition, 'with' ('*im*), has already been explained in 1 Chron. 11.9; it enshrines central affirmations of Jerusalemite 'Immanuel' theology. There is but one sovereign LORD and the Davidic king is his sole representative and agent on earth; the hosts led by the Davidic king are the sacramental representation on earth of the cosmic hosts that the LORD has at his disposal. The north, as a schismatic and apostate kingdom, has forfeited its status of belonging to that people; it can thus play no part with Judah and Benjamin, the remnant of the true host of Israel; its 'host' is a non-power, indeed, a negative force, which, because it has lost its sacramental status, can only bring disaster on Amaziah.

There must be another factor in the prophet's reaction. The point of paying the 'redemption' money of half a shekel per head to the sanctuary when the host of Israel is mustered for battle is to secure the safety of the army. It is to protect them, so that no 'blow' befalls them (Exod.30.12), from God and their foes. To use the redemption money to secure protection against God by hiring an army from the non-power of the north is an absurdity.

Once again the choice for the sacramental figure is a stark either/or (2 Chron. 15.2). Amaziah must 'go' alone (v. 8), in which case he will be 'strong' (the key word of 1 Chron. 22.13) in battle; if not, the LORD will inevitably cause him to 'stumble' (the verb is used again in 2 Chron. 28.23). The fundamental theological truth is that mere numbers, in this case an extra 100,000, count for nothing (1 Chron. 14.15; 2 Chron. 14.11); the will of the cosmic God (the universal title of deity is used here) must prevail, no matter what forces are deployed on the field of battle.

What, then, is Amaziah to do with his costly investment in this raiding party (1 Chron. 12.18) from the north? He is told simply to cut his losses. Here is a colossal challenge to normal scales of human values: better to sever connections made even at high cost, if these relationships are illicit, and to rely on 'the power of the LORD to provide still more'.

Thus there follows (v. 10) the response of Amaziah which, to C, merits the positive evaluation in v. 2, that 'he did what was right in the eyes of the LORD'. He reverses his reliance on dubious human support and depends on the LORD alone. He dismisses the Ephraimites from the ranks of his troops, despite the enormous cost and the humiliation in the eyes of the enemy and of his own troops that the reversal of policy must mean. The Ephraimites, filled with indignation at this slight, do not wait long to wreak vengeance (v. 13).

3. 2 Chronicles 25.11-16: The Campaign against Edom and its Consequences

MT subdivides into three sections.

2 Chronicles 25.11-12: The Successful Campaign against Edom
Verse 11 picks up v. 3: Amaziah is truly 'established' on the throne by his exclusive reliance on the LORD, even when that reliance, by any human reckoning, could only seem to have weakened his position.

The consequences of this 'being established' are soon revealed: a renewed demonstration of the authority of the Davidic house over a recalcitrant neighbour. The phrase, 'Amaziah...led his people' (v. 11) as of a shepherd his flock, uses one of the standard metaphors for monarchy in the ancient Near East (2 Chron. 18.16; cf. 1 Chron. 20.1).

C finally informs the reader of the goal that Amaziah has been pursuing—an expedition against the kingdom of Edom, Judah's neighbour to the south. No immediate motive for the attack is given. It is now more than half a century since, in the time of Jehoshaphat, Edom had actually invaded Judah (2 Chron. 20.10-23) and, in the time of Jehoram, had finally regained its independence (2 Chron. 21.8-10; no incident in the interim is recorded by Kings either, to explain the conflict). The scene of the engagement in 'the Valley of Salt' may give a clue: this is presumably the rift valley south of the Dead Sea ('the Sea of Salt', Gen. 14.3, etc.). In realistic, historical terms, the campaign is likely to have been envisaged as the reopening of Judah's trade route south to the Gulf of Aqaba (an aim only accomplished by Amaziah's son and successor, Uzziah, 2 Chron. 26.2). But there was recurrent border friction. The territory of Judah, the southernmost tribe of Israel, abuts the territory of Edom at Mt Seir: in some contexts that southern frontier is defined as 'Mt Halak which ascends to Seir' (Jos. 11.17; 12.7). 1 Chronicles 4.42 has already recorded how 500 Simeonites settled Mt Seir, having driven out the remnant of fugitive Amalekites.

The fury of Judah at the gloating pleasure of Edom over the sack of Jerusalem in 587 BCE might be another factor in the way in which the narrative is written up (cf. Obadiah).

To the modern reader the treatment meted out on Edom by Amaziah is horrifying (cf. 1 Chron. 5.22): 10,000 slaughtered in battle (v. 11); a further 10,000 taken prisoner and summarily executed by throwing them down from a crag (v. 12; the word 'crag' may cross-refer to the equally horrifying ending of Ps. 137.9; cf. 1 Chron. 20.3). The episode appears to be nothing less than a war crime. The narrative has, however, to be read within its own terms. Israel's relations with Edom can only be understood in the light of Jerusalemite theology (v. 12 has no parallel with Kings and must be taken as a reflection of C's point of view). In Genesis 27 the relationship between Edom and Israel has already been portrayed in terms of the two brothers, Esau (equated with Edom) and Jacob (equated with Israel). Esau surrenders to Jacob the rights of the first-born; Jacob usurps the blessing of their common father—it is he who shall have dominion over his brother (Gen. 27.29, 37). This narrative has been transposed into monarchical terms by C: Edom had kings before Israel (1 Chron. 1.43-51), but, once the monarchy of the house of David is established, primacy passes to Israel; Edom is subjugated by David (1 Chron. 18.11-13); the rights of dominion are conferred by God himself. It is thus a particular exposure of the weakness of the Davidic house that subsequent generations have been unable to exercise this dominion over Edom. It is not a matter of conquest, but of recognition. Both Israel and Edom have equal rights to their respective territories and neither should encroach on the other. But a successful campaign led by Amaziah is a significant reassertion of the status and role of the Davidic house and a putting to rights of earlier neglect, indeed infringement, of that status. The unfortunate Edomites are props (in all probability largely unhistorical props, it may be said) in the dramatization of this truth: dominion and justice, the effectiveness of the divine regime through the Davidic house, stand in the forefront and woe betide any who resist or detract. That is an uncomfortable truth that remains, as this drastic narrative illustrates.

2 Kgs 14.7 uses 'Edom' for 'Sons of Seir': for C the terms appear to be interchangeable—'Edom' in vv. 14, 19, 20, 'Seir' in vv. 11, 14 (so again, e.g., 1 Chron. 1.38 'Seir'; 1 Chron. 1.43, 51, 54 'Edom'). In the Hebrew Bible, Mt Seir was originally inhabited by the Horites. They were

displaced by the Edomites, viewed as the descendants of Esau, just as the indigenous population of Canaan were displaced by Israel (Gen. 36.20; Deut. 2.5, 12).

For v. 12, 2 Kgs 14.7 has: 'he captured Sela in battle and called it Joktheel to this day'. Sela is the capital of Edom. C may be exploiting its meaning simply as 'rock' in this context, not necessarily equating the place of execution with the Edomite capital. If 'Joktheel' could by something of a pun or popular etymology be held to mean, 'may God kill', that might have given C the idea for the development of the story as a theodicy.

2 Chronicles 25.13: The Looting of Judah by the Disaffected North

The northern troops, whom Amaziah had hired for the campaign against Edom only to dismiss, vent their rage at being thus humiliated and denied share in the possible booty by plundering (1 Chron. 10.8; 14.9) and murdering in 'the cities of Judah from Samaria to Beth-horon'. There may be a certain ridicule implied by the geography. These cities belong to the north. In 1 Chron. 6.68; 7.24 Beth-horon is located in Ephraim (and if Beth-horon, all the more Samaria, which lies still further north). Now, admittedly, some modest gains in territory at the expense of the north have been attributed to Judah (2 Chron. 13.19). But on the whole the impotent fury of the rejected troops must have been directed against their own people, however much in principle or in practice these lands belonged to Judah. The cowardly barbarity of the north has thus been exposed as they make off with easily pickings from the civilian populace which it should have been their job to defend.

The incident (unrecorded in Kings) provides the occasion for the encounter between Amaziah and the north that follows in vv. 17-24.

2 Chronicles 25.14-16: Amaziah's Worship of the Gods of Edom

Now follows an extraordinary incident (again unrecorded in Kings) that C uses for the exposition of the negative side of the theological evaluation of Amaziah's reign omitted between vv. 2 and 3. Amaziah brings the gods—presumably, the idols, as the verb 'to set up' implies (2 Chron. 33.19)—of the defeated Edomites home, instead of destroying them (v. 14). He acknowledges them as his gods, prostrates himself to them and offers burnt offerings (the verbs imply continual action). These actions suggest that a sanctuary must have been constructed for them (there is no hint that these rites were performed in the Temple of the LORD; at least there is that limit to his unfaithfulness).

The anger of the LORD is aroused (v. 15; 1 Chron. 13.10). He commissions a prophet (2 Chron. 24.19)—again unnamed—to confront the king. The prophet has time to ask but one rhetorical question: Why do you resort to (*drš*) the gods of another people, when they were powerless against you, when you were commissioned by the LORD himself? Here is a yet further example of Israel's archetypal sin that is as foolish as it is inexplicable: resorting to (*drš*) a god other than the LORD (1 Chron. 10.13-14).

Amaziah cuts him short (v. 16, 'while he was speaking to him') with a petulant rhetorical question in return, 'When did we appoint you as the king's adviser [cf. 1 Chron. 27.32-33]?' Amaziah is wilfully blind to the truth that the one commissioned by God needs no official position to influence the course of affairs. Like a latter day Ahab against Micaiah (2 Chron. 18.25-27), he backs up his words with a threat to the prophet's life. The prophet can only reply that, though the king rejects his advice, he knows what God's advice is and that is—again using the vocabulary of the 'negative Passover' (1 Chron. 21.12)—the king's 'destruction'. By using the term 'advice', C links together the word of the prophet, the guilty response of the king, and the divine verdict upon him—and the opening (which he supplies) of the next section, which begins the account of his destruction (vv. 17-24).

4. 2 Chronicles 25.17-24: Amaziah's Disastrous Campaign against the North

Amaziah now regards the moment opportune to settle his accounts with Joash, king of the north, not least, in context, for the incident recorded in v. 13. He takes advice in the apparently approved manner (1 Chron. 13.1); with whom is not stated, presumably a faction of like-minded leaders (cf. v. 27), unless C wishes to suggest that Amaziah has succeeded in seducing the whole populace. He issues his challenge to Joash: the verb used, 'sent', exploits another thematic term in the context; it echoes the 'sending' of the prophet by the LORD in v. 15; it recurs at the beginning of v. 18 to introduce Joash's response and also at the beginning of his parable about the thorn in Lebanon; it is to recur, Nemesis-like, in v. 27. This 'sending' to the house of Jehu is analogous to other ill-judged and ill-fated encounters by the anointed of the LORD with the kings of the nations (cf. 2 Chron. 10.1). The challenge to Joash is issued in terms of direct personal trial of strength (this form of the verb occurs outside this passage only in the uncertain context of Gen. 42.1).

Joash's reply (vv. 18-19) is a fine example of diplomatic vituperation, all the more insulting for being expressed in memorable story form, decipherable by all. The thorn, the lowliest form of scrub life in Lebanon, proposes a marriage alliance with the cedar of Lebanon, proverbial as the most magnificent specimen in the forest. A wild beast trampling the thorn down is enough to demonstrate the preposterously ill-matched nature of the proposal. Amaziah's triumph against the Edomites has gone to his head; he, the thorn, is no match for Joash, the cedar, and had better withdraw before he is destroyed, along with his kingdom, by any passing force (of which no identification is offered). Joash gives Amaziah advice that perfectly befits his status as Davidic king: 'stay in your palace' (cf. Pharaoh Neco in 2 Chron. 35.21). The further advice, 'do not commit aggression', uses the vocabulary of Deuteronomy 2 (vv. 5, 9, 19, 24) of the conquest of neighbouring peoples. Such an attempt at armed conquest will only rebound on Amaziah—which is precisely what happens.

> C remains usually very close to the parent text of 2 Kgs 15.9-10 in this passage. Joash's advice is rendered slightly differently in Kings: 'you have indeed smitten Edom and your heart has lifted you up; be content with that distinction and stay in your palace'. C reads, altering some words and punctuation: 'You say that you have smitten Edom and your heart has incited you to seek further glorification. Now stay in your palace'.
>
> There are reminiscences of Jotham's parable in Judg. 9.7-15 (there, the bramble is the cause of the destruction of the cedars).

Amaziah is unwilling to take the correct advice from such a quarter (v. 20; cf. Josiah in 2 Chron. 35.22). C adds to the parent text the theological explanation for the impending humiliation, using his standard categories. It is God in his nature as sovereign, cosmic deity who has brought about this turn of events (cf. 2 Chron. 22.7); the reason for the disaster is Amaziah's unfaithfulness in that he denied the LORD his rights by consulting (*drš*, 1 Chron. 10.13-14) the gods of Edom (v. 14).

Now it is Joash who takes the initiative (v. 21). He invades Judah and the encounter which Amaziah sought takes place at Beth-shemesh, a levitical city given to Aaron (1 Chron. 6.59) in the Shephelah, on the north-west frontier of Judah, at the western end of one of the major access routes to Jerusalem itself. Judah is defeated; its army flees (cf. 2 Chron. 10.16); Amaziah is taken captive and brought back to Jerusalem in humiliation by Joash, who then proceeds to demolish 200 metres of the northern part of the city wall 'from the Ephraim Gate to the Gate of the Turning' (vv. 22-23).

> The topography of Jerusalem is a subject fraught with difficulty: once again, the Hebrew Bible does not provide enough material for precise reconstructions (cf., e.g., Grollenberg, map 24, p. 96). The most complete description of the walls and gates of Jerusalem is to be found in Neh. 2.13-15; 3.1-32; 12.31-39. A preliminary question to be decided is whether C is presupposing the Jerusalem known to himself, which must have been very similar to that portrayed in Nehemiah, or whether he is describing, with whatever degree of accuracy, the Jerusalem of four hundred years earlier. This account presumes the former. The matter is slightly eased for the reader of C in that only half a dozen locations in the city gates and walls are referred to in this and the subsequent chapters. It is convenient to draw these references together here: besides (1) the Ephraim Gate and (2) the Gate of the Turning in this context, (3) the Gate of the Corner, and (4) the Angle, in 2 Chron. 26.9, (5) the Wall of the Ophel in 2 Chron. 27.3, cf. 33.14, (6) the Gate of the Valley, again in 2 Chron. 26.9, (7) the Fish Gate in 2 Chron. 33.14, and, more vaguely, (8) the square of the gate of the city in 2 Chron. 32.6 (cf. 2 Chron. 29.4, the Square of the East).
>
>   (1) In Neh. 12.39, following the circuit from west to east, the Ephraim Gate comes after the Broad Wall and before the Fish Gate, that is, on the north side of the city, as its name implies. It is likely to be in the vicinity of the present Damascus Gate.
>   (2) The Gate of the Turning may involve a textual problem. It does not recur elsewhere but is almost identical in consonantal outline (*pnh*) to (3), the Gate of the Corner (so 2 Kgs 14.13 reads). That too is uncertain: in Neh. 3.31-32 the 'upper chamber of the Corner' is referred to, following the circuit east to west, just before the Sheep Gate in the north east corner of the city, but no tower is mentioned with it (cf. 2 Chron. 26.9).
>   (3) Whether 'Gate of Turning' or 'Gate of the Corner', the reference is likely to be to the eastern end of the northern wall of the city.
>   (4) The Angle recurs in the difficult text of Neh. 3.19, 20, 24, where it is clearly on the eastern side of the city, in the vicinity of the palace, south of the Gate of Horses, Neh. 3.28; see sketch at 2 Chron. 23.5.
>   (5) The Wall of Ophel in Neh. 3.27 comes just before, that is, south of, the Gate of the Horses on the east side of the city.

(6) The Gate of the Valley (of the Son of Hinnom?, 2 Chron. 28.3) is on the south-west side of the city: it is where Nehemiah began his tour of inspection (Neh. 2.13; cf. 3.13), and is the implied point of departure of the two choirs in Neh. 12.31-39.

(7) The Fish Gate recurs in Neh. 3.3; 12.39 to the east of the Ephraim Gate and to the west of the Tower of Hananel on the north wall.

(8) From Neh. 8.16 the square of the gate of the city may be at the Water Gate on the East, one of the two major concourses of the city (the other being the Ephraim Gate).

With the breaking down of a sizeable stretch of its northern wall Jerusalem is now defenceless on its weakest side; it lies symbolically open to Ephraim and the north. As token of its submission, Joash raids the treasuries of Temple and palace (v. 24): the store-chambers, where all the tokens of the people's commitment to the LORD and of the nations of the world's submission to his vicegerent on earth (1 Chron. 18.11) have been stored, are emptied and their contents carried off to Samaria. The point of loss of sovereignty is emphasized by C's addition to his parent text that these treasures were in the safe-keeping of Obed-edom. It was to Obed-edom's care that the ark, that symbol *par excellence* of God's dominion on earth exercised through the Davidic house, had originally been entrusted (1 Chron. 13.13-14; 15.18, 21, 24-25; 16.5, 38; cf. 26.4, 8, 15).

> Using 'Temple of God' for 'Temple of the LORD', as in 2 Kgs 14.14, C with deliberate irony gives God his title of cosmic sovereignty. He also changes the 'in the treasuries' of Kings to 'the treasures' to emphasize the loss of the items not merely as financial but as symbolical (cf. 2 Chron. 12.9).
>
> Mandelkern suggests that the Obed-edom here must be a descendant of the Obed-edom of the time of David. It may be, rather, that C is simply using the progenitor to indicate the house as a whole, or, perhaps better, that there is here another example of C's 'timeless contemporaneity' (cf. 1 Chron. 9).

The 'hostages' are also returned to the north. Who these are is not explained in either C or Kings. The implication is that Amaziah had secured some northerners who were detained under his control as a guarantee of good conduct on the part of the north. The only information that has been given of such an act is the cities in southern Ephraim that Asa had annexed, already referred to under v. 13. At all events Judah is deprived of every bargaining counter. The symbols and the reality of sovereignty have passed to the north: what the house

of Ahab had tried to do has now been accomplished by the house of
Jehu.

5. 2 Chronicles 25.25-26.2: The Assassination of Amaziah

With consummate terseness, C records (v. 25) that Amaziah 'survived'
the death of his vanquisher by 15 years (i.e. for more than half his
reign). That is the most notable thing that he achieved in that period.
If one needs confirmation (v. 26), all one has to do is to consult the
standard prophetic midrash on the reign (see Introduction to 2 Chron.
10–36). As a direct consequence of his worsting by Joash (v. 27)—or,
more accurately, as C makes clear by his addition to the Kings text, as
soon as he was guilty of unfaithfulness, defined in this context as
'turning away from following the LORD' (2 Chron. 8.15)—he
becomes the object of a conspiracy by his own people. Amaziah is
obliged to seek refuge in the lowlands of western Judah, in provincial
Lachish (one of Rehoboam's fortified cities, 2 Chron. 11.9). But there
is no hiding place: they 'send' (a thematic term of the chapter, v. 17)
and execute him (the term used is that of the carrying out of a legitimate judicial sentence). At least he is then given burial in the royal
sepulchre (unlike his father Joash, 2 Chron. 24.25).

It would appear that the conspirators, 'all the people of Judah' (cf.
2 Chron. 22.1) took the initiative in the appointment of his successor,
Uzziah ('The LORD is my strength'; Kings usually uses 'Azariah', 'the
LORD has helped', except in 2 Kgs 15.13, 30, 32, 34; C uses 'Azariah'
only once [1 Chron. 3.12] perhaps because the High Priest is so called,
2 Chron. 26.17, 20). The concerted action (already indicated by the
judicial sentence) perhaps explains why there are no reprisals against
the assassins, as in 2 Chron. 25.3-4: this was no individual initiative,
but a corporate act, whereby the unfaithful, and therefore unsuccessful, king was removed.

2 CHRONICLES 26.3-23: THE REIGN OF UZZIAH

MT presents its account of Uzziah's reign in three sections:

1. vv. 3-5: elements (1)–(4)—and development—of the standard annalistic framework;
2. vv. 6-10: Uzziah's successes in war and peace;
3. vv. 11-23: Uzziah's success turns to presumptuousness, with disastrous results.

C's account relates to material in 2 Kgs 15.2-7 only at the beginning and the end: vv. 5-20bα are independent.

1. *Verses 3-5: Elements (1)–(4) of the Standard Annalistic Framework*

Verse 3 provides standard elements (1)–(3) of the annalistic framework: Uzziah's age at accession, the length of his reign, and his mother's name. The first of these has already been given in v. 1, anticipated there in order to record the accomplishment of what had been the main objective of his father Amaziah's reign, but only achieved by Uzziah: the reopening of the trade route to Aqaba. The imposing length of Uzziah's reign of fifty-two years is about to be matched with a full record of positive achievements. Like his father (2 Chron. 25.1), Uzziah has a Jerusalemite mother (Jecoliah, 'May the LORD sustain', as the *kethib* suggests, rather than the alternative, 'The LORD has been able' [BDB]), of whom nothing further is known, but who was no doubt steeped in the hopes and the pathos of the Davidic house.

Verse 4 begins the theological evaluation of Uzziah's reign. At first sight, by the suppression of the qualification of Uzziah's reign in 2 Kgs 15.4, C's evaluation appears to be wholly positive. But the impression is misleading: how could C's view of Uzziah be unreservedly favourable when the standard of comparison is his father Amaziah? As in 2 Chron. 24.2; 25.2, C breaks off from the text of Kings before the qualification in order to expound the evaluation in two parts, first the positive (vv. 6-10), then the negative (vv. 11-23).

> The resumption of the evaluation in vv. 11-23 is hardly, however, in
> terms of 2 Kgs 15.4: 'only the high places were not removed; the people
> were still sacrificing and burning incense [or holocausts?] on the high-
> places'. Nonetheless, there may be a link between these negative evalua-
> tions: for C, it was precisely Uzziah's burning of incense in the Temple
> that was his undoing.

The nature and the results of Uzziah's 'doing right in the eyes of the
LORD' are previewed in v. 5. 'Doing right' is interpreted in the standard terms of 'seeking God' (*drš*, 1 Chron. 10.13-14; recognizing the
Deity, here in his sovereign dominion). A qualification is added, however, which both is a premonition of ultimate failure and places a
condition upon Uzziah's reign. Uzziah sought God only 'during the
days of Zechariah' (he was, after all, only a youth of sixteen when he
came to the throne). Unfortunately, it is not known who this
Zechariah was: the relation between king and mentor must have been
as that between Joash and Jehoiada (2 Chron. 24.2; could there be
some confusion with Jehoiada's martyred son, Zechariah, 2 Chron.
24.20-22?). What he instructed him in is also uncertain: the text
appears to read, 'in the seeing of God', which JPSV takes to mean,
'visions', in which case Zechariah would be a prophetic figure; others
(e.g. NRSV) adjust the text slightly to read, 'in fearing God', in which
case he might be a priestly teacher. Obedience to Zechariah's teaching
also attaches a condition to Uzziah's reign: only for so long and in so
far as he 'sought the LORD'—now the term for the Deity is the special, relational, Israelite one—did 'God cause him to prosper' (another
thematic term, 1 Chron. 22.11).

> This passage gives a good example of C's concept of the Deity: one God,
> in a duality of cosmic transcendence and sovereignty—'God'—and of
> immediate, personal relationship to his chosen people—'the LORD'.

2. *Verses 6-10: Uzziah's Successes in War and Peace*

Uzziah successfully imposes his authority, that is, the authority of the
LORD of hosts, whose vicegerent on earth he is, on an appropriately
representative list of those neighbouring peoples who are ever ready
to encroach on Israel's territory. The Philistines, as the nearest and
archetypal invaders from the world of the nations (1 Chron. 1.12),
are mentioned first (v. 6). As the agents of the destruction of Saul

(1 Chron. 10), they are of special significance in the endeavour of the royal house of Israel to establish itself. As David had once annexed Gath (1 Chron. 18.1), so now the latest Davidic king asserts his authority by 'sallying forth' himself (1 Chron. 1.12; 14.15), the spearhead of the counter-offensive in the name of the LORD of hosts, and removes the fortifications not only of that inland city, but also of those on the Philistine coast, Yabneh (mentioned for the first and only time in the Hebrew Bible) to the north and Ashdod (only here in C) in the centre. What the north had just done to Jerusalem in his father's reign (removal of part of the city wall, 2 Chron. 25.23), in expression of the loss of Amaziah's status as God's vicegerent, Uzziah now succeeds in doing to Israel's arch-foe. In token of the re-annexation of Philistia (it is assigned to the territory of Judah, according to Josh. 15.45-47), Uzziah constructs settlements throughout its territory.

C attributes Uzziah's success (v. 7) entirely to God's help (again a keyword, 2 Chron. 14.11); the monarch, as sacramental figure in tune with God, necessarily wins the field in battle. The context suggests that Uzziah was helped in battle not just against the Philistines, but also against other potentially unruly immediate neighbours to the south and south east, the Arabs (2 Chron. 9.14; who, like the Philistines, can act on Egypt's behalf, 2 Chron. 21.16) and the Meunites (1 Chron. 4.41).

> Gur-baal, the locality mentioned in this verse where the Arabs live, does not occur elsewhere in the Hebrew Bible. KBS equates it with Jagur (a verbal form from the same root), mentioned in Josh. 15.21 as one of the towns marking the southern boundary of Judah; if that is so, the victory represents the regaining of control of territory regarded as belonging rightfully to Israel.

The Ammonites (v. 8), to whose land Israel had no claim (Deut. 2.19), send tribute in token of their recognition (1 Chron. 16.29; 18.11). Thus, Uzziah's 'name reaches as far as Egypt': the 'name' is the reputation, the regard in which the bearer of the name is held (1 Chron. 13.6). But it is also the means of laying claim to property (2 Sam. 12.28): Uzziah's claims to status and possessions are both acknowledged.

By means of this success, Uzziah 'shows strength': the phrase is a variant on the verb 'to become established', the standard term for the confirmation of the contemporary successor to David in office (2 Chron. 1.1). Once again it is tempting to see in 'exceedingly' (*'ad l^{e}mā'lâ*) a pun on *ma'al*, 'unfaithfulness' (1 Chron. 14.2): the two express the polar opposites of the success that comes from loyalty to God and the ruin that is the immediate consequence of disloyalty— soon to befall Uzziah.

The same consolidation of his position is to be seen in his internal measures. It is an idyllic picture of security under which the arts of husbandry of flock, field and vine can flourish, under the patronage of a king 'who is a lover of the soil' (vv. 9-10). The walls of Jerusalem (v. 9) are fortified ('strengthened', picking up the verb 'to show strength' in v. 8) with towers at points on the north-east, south-west and east (2 Chron. 25.23); so also in unspecified places in the 'wilderness', presumably in the east and south of the country. Cisterns are hewn for the watering of the growing flocks and herds in the western lowlands and coastal plain. Farmers and wine-growers culti- vate the slopes and the valleys. The land is at peace from threats from without or within; prosperity is the fruit of this peace. The ideal has to that extent been realized.

3. *Verses 11-23: Uzziah's Success Turns to Presumptuousness, with Disastrous Results*

The final section breaks at v. 16. The celebration of Uzziah's confirmation in his position, which is further expounded in vv. 11-15, turns in v. 16, with an ominous, 'when he became strong', which echoes the verbs in vv. 8-9 and the climactic position of the same root in v. 15, to the record of his act of presumptuous violation of the sphere of the holy (cf. David, in 1 Chron. 13; 17; 21).

The function and strength of the citizen army are described in vv. 11-15. They go out (1 Chron. 1.12; 14.15) on raiding-parties (1 Chron. 12.18) as the 'host' (v. 11; 1 Chron. 5.18). They are noth- ing less than the earthly counterpart of the cosmic 'hosts' that the LORD possesses to execute his will on earth as in heaven (1 Chron. 11.9). For that purpose Israel is mustered as a sacral host (the tech- nical term, *pqd*, as in 2 Chron. 17.14). As David stipulated in 1 Chron. 26.29-30, the officials who oversee and validate the muster for holy war will be Levites (1 Chron. 18.16). All are placed under the leader- ship of a lay royal official as commanding officer.

> None of the individuals named is known from other sources. For compar- ison of the numbers mustered by Uzziah (vv. 12-13)—similar to those of Amaziah, 2 Chron. 25.5—see table at 1 Chron. 5.18.

The function of this host is 'to help' the king (v. 13; 1 Chron. 5.20): it is through their assistance to him as the divinely appointed leader that they realize their identity and purpose as God's people. In return, Uzziah enables them (the key term, *kûn*, 1 Chron. 14.2) to fulfil their role by ensuring that they are fully equipped (v. 14), indeed, seemingly better than at any time during the monarchy: beyond the standard lance and the shield of the infantryman and bow of the archer (1 Chron. 5.18), are itemized here helmet, breastplate (but cf. 2 Chron. 18.33), and slingstones for the only time in C (it is notable that Judah and Benjamin are not itemized separately in this muster; often it has been Benjamin that has supplied the archers; see 2 Chron. 17.14-19; for Benjaminite slingers, see Judg. 20.16). In addition, Uzziah contrives engines for the hurling of arrows and stones from the defence works he adds to the walls of Jerusalem (v. 15). These defensive measures at home spread his fame still further than his successes in the field of battle. By such measures he ensures in brilliant fashion that he is indeed 'helped' (the thematic term as in v. 13). Thus he truly becomes 'strong' (cf. v. 8).

The watershed of the reign has now been reached. Uzziah has been confirmed on the throne by all these actions; the ideal goal of every reign has been attained. What will he do with that 'strength'? The outcome is arrogant self-reliance ('his mind became inflated', contrast 2 Chron. 17.6), which brings down destruction on himself (v. 16). C uses the verb related to the term 'the destroyer' of the 'negative Passover', which he has employed in similar fashion in 1 Chron. 21.12 in his account of the hinge event of David's reign. To convey the enormity of the offence, C introduces one of the principal key terms of his whole work, *ma'al*, violation of the rights of God (v. 18; 1 Chron. 2.7).

In Uzziah's case the *ma'al* consists in his entry into the nave of the Temple and his offering of incense on the incense altar (1 Chron. 28.18). There is no indication of the occasion on which Uzziah is guilty of this breach of the holy, whether on one of the routine daily offerings of incense morning and evening or on the Day of Atonement; the reference to the fact that it is the priests in the plural who have the role of burning incense (v. 19) may suggest the daily rite rather than the once per year, associated with the High Priest alone.

Uzziah's successes have gone to his head and cause him to misread the situation. There must have been a strong desire on the part of the monarchy to reassert the right of the king to act as High Priest for his people: perhaps this is one of the attractions of the old Canaanite religion—that the king could officiate directly in the cult (so Amaziah in 2 Chron. 25.14, or Ahaz in 2 Chron. 28.3). The blessings of peace on all sides are signs of divine favour. Could it be that these successes merit an affirmation of the rights of kings to have immediate access to God without priesthood? David as a man of blood—as presumably was Uzziah, vv. 6, 11—had not had that right. For C the role of the priesthood in maintaining the awesome transcendence of God, represented by the wreathing smoke of incense twice per day in the sanctuary, and the holiness of the people marked by the exclusion from the sanctuary of those not consecrated, remains paramount; it cannot be set aside no matter how successful any particular king has been in realizing the task of his people among the world of the nations. The legislation going back to Moses remains intact (1 Chron. 6.49). Even though hitherto he has been loyal to 'the LORD his God', he is now guilty of *ma'al*.

The High Priest, Azariah (he reappears in 2 Chron. 31.10), and eighty other priests (how had he eluded the levitical guardians of the thresholds to gain access to the shrine?) surround Uzziah in the Temple (vv. 17-18). They are described as 'sons of valour', a term elsewhere applied to warriors (e.g. Deut. 3.18 and 1 Sam. 18.17): the need to use force to eject the erring king must have been present in their minds.

> The singular notion of priests' bearing arms leads the English versions to adopt more restrained translations, such as 'brave priests' (JPSV), 'courageous men' (NEB). But in any event force might have been needed. For warrior priests in David's retinue, see 1 Chron. 12.27-28; cf. 2 Chron. 23.7.

They do not mince words from the start of the confrontation (v. 18): first, a direct statement that the right to burn incense belongs to the consecrated Aaronic priesthood alone; then a curt command to leave; and an explanation that his act is sacrilegious—defined again in terms of *ma'al*, an infringement of the holy—and can bring him no honour from God.

No human force is needed (v. 19). Uzziah rounds on the priests in self-justifying fury (the opposite of the self-abasement required as the first step to rehabilitation in a situation of *ma'al*, 2 Chron. 7.14; compare the fate of Asa in 2 Chron. 16.10). At that very moment, with an accuracy of timing that matches the king's sacramental status and his forfeiture of it, as he stands with the censer in his hand beside the incense altar, he is smitten with leprosy in his forehead.

There must be a cross-reference here to Exod. 28.36-38. There is legislation there for the making of a gold pendant, engraved, 'Holy to the LORD', which is to hang on a cord on the High Priest's turban on Aaron's forehead. It is to be worn, 'so that Aaron may bear the guilt attaching to any shortfall in the offerings of holy things which the Israelites make. It shall lie on his forehead for ever as a means of securing acceptance for them from the LORD.' So far from the priestly pendant announcing that the requirements of the laws of holiness have been strictly observed and with a genuine intention, leprosy has broken out on Uzziah's brow as a statement of the total unacceptability of the king's burning of incense. Not only is it unacceptable; it is a pollution of the Temple (for the rites of purification of leprosy, see the very extensive legislation in Lev. 13–14). So far from Uzziah being able to officiate on behalf of his people in the Temple, he is an outcast; were he ever to be pronounced cleansed of his condition, he would need the services of the priesthood, not least for the guilt offering (Lev. 14.13).

Uzziah scarcely needs to be bundled out of the Temple (v. 20); he himself rushes from the Temple horror-stricken, 'that the LORD has smitten him' (cf. 2 Chron. 6.28). As a leper to the day of his death he does indeed dwell apart in a 'house of isolation', 'cut off from the house of the LORD' (v. 21, the last point pushed home by C, who now returns to the Kings text; see Lev. 13.46: 'For the whole period that the affliction is upon him he shall be unclean. He shall reside apart; his residence shall be outside the camp'). His son, Jotham, takes over the regency until his death. Even in death, Uzziah, as a leper, is lodged apart in the graveyard, but not in the sepulchre of the royal house (v. 23, again a point made by C beyond 2 Kgs 15.7).

Further discussion is, as usual, available in the prophetic midrash (v. 22); but this time it is associated with the awesome name of Isaiah (2 Chron. 32.20, 32), the exponent above all of Jerusalem theology (cf.. e.g., 1 Chron. 11.9; 2 Chron. 20.20).

2 CHRONICLES 27: THE REIGN OF JOTHAM

C's presentation of the reign of Jotham is very brief—only nine verses long, and even one of these, v. 8 (= v. 1a [virtually]), is a repetition.

It follows the standard pattern of the editorial framework (see Introduction to 2 Chron. 10–36): elements (1)–(4) (vv. 1-2aβ), element (5) (v. 7) and elements (6)–(7) (v. 9). In the middle comes the main point of the presentation—element (4), the evaluation, elaborated in vv. 2aγ-6.

The effect of the repetition of elements (1) and (2) in v. 8 almost verbatim from v. 1a (for a similar repetition, see 2 Chron. 21.5, 20a) is to give a very clear framework to element (4), the evaluation. There may be another reason for the repetition: v. 8 substitutes for a verse in 2 Kgs 15.37 which speaks of impending invasion from the north, a topic that C is about to exploit in 2 Chron. 28.5-25 in connection with the next reign.

C's main interest lies in the elaboration of element (4), the theological evaluation of the reign. In the light of the presentation of the immediately preceding reigns, one would expect an exposition of the reign in two parts: first the positive achievements, then the negative features. But the brief data on Jotham in 2 Kgs 15.33-38 hardly gives C much scope for his elaboration. An alternative structure is therefore employed by MT:

1. vv. 1-5bα, the achievements of Jotham's reign, with qualifications included;
2. vv. 5bβ-9, the resulting confirmation of Jotham as ruler.

It is to be noted how v. 5 is divided in this structure. The words 'and in the second year and in the third', which relate to the payment of tribute to Jotham by the Ammonites, have been detached in MT and linked with what follows—Jotham's confirmation as ruler. By this almost whimsical division, MT indicates very strongly where the main emphasis lies: the repeated payment is important not so much in itself as in its significance for Jotham's standing.

Once again C's account relates to material in Kings (2 Kgs 15.33-
38) only at the beginning and the end: vv. 3b-6 have no parallel in
Kings.

1. *Verses 1-5ba: The Achievements of Jotham's Reign (with Qualifications)*

C does not inform the reader whether Jotham's regency during the
illness of his father (2 Chron. 26.21) is being counted as part of his
sixteen-year reign (v. 1; the thorny chronological problems thrown up
by the cross-references between the kings of Judah and the north,
which suggest that it must [see table under 2 Chron. 28.6], do not concern him). His mother, Jerushah ('taken over'), is otherwise unknown
in the Hebrew Bible, but the name of her father, Zadok, is suggestive.
Most famously, this name was borne by David's priest, 1 Chron.
15.11. That it is a traditional priestly name is indicated by 1 Chron.
9.11. This may, then, be further evidence of intermarriage between
the royal and the priestly houses (cf. 2 Chron. 22.11).

Both the positive and the negative theological evaluations of
Jotham's reign are included in v. 2: in this case C does not break off
before the negative qualification, 'only', in the parent Kings text, as he
has done in the case of Joash and Uzziah (2 Chron. 24.2; 26.4; cf.
Jehoshaphat, 2 Chron. 17.6). Uzziah is the standard against which his
'doing right in the eyes of the LORD' is measured; indeed, most of
Uzziah's reign had been exemplary.

The qualification on Jotham's reign, that 'he did not go to the
Temple of the LORD', seems rather general, a sin of omission rather
than of commission. Nonetheless, in a figure who is meant to be the
representative of God on earth, the defect is of a fundamental kind.
The shortcoming may, however, not be a matter of Jotham's personal
preference, but of his standing: Jotham never did progress beyond the
status of regent to be king in his own right. Had Jotham been crowned
king, it is difficult to see how he could have avoided presenting himself in the Temple at his coronation (cf. 2 Chron. 23.13). But it may
be that one should not assume that Uzziah predeceased Jotham: not
only would this help to harmonize the chronological cross-references
between Judah and the north; it also matches the chronology implied
by Isaiah 6 and 7, which seems to pass straight from Uzziah to Ahaz,
while acknowledging that Ahaz is son of Jotham (Isa. 7.1). In terms of

the overall chronology of C's work (see Introduction to Volume I), however, which requires fifteen generations from Rehoboam to Josiah, Jotham's obscure little reign is essential.

The criticism against the people is equally non-specific: they are 'still acting destructively'. Here again the language of the 'negative Passover' is being used (1 Chron. 21.12). The technical term for 'the destroyer' of the Passover narrative is used here not of any outside agency, but of the people's own activity. They are instrumental in their own undoing.

2 Kgs 15.35 focuses all the criticism on the people—but in still more stereotyped terms: 'only they did not remove the high places; the people were still sacrificing and offering incense on the high places'.

The remainder of the presentation is positive. Jotham's creative acts as regards internal security are listed (vv. 3-4). Though he has not gone to the Temple (officially for coronation, on the above interpretation), he undertakes the construction (or reconstruction?) of the Upper Gate in the Temple, the main interchange between the inner and outer courts of the Temple (cf. at 2 Chron. 23.13 and the sketch at 2 Chron. 23.5). Like his father (2 Chron. 26.9; at this point C adds his own material to the Kings text), he was concerned with the fortifications on the eastern side of Jerusalem (see on 2 Chron. 25.23), specifically of Mt Ophel, the original city of David (cf. 2 Chron. 33.14). Similarly, he was involved in the construction of settlements in the hill country of Judah and fortresses (the word as in 2 Chron. 17.12) and towers in the virgin wooded areas. These are standard works of consolidation (e.g., 2 Chron. 8.5-6).

Only one incident as regards external security is recorded (v. 5): the encounter with the Ammonites (again like his father, 2 Chron. 26.8). He 'became strong' over them (the key term about to be used at the beginning of v. 6). They had paid an unspecified tribute to his father. The tribute to him is now defined in colossal terms: a hundred talents of silver (the amount Amaziah had used to hire troops from the north, 2 Chron. 25.6) and 10,000 *kors* of wheat and barley (for comparative amounts, see 2 Chron. 2.10).

2. Verses 5bβ-9: The Confirmation of Jotham as Ruler

The fact that this tribute is also paid by the Ammonites in a second and third year is of importance not so much in itself as an accession of wealth. It is detached from v. 5 and linked to v. 6 as testimony to a much more fundamental truth: Jotham was by these and other such acts (cf. his 'wars' v. 7) 'established' (v. 6; 2 Chron. 1.1). Put theologically, he 'directed [using another key term, *kûn*, 1 Chron. 14.2] his paths before the LORD his God'.

These doings by which Jotham 'was established' are merged (v. 7) with the notices in the concluding framework: 'all his wars and his ways' which are recorded, no doubt with approval, in the prophetic midrash on his reign.

These make-weight phrases for the balance of C's presentation are substituted for the even more uncommunicative, 'which he did' of 2 Kgs 15.36.

C replaces v. 8 for 2 Kgs 15.37 with its ominous reference to the gathering threat of invasion from the north: 'In those days, the LORD began to send against Judah Rezin, king of Syria, and Pekah, son of Remaliah [king of the north]'. Compare Isa. 7.1-6. This is to be made the substance of 2 Chronicles 28.

A generally successful, if unremarkable, reign is brought to an end with the endorsement of burial in the City of David (v. 9).

2 CHRONICLES 28: THE REIGN OF AHAZ

There is no doubt about the verdict to be passed on Ahaz's reign. From the start, he is guilty of outrage, and outrage is to grow upon outrage. There is, therefore, no exposition of how it is that the king has become 'established' (*ḥzq*, 2 Chron. 1.1; contrast v. 20) on the throne, only to fall away towards the end of his reign, as in the case of some previous reigns (e.g. 2 Chron. 13–16). The general drift of the narrative is clear: the announcement of the reign of an evil king and an indication of its consequences (vv. 1-5); humiliation at the hand of the north (vv. 6-15); an appeal for help to Assyria that only makes matters worse (vv. 16-25); conclusion (vv. 26-27).

But this is not quite how, in fact, MT divides the material. C is concerned not so much to portray events of political history as to identify the deeper theological factors at work in the life of God's people. MT thus divides the chapter into two main sections: vv. 1-15 and vv. 16-27. These sections are chiastically arranged: apostasy precipitates foreign invasion (vv. 1-15); the experience of foreign invasion leads to still greater apostasy (vv. 16-27). These sections again reflect C's sacramental view of life: inner disposition and outer manifestation are one; each mutually reinforces the other.

> Once again, 'sacramental correspondence' of the inner and the outer, rather than 'retribution', seems to do justice to C's thought. The second half of Ahaz's reign culminates in the ultimate outrage of the closure of the Temple in Jerusalem (v. 24), yet no subsequent punishment is recorded. The reign of Ahaz is, rather, presented in a wholly consistent light in which the basic theological disposition and the outward course of events are in immediate correspondence with one another, no matter with which side one begins. The following reign of Hezekiah still involves no retribution; only the necessary restoration of the Temple and its rites with the blessings that flow therefrom.

The MT subdivisions of the narrative aptly match this concern.

1. vv. 1-15: Apostasy, invasion by the north, clemency shown by the North

This material is closely subdivided into six subsections:

1. vv. 1-5: standard framework elements (1), (2) and (4), with initial exposition of element (4), the unfavourable verdict on the reign;
2. vv. 6-7: slaughter of Judah by the north;
3. v. 8: captivity of Judah by the north;
4. vv. 9-11: the speech of the prophet Oded to the north;
5. vv. 12-13: the faithful response of the leadership of the north;
6. vv. 14-15: the surrender of the spoils and the return of the captives by the north.

2. vv. 16-27: Judah's humiliation at the hands of nations of the world. MT treats this material as a single unit.

C has reworked his base source in Kings with such freedom that he presents virtually a new text. The following is only a rough comparison for initial orientation:

2 Chronicles 28		*2 Kings 16*
vv. 1-4		cf. vv. 2-4
vv. 5-15,	total reworking of	vv. 5-6
vv. 16, 20-25,	only remote echoes of	vv. 7-18
vv. 17-19		no parallel
vv. 26-27		cf. vv. 19-20

1. Apostasy, Invasion by the North and Clemency of the North (Verses 1-15)

Verses 1-5: Standard Opening Framework Elements, with Initial Exposition of the Unfavourable Verdict on the Reign
Ahaz's name is the same as that of Ahaziah (2 Chron. 22.2), with the dropping of the suffix 'Yah' referring to the LORD, the God of Israel. In every respect, as the following narrative makes clear, this dropping of the name of the national God, and leaving a blank to be filled by other deities, is an only too appropriate (if coincidental?) commentary on the reign as a whole.

Standard framework elements (1), Ahaz's age at accession, (2), the length of his reign, and (4), the theological evaluation (Introduction to 2 Chron. 10–36), are included (vv. 1-2). In the rush to record the scandalous events of Ahaz's reign, C does not stop (nor does Kings) to record item 3, the name of his mother.

The data given on items (1) and (2) raise a chronological problem. If he was only twenty at his accession and reigned for sixteen years, and if Hezekiah his son succeeded at the age of twenty-five (2 Chron. 29.1), Ahaz must have become a father at the age of eleven! There is MSS and Versions support to read 'twenty-five' for Ahaz's age at accession (*BHK* and *BHS*). His becoming a father at the age of sixteen would then necessitate the reduction of the age of his own father at his birth from twenty-one to sixteen (cf. 2 Chron. 27.1)—which appears to have been the age at the birth of their sons of two subsequent kings, Amon and Josiah (indeed, the latter had already fathered Jehoiakim at the age of fourteen, 2 Chron. 33.21; 34.1; 36.2, 5).

In the theological evaluation, C suppresses the 'his God' of 2 Kgs 16.2 after 'the LORD' at the end of v. 1. At no point in his reign and in no way could the LORD be affirmed as the God of Ahaz.

C retains from 2 Kgs 16.3 the summary evaluation of Ahaziah, that 'he walked in the ways of the kings of Israel' (v. 2). 'Walk' is a metaphor for a way of life that gives, or in this case fails to give, the LORD his rights (2 Chron. 6.16). Within the context of C's work, 'the ways of the kings of Israel' most likely to be referred to are those of the house of Ahab, for C the epitome of wickedness (2 Chron. 6.23; cf. 2 Chron. 18–24). It had pursued a policy ultimately aimed at the abolition of the Davidic house and the assimilation of Judah into an Israel that was conformed to the ways of international Canaanite religion, in which the LORD would be, at most, but one deity within the pantheon.

It is perhaps to indicate the full range of these policies that C uses the plural 'ways' of the kings of Israel for the singular, 'way' of 2 Kgs 16.3 (cf. 2 Chron. 22.3) and adds vv. 2b and 3a in order to emphasize the full heinousness of Ahaz's religious malpractice. For Kings it is 'Jeroboam, son of Nebat', who, as the founder of the schismatic and apostate kingdom, is the epitome of the sin of the north.

The assimilationist policy of the house of Ahab is revived precisely at this time under Pekah, son of Remaliah (v. 6), on the evidence of Isa. 7.1-6. It is ironical, then, that in this chapter (vv. 9-15), to the shame of Judah, it is the north which is to be the element of the ideal Israel that most displays the character of God's people. When his designated followers fail, God does not leave himself without a witness, sometimes a most unwelcome one.

The catalogue of Ahaz's misdeeds now follows (vv. 2-4), couched precisely in terms of the 'abominations' of the religious practices of the Canaanite nations dispossessed by God in favour of his people.

This reference to 'abominations' is now to be made insistently by C—leapfrogging the long section on the positively evaluated reign of Hezekiah, 2 Chron. 29–32—as the narrative of the history of Israel hastens to the disastrous climax of Israel's own dispossession because of their crimes, 2 Chron. 33.2; 34.33; 36.8, 14 (cf. the use of the related verb in 1 Chron. 21.6).

Ahaz made cast-metal images for the Baalim, the double fault of attempting to manipulate and control the deity by 'casting' it in physical terms (forbidden in Exod. 34.17; compare, using different vocabulary, the Decalogue, Exod. 20.4) and of replacing the LORD by his local Canaanite rivals (the term for 'cast-images' could, however, mean 'libations'; see Jer. 19.13, referred to immediately below). To compound the theological outrage, he committed the atrocity of offering his sons [2 Kgs 16.3 'son'] as burnt offerings to Baal (v. 3), a further attempt to manipulate the deity, by offering the most valuable possession one has. The practice is mentioned in the Hebrew Bible precisely in connection with a period of threat to national existence, such as Ahaz has to endure, whether for Moab in the time of Jehoram, son of Ahab (2 Kgs 3.27; for Jehoram see 2 Chron. 22.5-7), or, later, for Judah in the time of Jeremiah (Jer. 7.31-32; 19.1-13; 32.35). Again, it is expressly prohibited in connection with the worship of the LORD in Exod. 34.20 (cf. Mic. 6.7).

Child sacrifice as Canaanite practice is confirmed from archaeological excavations at the Phoenician colony at Carthage. The 'valley of the son of Hinnom' ('Hinnom' does not appear in the Hebrew Bible by himself[?] apart from this connection), with which it is associated here and in Jeremiah, is the traditional frontier of the territory of Judah with Benjamin (Josh. 15.8; 18.16); it runs immediately below the southern wall of Jerusalem (it is plausible to relate the 'Gate of the Valley' [2 Chron. 26.9] to it).

The list of Ahaz's acts of religious malpractice concludes (v. 4, cf. v. 25) with a conventionalized compendium, quoted verbatim from 2 Kgs 16.4, of the worship of the Canaanite male and female fertility gods at the symbols of their potency on 'high places and hills and under every green tree' (cf. 2 Chron. 11.15). This phrase is about to be used in Kings as part of the explanation for the downfall of the north (2 Kgs 17.10; used already of Rehoboam 1 Kgs 14.23 [neither in C]).

The penalty from the LORD for this flagrant apostasy is the simultaneous withdrawal from Ahaz of his status as God's sacramental representative amid the world of the nations (v. 5). Ahaz is immediately worsted on the field of battle; the nations of the world threaten to overwhelm the people whom God has intended to be his 'host' on earth. Specifically, it is into the power of Damascus and of the north that Judah is delivered. It is notable how in v. 5 both aggressors are described in parallel: it is 'into the hand of the king' of each that Ahaz is 'given' (same verb each time, if different conjugation); the one 'slaughters' and carries off a 'great' number captive to his capital, Damascus; the other 'slaughters' a 'great' number.

The parallel deportation to Samaria is reserved for the exposition that follows in vv. 6-8 (there is no further reference to the Aramaeans of Damascus until vv. 22-23).

> In 2 Kgs 16.5 the Aramaean and Israelite kings attack and besiege Jerusalem, but are not able to reduce it.

Verses 6-7: Slaughter of Judah by the North

The leader of the northern host, Pekah ben Remaliah, is introduced for the first and only time in C (v. 6). The fact that it is not even explained that he is the 'king of Israel [in the narrow sense]' referred to in v. 5, suggests that C presupposes both for himself and for his readers the further information on Pekah in 2 Kgs 15.25–16.5 and Isa. 7.1–8.8.

Pekah was an officer who, at the head of a conspiracy of Gileadites, assassinated the then king of the north, one Pekahiah, whose own father, Menahem, had led a similar coup. The highly disturbed situation in the north was caused or exacerbated by the many campaigns to Syria and Palestine from the 740s by the Assyrian king, Tiglath-pileser III (745–727 BCE)[1].

The major incident involving Judah took place around 734–732, the 'Syro-Ephraimite War' (so-called from Isa. 7.2), in which the Aramaeans of Syria, whose capital was Damascus, and the Ephraimites of the north, whose capital was Samaria, entered into an alliance and threatened Judah, who, by that time, were led by Ahaz.

1.	J. Bright, *A History of Israel* (London: SCM Press, 3rd edn, 1981).

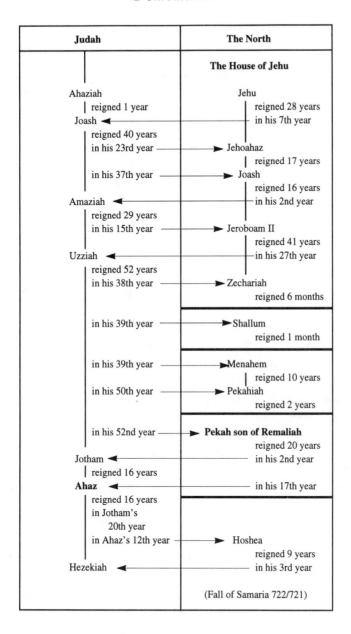

Judah	The North
	The House of Jehu
Ahaziah	Jehu
reigned 1 year	reigned 28 years
Joash ◀———————————	in his 7th year
reigned 40 years	
in his 23rd year ——————▶	Jehoahaz
	reigned 17 years
in his 37th year ——————▶	Joash
	reigned 16 years
Amaziah ◀———————————	in his 2nd year
reigned 29 years	
in his 15th year ——————▶	Jeroboam II
	reigned 41 years
Uzziah ◀———————————	in his 27th year
reigned 52 years	
in his 38th year ——————▶	Zechariah
	reigned 6 months
in his 39th year ——————▶	Shallum
	reigned 1 month
in his 39th year ——————▶	Menahem
	reigned 10 years
in his 50th year ——————▶	Pekahiah
	reigned 2 years
in his 52nd year ——————▶	**Pekah son of Remaliah**
	reigned 20 years
Jotham ◀———————————	in his 2nd year
reigned 16 years	
Ahaz ◀———————————	in his 17th year
reigned 16 years	
in Jotham's	
20th year	
in Ahaz's 12th year ——————▶	Hoshea
	reigned 9 years
Hezekiah ◀———————————	in his 3rd year
	(Fall of Samaria 722/721)

The complexities of the interrelationships between the kings of Judah and
the north are perhaps best indicated by a continuation of the table already
given under 2 Chron. 25.1 (opposite). The data are supplied by 2 Kgs
14.23–18.1, and are again here reproduced at face value. The horizontal
line in the north column represents the bringing to the end of a dynasty by
military coup.

This table, especially the north column, strikingly makes the point
once more that C is not, like a historian, interested in the mere complex interplay of events at the mundane level for its own sake (in
the case of Pekah, a military coup led by Gileadites, whose security
is under constant threat from Damascus, and the resultant diplomatic
and military pressures on Judah). C uses names and personalities
in the above list, but he does not explain in historical terms how they
interrelate with one another. For that he presupposes the narrative
in Kings. Rather, he wishes to use the data of history to illustrate
theological doctrine, specifically as that affects the life of his own
people.

Thus the record of Pekah's battle against Judah (v. 6) is expressed
in stylized form. 120,000 warriors of Judah are slaughtered in one
day; for the scale of the losses envisaged one can compare the army of
307,500, representing the whole military capacity of Judah, mustered
by Uzziah (2 Chron. 26.13; cf. table at 1 Chron. 5.18). As in the case
of Saul (1 Chron. 10.13-14), the reason for the catastrophe is no mere
military one; it has a theological cause and that cause is Judah's abandonment ('zb, cf. 1 Chron. 28.9; the word is central to C's vocabulary
of rejection) of the LORD. To push the point home, C adds the divine
title that emphasizes the whole tradition of Israel, both Mosaic and
Davidic, 'the God of their fathers' (cf. 1 Chron. 5.25). Judah has not
learned the lessons of the past, let alone profited from its heritage.

The three great Judaean heroes of the day perish (v. 7): three at the
hand of but one warrior from the north (contrast, e.g., 1 Chron.
11.22-23) All three bear programmatic—and, in the context, deeply
ironical—names: Maaseiah, 'The handwork of the LORD'; Azrikam,
'My help has arisen' (the key roots, 'zr, 1 Chron. 5.20, and *qûm*,
1 Chron. 17.11); and Elkanah, 'God [this time in the form of El, the
head of the traditional pantheon] has acquired'. The northern hero's
name, Zichri, 'My remembering', bears an equally chilling message,
if the 'my' refers to the LORD: all that happens on the plane of history, the world of appearances, is not a matter of chance, but of the
working out of processes determined by the intention of God himself

(cf. 2 Chron. 24.22). Zichri is dignified with the title 'warrior', the military agent of God on earth (cf. 1 Chron. 1.10; 11.17).

There is a frustrating lack of precision about the status of these Judaean heroes. Maaseiah 'the king's son' is presumably Ahaz's oldest (surviving? cf. v. 3) son and heir apparent. Azrikam is called the 'leader of the house'. If the reference is to the palace, he must be the highest state official (2 Chron. 19.11); indeed, he bears the old title, *nāgîd*, of the kings of Israel (1 Chron. 11.2) and might himself be the heir apparent (2 Chron. 11.22). More sensationally, the title may be a shortened form of 'leader of the house [of the LORD]' (1 Chron. 9.11; 2 Chron. 31.13; cf. 2 Chron. 35.8), in which case the reference is to the High Priest. The name Azrikam does not occur in the succession of High Priests in 1 Chron. 6.1-15 (indeed, none of these figures recurs elsewhere); but that list must be deficient—it does not include, for example, Uriah, the name of Ahaz's (subsequent?) High Priest (2 Kgs 16.10; he does not figure either in C's account of Ahaz's reign). Elkanah is described as 'the king's second'—either his immediate deputy (on the field of battle?) or, more likely, simply his second son (1 Chron. 5.12; cf., e.g., 1 Sam. 8.2, where the same word occurs). At all events, aside from the king himself, the status of these Judaean heroes could not be higher: these are individuals who above all could be expected to vindicate the claims of the Davidic house on earth, members of the royal house, indeed, through whom the promises were to be perpetuated.

Verse 8: Captivity of Judah by the North
The MT paragraphing makes the reader pause once more to take in the enormity of events. 'Captivity', a word pregnant with association with the bitterest experience of Israel—deportation from their land in 587 (cf. the climax of Solomon's prayer in 2 Chron. 6.36-40)—is now used of the action of one part of Israel, the north, against another, 'their brothers', Judah. The atrocity threatens to be compounded: it is 200,000 women, boys and girls who are deported, many of them humiliated by nakedness (v. 15), the traditional prize booty of brutalized soldiers for rape and enslavement. The lack of specification of adult males underlines the wholesale slaughter of Judah's army (v. 6). The wealth, too, of Judah is looted: what had once been symbols of Judah's status as the agents of the LORD (e.g., 1 Chron. 20.2) now become the tokens of their forfeiture of that status.

Verses 9-11: The Speech of the Prophet Oded to the North
An otherwise unknown prophet of the LORD, Oded (related to the
verb *'wd*, 'to testify'? cf. 2 Chron. 15.1), advances to encounter the
returning victorious army (v. 9; 'advances' echoes, no doubt deliberately, the vocabulary of the sallying forth of an army itself to battle,
1 Chron. 1.12). He delivers a speech, developed in six sentences as
terse as they are trenchant: (a) explanation; (b) accusation 1; (c) accusation 2; (d) interpretation; (e) instruction; (f) warning.

(a) By an inversion of the usual word order, the true cause of the
defeat of Judah is identified: it is 'the anger of the LORD, the God of
your fathers'. The Deity, personal to Israel and cosmic in his power,
affirmed in the traditions of Moses and David (v. 6), has been provoked to fury (2 Chron. 12.7, the fury that will eventually lead to the
final destruction of Jerusalem, 2 Chron. 36.16). The north have only
been commissioned as the interim agents of punishment.

(b) The first accusation is that the north have overstepped their
commission in the barbarity, the blind, irrational rage (2 Chron.
16.10), with which they have carried out their slaughter. They have
committed an atrocity that 'has reached the heavens', an expression
that not only conveys scale (cf. Ps. 57.10) but echoes Solomon's
prayer (2 Chron. 6.39): it is an outrage that has come to the LORD's
attention.

(c) The very first word of v. 10, which anticipates the first word of
v. 11, where it introduces the instruction proper (cf. 1 Chron. 17.7),
marks the stuttering anger with which the prophet speaks; he launches
himself into a further accusation. By a further inversion of normal
word order, the enormity of the action of the north is underlined
(v. 10a). 'It is the Judaeans and Jerusalem' that they are planning to
'reduce' (the verb is used of the indigenous population in 1 Chron.
22.18) to being slaves and slave-girls for their pleasure. Are they
aware of what they are doing?—committing the archetypal sin of
reducing the LORD's own people, God's chosen instruments of his
purpose, their own kinspeople, to slavery, and of being the agents of
an oppression from which they themselves have once been freed!

(d) Again an emphatic change of word order, with an emphatic
question, introduces the true interpretation of events: 'is it not only
you—to whom the guilt attaches of actions against the LORD your
God?' (v. 10b). Overstepping the mark against Judah is to overstep the
mark against God and so to incur guilt (the plural of a key term of C's

whole work, 1 Chron. 21.3) against their own God, which is the very point at issue (cf. v. 13).

(e) The instruction (v. 11) is introduced with the appropriate formula, 'So now' (1 Chron. 17.7), which links the message to the preceding argument. The instruction also opens with an appeal to the audience for a hearing (2 Chron. 15.2). The urgency of the message is reinforced by a three-fold play on words: '*Restore* your *exiled* brothers whom you have *exiled*'.

(f) The climax of the whole message is reached with the last word: 'the fury of the LORD's anger is now on *you*!'

Verses 12-13: The Faithful Response of the Leadership of the North
In model response to the words of the prophet, four members of the leadership of the north (of whom nothing further is known) confront their 'host' (v. 12; their army too no doubt marched out with presumed theological sanction; see 1 Chron. 5.18) as they 'return' (again a technical usage; see 1 Chron. 11.2).

> It is notable that the north is here referred to as 'Ephraim' as in Isa. 7.2 (cf. v. 7; 2 Chron. 25.7, 10, is the only other passage in C where 'Ephraim' is so used). Perhaps one should bear in mind the honorific status of Ephraim in 1 Chron. 7.20-29.
>
> Nothing further is known about the individuals named. Almost all of them bear names of high theological orthodoxy compounded with the name of Israel's God, Yahweh: Azariah (with the element '*zr*, cf. v. 7), Jehohanan ('The LORD has been gracious'), Berechiah ('The LORD has blessed'), Hezekiah (cf. 2 Chron. 29.1), Amasa (a shortened form of Amasiah, 'The LORD has borne', cf. 2 Chron. 17.16 [KBS]). For Meshillemoth and Shallum, see the levitical gatekeeper, Shallum/Meshelemiah (1 Chron. 9.17, 21)

Their response is in two parts, a prohibition and an explanation (v. 13). They forbid their fellow-countrymen to bring in captives from Judah. The reason is given in impeccable theological terms: the north is already incurring the wrath of the Lord for their sins (1 Chron. 21.8) and guilt (1 Chron. 21.3); there is no cause to add to that guilt still further (the key term, '*ašmâ*, is used no fewer than three times in v. 13; compare v. 10). Unspoken is the thought that the appropriate first stage in averting wrath is, rather, repentance for sin (2 Chron. 12.6-7). The sin they have already committed and the guilt they bear are not explained. In the immediate context, it must be their invasion of Judah and huge slaughter of their fellow-countrymen

(v. 6). But it is possible that they are taking a longer view and include the break-away of their regime as such (cf. 2 Chron. 10) in their national guilt. Thus it may be that in the phrase 'wrath upon Israel', with which the leaders' reply ends, it is Israel as a whole, Judah as victims and the north as aggressors, that is meant, and not simply the north alone. This war is yet another symptom of the general malaise under which the nation as a whole languishes.

Verses 14-15: The Surrender of the Spoils and the Return of the Captives by the North

The army of the north respond in an equally exemplary manner. They assent without demur (v. 14). They deposit the captives and the spoils in the presence of the leaders and of the community as a whole (notably called here by the sacral term, *qāhāl*; see 1 Chron. 13.2: there *are* occasions, when the north, through its acknowledgment of theological principles, can act as 'Israel'). Specified individuals (those named in v. 12?) take the captives, clothe the naked from the spoils, and convey them clothed, shod, fed, supplied with water and anointed, with the feeble on donkeys, back to their kinsfolk and territory to Jericho, the traditional southern boundary of Ephraim and Benjamin (cf. Josh. 16.1; 18.12). Never can the 'city of palm trees' have provided a more welcome oasis for re-entry into the land, reunion and recuperation (cf. 1 Chron. 19.5)!

2. Judah's Humiliation at the Hands of Nations of the World (Verses 16-27)

The second major section of the chapter deals with Ahaz's reaction to the emergency. The magnanimity on the part of the north and their faithful response to the prophetic word merely serves to highlight still further Ahaz's inadequacy on every front.

Ahaz's reaction begins in fateful fashion (v. 16): oblivious to his status as Davidic king and all that that should imply for his power on earth, he 'sends' for foreign assistance (cf. 2 Chron. 16.2). Any 'help' that he should seek should be from the LORD alone (1 Chron. 5.20; 2 Chron. 14.11).

> C generalizes the situation: he says 'to the kings of Assyria', where 2 Kgs 16.7 has 'Tiglath-pileser'. It is only in v. 20 that C introduces Tiglath-pilneser by name (cf. 1 Chron. 5.26). Again the details of historical

reconstruction do not concern C, nor considerations of how significant, militarily, such assistance might be. Perhaps, too, C heightens Ahaz's culpability by making him send personally; in Kings it is messengers whom he sends.

C now portrays the extremity of Judah's situation. Ahaz is under threat from all sides—not just from the Syrians to the north-east and Ephraim to the north, but also from Edom to the south and the Philistines to the west.

The Edomites invade, slaughter some Judaeans and carry off captives (v. 17; again no details are given).

> In Kings it is the Aramaeans who recapture Elath and drive the Judaeans out of the area. The Edomites take advantage of this to re-annexe Elath for themselves (2 Kgs 16.6).

The Philistines also sense Judaean weakness and launch raids (v. 18; the same pun on the name 'Philistine', as though they were lurking ever ready to live up to their name, is used as in 1 Chron. 14.9; compare 1 Chron. 10.8. In point of fact, this is the last occasion on which the Philistines appear in C). The territories that Uzziah had conquered in the lowlands and beyond (2 Chron. 26.6) are lost to Judah: a whole string of cities down the eastern limit of the lowlands, with daughter villages, is listed. While Gimzo occurs only here in the Hebrew Bible and Gederoth only once again (Josh. 15.41), others are rich in association: Beth-shemesh and Aijalon are levitical cities (1 Chron. 6.59, 69; Beth-shemesh has already proved to be a vulnerable frontier town in 2 Chron. 25.21, 23); Aijalon and Soco were fortified by Rehoboam (2 Chron. 11.7, 10); Timnah figures in the Samson tales of Israel's deliverance against the Philistines (Judg. 14.1, if it is the same site; there is another Timnah in Judah, Josh. 15.57).

The theological explanation for these crises is now given (v. 19). It is the LORD who has 'humbled' Judah: the verb in the reflexive, 'humble oneself', that is, admitting that one has been in the wrong, has already been used of the first necessary stage in rehabilitation (2 Chron. 7.14). This is not an optional spiritual exercise; it is the first essential step back to the recognition of the sole rights of God and how they have been infringed by human actions. As Ahaz has not been prepared to humble himself, there is no alternative to the necessary humiliation being brought upon him, in the hope of bringing him to his senses.

In terms of sacramental theology, humiliation is, further, the inevitable consequence of denying God his rights. C therefore adds his fundamental category (v. 19): Ahaz has been guilty of gross *ma'al* (1 Chron. 10.13-14), as vv. 1-5 have expounded. He has broken all bounds of restraint in Judah (the *parish* verb is used again in Exod. 5.4 of letting the people go free from the duties of their daily work; there may be a play between it [*hipria' bîhûdâ*] and the first phrase in the verse 'humbled Judah' [*hiknîa' et-yᵉhûdâ*]). His wilful violation of the LORD's claims to sole deity brings with it forfeiture of his status as the LORD's representative (notably, Ahaz is here called, 'king of Israel') and of Israel's status as the LORD's host on earth. That is why Judah is beset on every side by the nations of the earth.

The folly of appealing for 'help' to the Assyrian king now rebounds on Ahaz: Tiglath-pilneser comes to him (v. 20) but, instead of 'strengthening him' (a bitter play on the standard verb of the Davidic king being 'established' in his position; *ḥzq*, 2 Chron. 1.1), lays siege to Jerusalem. He is bought off (v. 21) only at the cost of Ahaz's stripping bare (so the meaning in context of the verb *ḥlq*; the usual sense is 'to divide') the treasuries of Temple, palace and even of his chief officers (there may be another play on words intended between *ḥzq* and *ḥlq*). Spoils and tribute, the symbols of recognition of Israel by the nations of the world in virtue of its status as the LORD's host on earth (1 Chron. 16.29; 20.2), have now been handed over to Assyria in recognition of its temporal sovereignty over it. 'He was of no help to him', C adds tersely, using again the key term, *'zr* (cf. v. 16).

These reverses still do not bring Ahaz to his senses. He now compounds his *ma'al*, his failure to accord the LORD his rights (v. 22), by turning in his extremity to the worship of the gods of the Syrians. C returns to the episodes to which he has alluded in v. 5. Ahaz reasons from the victories of the Syrians over him, not that he was at fault in his abandonment of the worship of the LORD, but that, since the Syrians have been superior in battle, their gods must be superior to his God. As the Syrian gods had 'helped' (the key word again, v. 21) them, so, if he worships them, they will 'help' him. Again C comments: they merely became the means of making both Ahaz and Israel 'stumble' (2 Chron. 25.8, where the same verb is used of God regulating the outcome in accordance with the intrinsic merits of the situation).

C records Ahaz's thorough actions not only in instituting the worship of the gods of Syria but in abolishing the worship of the LORD

(v. 24): the melting down of all the cultic utensils in the Temple, the closing of its doors, the construction of rival altars in every 'corner' (ironically picking up the word used of the means of fortifying Jerusalem, 2 Chron. 26.9, 15). Similarly, throughout the whole land (v. 25), he re-establishes the high places in every city: the increase of settlements achieved by Jotham (2 Chron. 27.4) serve now only to compound the apostasy. Thus he 'vexed the LORD, the God of his fathers' (cf. v. 6).

> The term 'vex' (2 Chron. 16.10) is much more characteristic of the interpretation in Kings of 'provoking God to anger', and is used again in C only in 2 Chron. 33.6; 34.25, both passages derived from parallels in Kings.

It is striking that further no punishment of Ahaz is described by C. The emphasis is on the comprehensive surrender by Ahaz of his status. The contrast has been prepared with the reign of Hezekiah, who is to be faithful in almost model terms.

The MT thus continues without break into the final framework section (vv. 26-27): the rest of Ahaz's acts are all of a piece with what has just been described and are recorded with due negative comment, one is left to assume, in the prophetic midrash (Introduction to 2 Chron. 10–36). But, when he dies, his subjects are still conscious enough of the unworthiness of his reign not to give him the honour of burial in the royal sepulchre.

> The account of the second phase of Ahaz's reign (vv. 16-27) is markedly more circumstantial in 2 Kgs 16.7-18. For example, Ahaz goes to Damascus to meet the Assyrian king; the High Priest, Uriah, is involved in the construction of a new altar for the Jerusalemite Temple itself, following the pattern of one which Ahaz sees in Damascus; it is duly installed in the Temple in Jerusalem, so that the altar of the LORD is set aside; the covered way between palace and Temple that gives the king access on the sabbath, and is no doubt the symbol of the Davidic king's sitting at God's 'right hand' (Ps. 110.1), that is, to the south of the Temple in his palace, is removed (see sketch at 2 Chron. 23.5).

2 CHRONICLES 29–32: THE REIGN OF HEZEKIAH

At 117 verses, C's presentation of the reign Hezekiah is the longest of the reigns of any of the kings of Judah after the break-up of the united kingdom. There are four main phases, which correspond to the chapter divisions: the purification of the Temple (ch. 29), the celebration of the Passover (ch. 30), the offering of holy things (ch. 31), and the invasion of the Assyrian king, Sennacherib (ch. 32). The sequence of these chapters—Temple, city, land, outside world—clearly reflects fundamental ideas C has been presenting, especially the concept of gradations of holiness (compare the sequence in Solomon's prayer in 2 Chron. 6.22-40).

In its systematic way, MT divides (and then, on occasion, still further subdivides) all this material into nine major sections:

1. 29.1-30: the purification of the Temple and the restoration of the cult;
2. 29.31-36: the celebration of the restoration of the Temple;
3. 30.1-9: the invitation to celebrate the Passover;
4. 30.10-27: the celebration of Passover and Unleavened Bread;
5. 31.1-8: the offering of holy things by the community;
6. 31.9-21: the reception of the holy things by the clergy;
7. 32.1-8: Sennacherib's invasion: the security of the land;
8. 32.9-20: Sennacherib's mockery of the power of the LORD;
9. 32.21-33: Hezekiah's deliverance, lapse and restoration.

Despite the amount of material in these chapters, the links between C and Kings are relatively few. To all intents and purposes, C's is a new composition. Only a dozen verses are parallel to Kings, and even then there are many variations. In summary, 2 Chron. 29.1-2 is parallel to 2 Kgs 18.1b-3; 2 Chron. 29.3 to the end of 2 Chronicles 31 is essentially independent; 2 Chronicles 32 is a drastic reduction and substantial modification of 2 Kgs 18.13–20.21.

Even more strikingly, essentially the first three chapters, or over 70 percent, of C's presentation relate to the first half of the first year of Hezekiah's twenty-nine-year reign (2 Chron. 31.7): the material in these

chapters (2 Chron. 29.3–31.21; 82 verses in all) is an elaboration of half a
verse in Kings (2 Kgs 18.4a).

2 Chronicles 29.1-30: The Purification of the Temple and the Restoration of the Cult

The section is subdivided into seven paragraphs.

Verses 1-11: Hezekiah's Summons to the Priests and Levites to Purify the Temple

C makes a striking beginning to his account of Hezekiah's reign (v. 1).
For the only time in his presentation of a reign, he opens directly with
the king's name. The reason for this unique opening must be that the
name, 'Hezekiah', 'May the LORD establish', contains the very verb,
ḥzq, 'to establish', which is one of the chief points at issue in C's
whole presentation of the monarchy (1 Chron. 22.13; 2 Chron. 1.1;
cf. 2 Chron. 32.5): how is a king 'established'?

> The inversion, by which C brings 'Hezekiah' to the fore—and the awk-
> ward adverbial construction, 'as a twenty-five year old' with the verb, 'he
> reigned', which confirms the deliberate nature of the inversion—is lacking
> in 2 Kgs 18.1.
>
> It is notable that the Kings narrative uses almost consistently through-
> out (43× to one exception) the form of the name Hezekiah in which the
> noun from the root *ḥzq* occurs ('the LORD is my strength [Hizkiyahu]'),
> whereas C almost always (37× to five exceptions) uses the form contain-
> ing the imperfect tense of the verb from the same root, 'May the LORD
> establish [Yehizkiyahu]'. C thus imparts a conditional overtone to the
> whole that is thoroughly in line with his overall purpose.

Hezekiah is about to be portrayed as true to the hopes expressed in his
name; with the exception of a couple of incidents (2 Chron. 32.25-26,
31), he is to be consistently commended.

This foreshadowing of the success of the reign through the name of
the king anticipates the standard theological evaluation (element 4) in
the annalistic framework with which each reign is introduced (Introduction to 2 Chron. 10–36). Thus, before returning to the exposition
of this commendable reign, C now quickly provides the first three elements of that framework. The data are derived from 2 Kgs 18.2. The
orthodox character of the names of Hezekiah's mother and maternal
grand-father may be noted: Abijah, 'The LORD is my father',
Zechariah, 'The LORD has remembered'. Neither of these personages

occurs elsewhere in the Hebrew Bible (apart from the Kings parallel).

The standard of comparison for Hezekiah is David (v. 2; only Jehoshaphat, 2 Chron. 17.3, and Josiah, 2 Chron. 34.2 are picked out for this accolade; contrast Ahaz, 2 Chron. 28.1). Indeed, he is to be a new David/Solomon. This is to be demonstrated pre-eminently in his care for the Temple.

The Temple, through altar and ark, enables and expresses what Israel is meant to be among the nations of the world. Hezekiah loses no time in ensuring that that institution, which can be the sole foundation of his reign, is reopened and restored (v. 3). In the very first month of his very first year, he sets about the task of re-establishing the Temple, which Ahaz has so catastrophically neglected. The reopening of its doors contrasts with 2 Chron. 28.24; his 'restoration [*hzq*] of them' picks up his own name (v. 1). As is to be clear from 2 Chron. 30.2-3, this reopening took place in the first calendar month, which should have been the month of Passover; the related pilgrimage festival of Unleavened Bread (2 Chron. 30.13) will certainly have been in abeyance under Ahaz.

But restoration is not just a matter of physical repairs. The Temple has to be purified of the contaminating uncleanness of the Ahaz regime (in C's account this has been a matter of violation, of stripping the Temple of its furnishings, rather than of importing any of the apparatus of an alien cult, as in 2 Kgs 16.10-16).

Hezekiah gathers the priests and Levites (v. 4) (as David had done, 1 Chron. 15.4) at the 'square of the east' (see location [element 8] under 2 Chron. 25.23). They proceed from the main access gate on the east side of the Temple to begin the work of purification.

Hezekiah's address to them (vv. 5-11) falls into six parts:

(a) An opening summons for a hearing (v. 5a), as in the prophetic mould (2 Chron. 13.4). The 'Levites' addressed must, in the light of the sequel, include the priests.

(b) An instruction (v. 5b): 'sanctify yourselves and the house'. The whole system of 'holiness' is to be reinstated: just as there is 'holy time', so there is 'holy space'—a system of physical separation and apartness expressing symbolically dedication to the exclusive use of God. Within that sacred space, there are gradations, expressing a hierarchy of holiness. The dedication of Israel's whole life is symbolically effected by the dedication of the appropriate offering by the appropriate Levite at the appropriate place.

The nature of the Deity in whose name the whole system is restored is solemnly reacknowledged and the significance of his tradition reaffirmed (1 Chron. 5.25; again v. 6). The obverse of sanctification is the removal of 'pollution' (*niddâ*, v. 5), caused whether through physical object or unauthorized access (various causes of *niddâ* are specified in much narrower senses in Lev. 12.1-8; 15.19-33; 18.19; 20.21).

(c) The explanation (vv. 6-7): the need for the purification is explained in terms of the violations perpetrated by Ahaz. The archetypal sin is, once again, *ma'al*, depriving God of his rights (1 Chron. 2.7). The vocabulary of rejection is used ('*zb*, 1 Chron. 28.9), here with a new metaphor, 'turning the back on' (cf. 2 Chron. 30.8; 36.13). The archaic term, 'tabernacle', with its early associations with Moses, which, since the construction of the Temple, has been obsolete (2 Chron. 5.5), is now used for effect (cf. 1 Chron. 6.32). The specific denials of God's rights are spelled out in v. 7: the closing of the doors (2 Chron. 28.24), which would inevitably involve the extinction of the lamps, the non-burning of incense, and the suspension of the sacrificial cult (1 Chron. 28.11-19).

Hezekiah reminds the Levites of the consequences of such neglect (vv. 8-9): defeat in battle and captivity of women and children, which Judah has just experienced (2 Chron. 28.5-8), are to be understood as evidence of the anger of the LORD (1 Chron. 27.24). The effects of these experiences have not been confined to Israel: as Israel in its faithfulness is meant to be a beacon to the world of the Gentiles, so, when it fails in its destiny, it becomes a spectacle to all nations, a source of horror and appalment (ideas which are very consistently attached to the word 'horror' in five out of its eight occurrences in the Hebrew Bible, for example, Deut. 28.25; Jer. 15.4, where 'to all the kingdoms of the earth' is explicitly added).

(d) Hezekiah now makes his declaration of intent (v. 10; for 'now', cf. 1 Chron. 17.7; so, again, v. 11). It is a striking coincidence that the formulation, 'It has been in my mind', with which Hezekiah begins his declaration, is used elsewhere in C only in connection with the building or refurbishment of the Temple (1 Chron. 22.7). Hezekiah may be reflecting the original resolve of David.

His resolve is 'to make a covenant with the LORD'. It can hardly be doubted that, in context, the covenant is to restore the Temple and its rites: it is reinstatement of the existing covenant between the LORD and his people, as first mediated by Moses and then institutionalized by David in the Temple, not some brand new agreement (see 2 Chron. 34.31, where Josiah makes a covenant to keep the Covenant!).

> In the phrase, 'make a covenant with the LORD', the preposition in Hebrew is actually 'to, for' (cf. 1 Chron. 11.3). But there are many occurrences of the phrase 'make a covenant for' in the Hebrew Bible where this preposition appears to be used synonymously with the preposition 'with' (e.g. Jer. 32.40, 'for'; Jer. 31.33, 'with'). If the force of the preposition is pushed, then the sense would be that Hezekiah is making a covenant with the Levites on behalf of the LORD.

The only way to reverse the fury of God, inevitably expressed through reverse on the field of battle when the divine agent has forfeited his status, as has Ahaz, is to reinstate the sacramental system.

(e) Hezekiah turns, therefore, in direct appeal to the Levites (v. 11). He is addressing them uniquely as his 'sons' (compare David to Israel as, 'my brothers and my people', 1 Chron. 28.2): 'do not be idle' (the reflexive of the verb 'to be at ease').

(f) The reason for appeal to them is then given: as the LORD has chosen them alone to officiate in the Temple, they alone possess the sanctification necessary for the task of purification of the Temple (the specification, 'assistants' and 'sacrificers', covers both the Levites and the priests).

Verses 12-13: The Response of the Levites of Kohath,
Merari, Gershon, Elizaphan and Asaph
The Levites in their response are separated into two groups by MT (vv. 12-13; 14). At first sight this seems to be another example of arbitrariness on the part of MT (cf. 2 Chron. 27.5), but there may be an important factor in this division. The first group comprises representatives of the three major families of the Levites, Kohath, Merari and Gershon (1 Chron. 6.1).

> There are resemblances in the names of individuals in this list to those of Levites elsewhere (e.g. Mahath, Amasai, Joel and Azariah occur in 1 Chron. 6.35-36, Kish and Abdi in 1 Chron. 6.44, Joah and Zimmah in 1 Chron. 6.20-21, but identity can hardly be intended).

Since all Levites are derived from these three families, it is again surprising that further groups are specified separately (cf. 2 Chron. 20.19). Thus El[i]zaphan is a son of Uzziel, Kohath's fourth son (Exod. 6.16-22). But there is reason to specify him in particular in connection with the purification of the Temple: he shared in the disposal of the corpses of Nadab and Abihu from within the Tabernacle when they offered 'strange fire', the ultimate in contamination (Lev. 10.4-5).

There is a particular reason also for including Asaph in the first group of Levites, as opposed to Heman and Jeduthun in the second. When these three families of musicians were designated to their tasks by David in 1 Chronicles 16, Asaph (from Gershon) was assigned to the praise of the LORD at the ark in Jerusalem (vv. 1-7, 37), while Heman (from Kohath) and Jeduthun (from Merari) were appointed at the altar in Gibeon (vv. 39-42). The reason for the distinction between these two groups of Levites is now clear: the first group are those concerned with the interior of the Temple itself, above all with the ark of the covenant, the primary focus of Temple worship (see 1 Chron. 15.8 for further association of Elizaphan with the ark). The second group are concerned with the purification of the inner court of the Temple, where the altar of burnt offering was situated, where the preparatory rites were performed. Though these groups of musicians are later brought together in Temple worship (2 Chron. 5.12), they may not have lost their specific associations.

Verses 14-17: The Response of the Levites of Heman and Jeduthun; Purification of the Temple by the Sixteenth Day
The rites of purification of the Temple thus proceed with due regard to the degrees of holiness of the complex and to the degrees of sanctification of the personnel involved. How the priests 'sanctify themselves' is not disclosed: it is done there and then, for they too begin their work on 'the first day of the first month' (compare the seven days of the ordination ritual of Exod. 29; Lev. 8.33). All is thus done not just 'in accordance with the command of the king' but 'by authority of the words of the LORD'. The priests alone have access to the Temple proper. The Levites receive from them the pollutions and consign them to the water-course in the Kidron Valley to the east of the city (2 Chron. 15.16).

The procedures for dealing with the pollution of the Temple are not described in detail (the role of the levitical musicians at the rededication of the walls of Jerusalem in Neh. 12.27 may be compared). The abhorrence at the whole notion of the pollution of the house of God may be gathered from the general horror with which pollution is regarded, for example in Leviticus, underlying which is the principle of holiness (Lev. 11.44; compare the prescribed rites for the purification of a domestic house in Lev. 14.34-53 or the rites for the purification of the sanctuary on the Day of Atonement, Lev. 16.16). It is that pollution with which C's work in part culminates in 2 Chron. 36.14.

Verses 18-19: Report to Hezekiah
The rites of purification systematically undo the pollutions of Ahaz. The use of C's stock vocabulary shows how the reigns of Ahaz and Hezekiah are being presented as polar opposites, signal examples of failure and ideal: what Ahaz had 'rejected' (1 Chron. 28.9) through his 'unfaithfulness' (1 Chron. 2.7), has now been 'reinstated' (the verb is *kûn*, as in 1 Chron. 14.2) and 'hallowed' (the act enabling the destiny of Israel as holy, 1 Chron. 6). The two major areas of the Temple are itemised, as in v. 17: the court, where the altar stands as place of burnt offering, 1 Chron. 22.1; the nave of Temple, where the twelve loaves of the showbread are laid out, 1 Chron. 9.32. The actions of Ahaz have been reversed (2 Chron. 28.24). The priests and Levites accordingly report to the king that all is now in readiness: the focal point of national life has been restored; the necessary round of sacral observance can recommence.

Verses 20-25: Hezekiah and the Leaders of the People Provide the Burnt Offerings and the Sin Offering
The first act in the purified Temple must be one of purification of the nation ('all Israel', v. 24). As leader of the community, Hezekiah 'gathers' the other leaders for concerted action (v. 20; cf. the precedent for such a 'gathering' under David, 1 Chron. 23.2). Together, they provide the sacrificial animals for the national burnt offering (seven bulls, seven rams, seven male lambs, cf. v. 24) and sin offering (seven he-goats, v. 21). They ascend from the palace, driving these animals with them to the Temple, where they are met by the priests.

> The provision for this rite of national purification is unique. For comparison, one may cite David's offering at the bringing of the ark into Jerusalem (1 Chron. 15.26): seven bulls and seven rams, as an act of national celebration (no goats for a sin offering were required on that occasion of national harmony). Again for comparison, one may note the sacrifices which by coincidence were appropriate to the seventeenth day of the first month (presumably the date in view here: Hezekiah 'rises early in

the morning', v. 20, after he has been told that the sixteen days of purification of the Temple in the first month have been completed, v. 17). That day falls within the context of the Festival of Unleavened Bread, though as Unleavened Bread was due to start on the fifteenth, when the Temple was still being purified, that Festival could not have been observed in Hezekiah's first month; see the Passover in 2 Chronicles 30. These offerings were: two bulls, one ram, seven yearling male lambs as burnt offerings, in addition to the two daily yearling male lambs, and a goat as a sin offering (Num. 28.16-25). For statistics for other offerings, see table at 1 Chron. 29.21.

The laying of hands on the head of the victim by the offerer as a rite of substitutionary identification corresponds to the rite for the whole burnt-offering in Lev. 1.4; it is not quite clear in v. 22 whether as in Leviticus it is the laity who slaughter, not the priests (contrast Ezek. 44.11). As in Leviticus, the blood of the burnt offering is poured out by the bowlful over the altar of burnt offerings (1 Chron. 28.17).

This is the only time when the sin offering is mentioned in C. Again, this sin offering matches no specific legislation in the Pentateuch. In Lev. 4 the appropriate sin offering is one bull for the high priest (vv. 3-12) or for the people as a whole (vv. 13-21), one he-goat for the prince (vv. 22-26), and one she-goat or female lamb for the individual (vv. 27-35). Again for the sake of comparison, one may note that on the Day of Atonement (on the tenth of the seventh month, therefore not in view here) the victims were a bull as a sin offering and a ram as a burnt offering for the high priest and his family, and two he-goats, one as sin offering and one as the 'scape-goat', and a ram as a burnt offering for the people (Lev. 16.3, 5). One can only assume that seven, the number of sacrificial animals of each variety prepared by Hezekiah, represents a perfect, complete offering; there is nothing in the text to imply that it represents a week of observances (compare the dedication of the altar in Num. 7.87-88, where twelve of each—one per tribe of Israel—were offered).

The slaughter and the handling of the blood in vv. 23-24 contrasts with the legislation in Leviticus 4. Here it is not the offerers, but the priests, who sacrifice; none of the blood is taken into the nave of the Temple. This distancing of the laity, including the king, from the sacrificial rites thus lays greater weight on the priests and the adequacy of the rites of purification already carried out by them.

There is a further important difference to be registered between Hezekiah's actions here and the stipulations for the normal sin-offering in Leviticus 4. There, the problem envisaged is *inadvertent* infringement of the laws of pollution (such as bodily discharge, contact with a dead body; the offence is summed up in the general expression, as doing 'any of the things commanded by the LORD, which ought not to be done', Lev. 4.2). In Israel's present case, the predicament is of a different order. The pollution caused by King Ahaz has been deliberate, systematic and sustained. This application of the law of the sin offering to *deliberate* offences covering the life of the people as a whole thus represents a radical extension by C of the legislation of the Pentateuch (it is similar to the way in which he applies the law for the individual guilty of *ma'al* in Lev. 5.14–6.7 to the life of Israel as a whole, 1 Chron. 10.13-14). Its application to a situation unimagined by the legislation represents an equally radical extension of the understanding of divine grace.

As the restorer of the Davidic system, Hezekiah completes the act of restitution by reinstalling the Temple musicians (v. 25; for the verb, cf. 1 Chron. 6.31). The action of the cult is accompanied and complemented by music and words; the cymbals, the lutes and the harps are the instruments of the Levites as in 1 Chron. 15.16. Music-making is a form of prophecy in C (1 Chron. 25.1); thus it stands under the authority of the two prophets associated with the later career of David, Gad (1 Chron. 21.9) and Nathan (1 Chron. 17.1). Even David is here subordinated to the prophets as mediums of revelation.

Verse 26: The Levites and the Priests are Installed with their Respective Musical Instruments
The emphasis MT places upon the musical role of the Levites and priests by giving it a separate paragraph of six words is notable. The priests with their trumpets are now added to the Levites. Whereas the music of the Levites accompanies Psalms that verbalize the actions of God in the past, the trumpet, with its unvarying note sounded by the priests, announces the arrival of God now in triumph with the ark (1 Chron. 15.24). As in the cult the actions of priest and Levite are complementary, so in the music accompanying the cult the one is not complete without the other (2 Chron. 5.13). It is that joint celebration by the combined forces of Levites and priests that the MT pauses to contemplate.

C stresses that the priests and Levites play the 'instruments of David', not just to claim Davidic authority for their music but to contrast the destruction of the 'instruments' by Ahaz in 2 Chron. 28.24.

Verses 27-30: The Recommencement of the Daily Whole Burnt Offering

Now that the Temple has been duly purged and purified, the perpetual ordinance of the twice daily whole burnt offering (Num. 28.3) can begin again. Hezekiah issues the command for the restart (v. 27).

> A notable absence is that of fire from heaven to re-inaugurate the cult (contrast 2 Chron. 7.1)

But the cult is no mere routine, mechanical round of observance. It can only recommence if the liturgy is also ready to recommence; sacrifice is accompanied by the song of the Levite and the trumpet blast of the priest. During the ceremony of the kindling of the burnt offering, the whole sacral assembly (1 Chron. 13.2) prostrate themselves. After the ceremony, king and people in an extremity of emotion (using the same vocabulary as at the moment of exaltation at the designation of Solomon, 1 Chron. 29.20) again prostrate themselves; praise redoubles to the highest pitch of fervour 'in the words of David and of Asaph' (1 Chron. 16.7).

The scene is now set for an expression of devotion that surpasses the stated round of obligations: the presentation of thanksgiving and free-will offerings. To signal that expression of extraordinary devotion MT now puts it in a separate section.

2 Chronicles 29.31-36: The Celebration of the Restoration of the Temple

In celebration of the restored Temple, Hezekiah summons the sacral assembly to give free rein to their devotion. He uses the striking figure of 'ordination' (v. 31; as David has already done in 1 Chron. 29.5): it is not just the priests, to whom ordination properly belongs, who have 'filled their hand'; it is the whole community who, by their united purpose and commitment, have shown their common zeal. They can, therefore, 'draw near' to present their offerings (a verb used of priestly activity, e.g. Exod. 19.22). That shared commitment finds natural expression in the offering of sacrifices that are over and above those required for the day-to-day servicing of the cult: communion sacrifices that by the sharing of the victim between God, priest and participant in the sacrificial meal are an unsurpassed expression of community solidarity (1 Chron. 29.21); thank offerings (mentioned here for the first time in C; cf. 2 Chron. 33.16) in response to special favour of God (cf. Lev. 7.11-15); and free-will offerings (again, 1 Chron. 29.5), appropriately in the form of whole burnt offerings, as an expression of selfless gratitude.

> The scale of the free-will offerings thus presented—whole burnt offerings, 70 cattle, 100 rams and 200 male lambs; 'holy things', 600 cattle and 3, 000 sheep (not to mention the further enormous provision in 2 Chron. 30.24)—can only be gauged from other comparable occasions: see table at 1 Chron. 29.21.
>   The 'holy things' are distinguished from the 'most holy things': the latter relate to those offerings that are brought into the interior of the sanctuary (e.g. cereal offering, Lev. 2.3; sin offering, Lev. 6.18; showbread, Lev. 24.9); the former to those which do not, in this case, thank offerings (Lev. 7.31; Num. 18.11-19).

Scarcely surprisingly, such a colossal scale of sacrifice far outstrips the capacity of the priests to cope. The only possible reservation ('only', the first word of v. 34) in the whole restoration is that the priests are not adequate to the task in number or sanctity (the priests are in any case the means not the end). In C's view, the Levites, as faithful teachers and monitors, are the ultimate expression and guardians of holiness; they stand ready to assist the priests in the task (the key term, 'strengthen', 1 Chron. 11.10, is used). For the occasion, they help at least in the flaying of the victims, but not presumably in the pouring of the blood at the altar (for normal procedure in sacrifice—ritual slaughter, presenting of blood, flaying, dismembering, arranging parts on altar, see Lev. 1.5-9).

It is striking how in this passage groups are moved up in the scale of holiness. The people have already been addressed as though they were priests (v. 31); now the Levites are given temporary promotion. The whole account is designed to express how to the ultimate degree—if not beyond—Hezekiah's action marks the absolute reversal of Ahaz's reign. As Ahaz's reign has represented a high point of *ma'al*, so Hezekiah's an equally high point of holiness (the key root *qdš*, deliberately recurs in vv. 33, 34 [twice]).

The colossal scale of the sacrifices is again underlined in v. 35. Not only was there this vast number of whole burnt offerings for the priests to cope with; there were the communion sacrifices, which demanded careful butchering for the burning of only certain parts of the victims (e.g. Lev. 3.3-4); there were the libations of wine that accompanied the whole burnt offerings (e.g. Num. 15.1-12).

Thus the whole 'worship of the House of the LORD', the system of cult and liturgy, is reinstated. The response of king and people is one of joy (1 Chron. 12.40), as intense as it is instant; the harmony intended by God has been attained. It has all happened at a stroke— necessarily so, given the affirmations of sacramental theology: to reinstate the symbol and the vehicle with a perfect intention is by that act to reinstate the reality. As the worship was undertaken, so, sacramentally, God undertook for the people (see the matching use of the key term, *kûn*, 1 Chron. 14.2: it is used both for the fact that worship was 're-established' in v. 35 and for what God 'established' for the people in v. 36).

2 Chronicles 30.1-9: The Invitation to Celebrate the Passover

Meantime, the date for the celebration of Passover, the annual, national commemoration of Israel's status as a free people through their original deliverance from Egypt, has elapsed (see C's play on 'negative Passover', 1 Chron. 21.12, and on the continuing potentiality of Egypt/Cush, 1 Chron. 1.8, to be the power of the nations of the world to re-enslave Israel, for example, 2 Chron. 12.2-12). The Passover should be held on the night of the 14th–15th of the first month (Exod. 12.6), but at that time the priests and Levites are still in the process of purifying the sanctuary (2 Chron. 29.17). Nonetheless, as in the emergency conditions provoked by uncleanness envisaged in Num. 9.6-12, the plan is to observe the Passover in the second month.

Verse 1 gives a summary of the action: the summons to both north and south, reinforced by letters to the immediate neighbours in the northern hill country, 'to come to the house of the LORD in Jerusalem, to observe Passover in honour of the LORD, the God of Israel'. C uses all the loaded terms: the names of God in his personal, relational nature and in his cosmic, transcendental one; 'Israel' in the ideal sense of the twelve-tribe system. 'Passover' is also (as not uncommonly in the Hebrew Bible) used absolutely, without the definite article (it is subsequently used interchangeably with and without the definite article in this chapter).

Verses 2-5 provide a 'flash-back' describing how Hezekiah set in train the planning for holding the Passover in the second month. He 'took counsel' (v. 2; 1 Chron. 13.1; cf. his earlier corporate act in 2 Chron. 29.4) with the leadership and with the sacral assembly (1 Chron. 13.2). The reason for not having held it in the first month is now given in slightly different form (v. 3): again, it is deficiency on the part of the priests—'they had not sufficiently sanctified themselves'—nor had the people come up to Jerusalem to observe the pilgrimage festival. The support for the plan is enthusiastic; messages, 'a voice', are to be sent out throughout the ideal extent of the settlements of Israel from Beer-sheba in the south to Dan in the north (v. 5; the sequence as in 1 Chron. 21.2).

There are significant resonances in that expression 'to send a proclamation throughout all Israel' (v. 5), especially when it is taken in conjunction with the conclusion of the whole Passover narrative in 2 Chron. 31.1, 'All the Israelites returned each to his holding'. The proclamation throughout the land of the return of each to his ancestral holding is part of the eschatological expectations associated with the Jubilee (Lev. 25.9-10). There are echoes of that expectation in the conclusion of C's whole work in the proclamation of Cyrus (2 Chron. 36.22; cf. 1 Chron. 9.2). Here, in the celebration of the Passover in the time of Hezekiah, there is an interim realization of that hope and an anticipation of that final home-coming, just as every Passover is an anticipation of 'next year in Jerusalem'.

A further reason for the proclamation is given at the end of v. 5: the consciousness of how incomplete as yet is the implementation of all the requirements of the written Law.

> The ambiguity of that last phrase is well indicated by the variety of renderings in the English Versions:
> NEB: 'Never before had so many kept it according to the prescribed form';
> JPSV: 'not often did they act in accord with what was written';
> NRSV: 'for they had not kept it in great numbers as prescribed' (NIV similar).
> The last seems to be on the right lines, in the light of the recurrence of a similar phrase in v. 13.

The messengers (2 Chron. 12.11) speed with the letters from the king and his leaders throughout north and south (vv. 6-9; the reverse geographical direction [contrast v. 5] may represent the envisaging of the action as a return to the ideal primal time). The message is, however, in the main addressed to the north; it is a summons to learn the lessons of history and an invitation to return to the worship of the LORD by coming to Jerusalem to share in the Passover. It affects Judah only in the solidarity of the nation ('your brothers', v. 7), in so far as the experience of the north provides an object lesson from which all can

profit. The message is an exposition, in five parts, of sacramental theology: the response of God is directly co-ordinated with human action
(cf., e.g., 2 Chron. 15.2b). At its heart (parts 2 and 3) stands the central theme of C's work: God is constant and consistent; those who
commit *ma'al*, 1 Chron. 2.7, who defraud God of his rights, forfeit
their share in his land; those who acknowledge his rights, find that he
is gracious and compassionate. In bald outline the five parts run:

1. if you return to him, he will return to your survivors
   (v. 6b);
2. as they defrauded him, he made their land a desolation (v. 7);
3. if you acknowledge his rights, his anger will be turned away
   (v. 8);
4. if you return to him, your exiles will return to this land
   (v. 9a);
5. he will not turn from you, if you return to him (v. 9b).

The parts are closely interconnected structurally with one another. 1 and 5
form the outer framework; the two phrases of 5 have been inverted so that
the last phrase of the whole composition corresponds directly with the
first. The verb 'to return' [*šûb*] is a major linking theme (vv. 6b [2×], 8, 9
[3×]. The force of the verb is sacramental: 'as you turn, so he turns'; see
the prayer of St Augustine cited at 2 Chron. 15.2). The play on the
meaning of the verb *šûb* is coupled in v. 9 with a play on the noun/
participle for 'captors', *šôbîm*. The actions of 'your fathers and your
brothers' (vv. 7, 8) are linked to the fate of 'your brothers and your children' (v. 9). The defrauding of God in v. 7 can be made good by the
recognition of God's prerogatives, 'his holy place which he has made
holy for ever' (v. 8).

As befits an invitation to Passover, the whole is an impassioned plea
based on shared Israelite tradition. It is addressed to 'the sons of
Israel', Israel in its ideal, unified, genetic descent. It is in the name of
the personal God of Israel, the LORD, the God of the tradition of the
patriarchs (1 Chron. 5.25), Abraham, Isaac and, significantly, 'Israel',
that the messengers speak. The bitter experience of deportation of the
north at the hands of the Assyrian kings—again the plural is used, as
in 2 Chron. 28.16—is presupposed (cf. 2 Kgs 15.29; 17.6, the latter
depending on how strictly C adheres to the chronology implied by
Kings; see on 2 Chron. 28.6). The experience is all the more bitter for
being in C's view unnecessary. If only Israel had acknowledged the
LORD, they would not have been left a tiny remnant (2 Chron. 12.7)

and his land would not have been devastated (Judah, too, has not escaped, 2 Chron. 29.6). The only way to reversal of fortunes is 'to give hand to the LORD' (v. 8), a turn of phrase already used of acknowledgment of authority (1 Chron. 29.24). It is only by the faithful response of the present generation ('serve' in cult and in life, 1 Chron. 28.9) that the adversity of the past can be undone and hope of restoration can be kindled.

2 Chronicles 30.10-27: The Celebration of Passover and Unleavened Bread

Again the MT subdivides the section quite unequally, but that inequality serves to highlight the relative significance of the elements of the narrative.

Verses 10-19: The Zeal of those who Come Outruns their Discretion
The first sections of the presentation of the reign of Hezekiah have told of the purification of the Temple and its personnel; this section records the purification of the city of Jerusalem and the populace who come on pilgrimage.

The king's messengers find only limited response in the north (though in absolute terms still a sizeable number, v. 18). They are met with ridicule in the immediate territories to the north, Ephraim and Manasseh in the central hill country and in Zebulun in southern Galilee (v. 10).

> The unique conjugation of the verb, 'to make sport of', is perhaps to distinguish this negative reaction from the use of the same root in a different conjugation of the approved action of David in 1 Chron. 13.8; 15.29.

Yet there are some from Manasseh and Zebulun, and Asher on the far north-west coast, who 'humble themselves'—the first step in rehabilitation (2 Chron. 7.14)—and who come as pilgrims to Jerusalem (v. 11).

By contrast, the response in Judah is unanimous (cf. 1 Chron. 12.38): what God has planned through his faithful agents, he enables (v. 12).

The vocabulary of approved concerted action by the sacral community is now used in v. 13: 'they assemble' (1 Chron. 11.1, 13; 13.2) in numbers more appropriate to the occasion (contrast v. 5). In anticipation of the main point of the section, the occasion is now called

'Festival of Unleavened Bread', normally a seven-day festival from the fifteenth to the twenty-second of the month, rather than the one night of 'Passover'.

As lodging-place for the pilgrimage festival, the city has itself now to be purged of all the remnants of Ahaz's regime (v. 14). The altars and incense burners (?; the nominal use of this feminine participle is unique in the Hebrew Bible) which he had installed throughout the city (2 Chron. 28.24) are torn down and, like the pollutions within the Temple, thrown into the water-course of the Kidron (2 Chron. 29.16).

The pilgrims slaughter their Passover victims (v. 15). The text then takes a surprising turn: the priests and Levites 'are ashamed'. At first sight, it is as though they were put to shame by the zeal of the pilgrims. But the more likely explanation is given in vv. 17-18: inevitably, among such a large influx of pilgrims, of whom the majority are from the polluted north, there are many who are not in a state of ritual cleanness. The priests are scandalized. Verse 16 may refer, not be the precautionary measure they now take to make atonement (whole burnt offerings are surprising in connection with Passover), but, rather, to the measures they have already undertaken to sanctify themselves and the sanctuary by offering whole burnt offerings at the altar in the approved manner (2 Chron. 29.15-35). Their preparations do not avail in face of this influx from the north. The Levites do what they can by undertaking the slaughter of the victims on behalf of those ritually unclean. But, even so, the pilgrims 'do not eat the Passover in accordance with the written Law'.

At this critical moment (vv. 18b, 19), Hezekiah appeals to the principle he has already laid down in his letter (cf. v. 9): each one who seeks the LORD 'the God of his fathers' with a pure intention will find that the LORD is gracious and forgiving (Hezekiah uses the key terms, *kûn*, 'to set', 1 Chron. 14.2, and *drš*, 'to seek', 1 Chron. 10.13-14). The LORD is 'good' (1 Chron. 16.34) and can himself, beyond any rites of the sanctuary, effect atonement.

> Quite what is the legislation of 'Moses the man of God' that C has in mind (v. 16) is also unclear. The emphasis on ritual purity suggests an observance of Passover as envisaged in Deut. 16.1-8, where the slaughter of the sacrificial victims should take place at the Temple, with the Levites and the priests officiating as at any regular sacrificial offering, rather than in Exod.12, where the official clergy have no overt role.

Verse 20: The LORD *Heals the People*
Again in one brief, pregnant, sentence, MT pauses to signalize
the gracious response of the LORD. He 'hears' Hezekiah's prayer
(2 Chron. 6.19): he stands by the terms of Hezekiah's invitation. He
'heals' the people (2 Chron. 7.14): the life-giving properties of the
relationship realized are available even to the people of the north.

Verse 21: The Festival of Unleavened Bread Is Held
The fact that the pilgrims went on to observe the festival of Unleavened Bread after the Passover has already been anticipated in v. 13.
Here is it formally recorded. The seven days of the festival correspond to the legislation of Exod. 23.15; Lev. 23.6-8; Deut. 16.8.

The keynote of the celebration is joy (1 Chron. 12.40—strikingly in
another context of participation by the north): primarily, joy in the
renewal of the fruits of the earth at the beginning of harvest. But this
joy is linked to the knowledge that those who had once been slaves in
Egypt now enjoy freedom through the gift of the LORD's own land.
That joy is also the foretaste of the restoration of the Jubilee (cf. on
v. 5).

The daily hymn of praise is sung to the LORD by priest and Levite
as in 1 Chronicles 16 to the accompaniment of 'instruments of power'
(a unique phrase; perhaps read 'with all power' [*BHK* and *BHS*] as in
1 Chron. 13.8?).

Verse 22: The Essential Role of the Levites in that Celebration
Hezekiah encourages the Levites ('speaks to the heart' in reassurance
and comfort, e.g. Gen. 50.21; Isa. 40.2).

Their role is defined in the next three phrases, but each is somewhat
elusive in meaning. The first may mean either, 'who impart good
understanding for the LORD', referring to their teaching role (e.g.
Deut. 29.9); or, 'who sing psalms with good understanding to the
LORD', referring to their role as musicians (a dozen Psalm titles, e.g.
42, 44, 45, 52, use the same term); or simply, 'who showed understanding as regards the LORD', referring to their innate qualities (so
of Hezekiah himself, 2 Kgs 18.7; cf. Solomon, 1 Chron. 22.12;
2 Chron. 2.12).

The following phrase is equally obscure: 'they ate the Festival for
seven days'. At face value, this refers to their role as recipients of
'holy things' (2 Chron. 29.33); that is, as was their right and duty,

they ate their share of the sacrifices of the people (specified in the next phrase as communion sacrifices).

The final phrase ought to mean 'making confession [of sin] to the LORD' (compare the High Priest confessing the sins of Israel over the scapegoat in Lev. 16.21; cf. Lev. 5.5; or, suggestively, in the context of *ma'al*, Lev. 26.40; Num. 5.7). The title, 'the God of their fathers', picks up vv. 7 and 19.

These last two definitions of role would, however, be restricted to the priests, and there is no suggestion in the text that C is using 'all the Levites' in the narrow sense of 'levitical priests'. Accordingly, proposals have been made to read the text more broadly to refer to the Levites: thus in the second phrase, 'they carried out the festival for seven days' (*BHK* and *BHS*: *way^ekallû* for *wayyō'k^elû*, the same verb as that with which 2 Chron. 31.1 begins); and in the final phrase, 'giving thanks to the LORD'[1] (*môdîm*, a different conjugation of MT's *mitwaddîm*), that is, performing the levitical task of music as laid down in 1 Chronicles 16.

Verses 23-24aα: The Decision to Hold the Festival of Unleavened Bread for a Second Week: The Contribution of the King
As at the rededication of the Temple in 2 Chron. 29.31-36, the devotion of the people is expressed in spectacularly lavish provision for the altar, so again in the celebration of the first Festival of Unleavened Bread after that rededication the joy of the people (1 Chron. 12.40) spills over into still more exuberant fervour. A decision, again by the sacral assembly (1 Chron. 13.1-2), is taken to observe the Festival for a second week. Hezekiah now adds a further free-will offering of gigantic proportions—1000 bulls, 7000 sheep (cf. 2 Chron. 29.32-33; the verb used of Hezekiah's offering comes from the root from which the 'elevation offering', *t^erûmâ*, is derived, e.g. Exod. 29.26-27; Lev. 7.28-34, which is to be prominent in the next chapter, 2 Chron. 31.10, 12, 14; also 35.7-9).

Verses 24aβ-26: The Contribution of the Leaders and the Celebration of the Whole Community
To allow time for the stunning amount of the free-will offerings to sink in, MT again inserts a paragraph marker in mid-verse. It is now

---

1.   J. Milgrom, *Cult and Conscience: The Asham and the Priestly Doctrine of Repentance* (SJLA, 18; Leiden: Brill, 1976), n. 406.

the turn of the leaders of the community and they contribute a further 1000 bulls and 10,000 sheep as 'elevation offering'.

A terse note adds that, in contradistinction to 2 Chron. 29.34, the priests had now, a month later, sufficiently caught up with the requirements for their dedication.

A comprehensive list of participants is given (v. 25): the sacral assembly of Judah is listed separately from the sacral assembly of those from the north who had responded to the invitation: the priests and the Levites; the sojourners from the north, again noted separately from those resident in Judah (1 Chron. 22.2). As in the legislation on the Passover, the resident alien has a right to participate in the Festival (Exod. 12.48-49).

The high-water mark of piety that Hezekiah's reign represents is indicated by the comparison with Solomon (v. 26): the occasion and the joy engendered by it are without parallel since Solomon's time. What had been intended at the beginning has now been brought once again to realization.

Verse 27: The Prayer of the Priests and Levites is Accepted
The whole narrative is rounded off with the acceptance of the prayer of the priests (cf. Hezekiah's prayer, vv. 18-20). It is called a 'blessing', but, though blessing the people is one of the prerogatives of the High Priest (1 Chron. 23.13), it may rather have been a prayer for the blessing of the people rather than a direct blessing of the people themselves (cf. 1 Chron. 29.10; 2 Chron. 6.3). Thus, it is immediately called a 'prayer', which reaches to 'his holy dwelling [used again in 2 Chron. 36.15], to the heavens' (for the phrase, see, for example, Deut. 26.15, precisely in connection with the payment of tithes, which is to be a subject in the next section, 2 Chron. 31.5); for the heavens as the place sacramentally linked to Temple, city and land, where the LORD hears prayer, see Solomon's prayer, 2 Chron. 6.21.

*2 Chronicles 31.1-8: The Offering of Holy Things
by the Community*

The sub-division of the MT again makes the sequence of the action clear.

Verse 1: The Purification of the Land
'After all this has been completed': the systematic purification of the whole system of holiness and its re-establishment as vehicle of the continuing life of holiness proceeds to the next phase: first, it has been the Temple for the daily rites; then Jerusalem for the thrice-yearly pilgrimage festivals; now it is the land for the annual round of payment of 'holy things'.

The agents of purification of the land are 'all Israel who were found'—'all Israel', as the ideal extent of the community, is recognized. 'They went forth' with overtones of the host of the LORD on the march (1 Chron. 14.15). But, the object of their campaign is 'the cities of Judah': the present practical limits of that ideal are acknowledged.

In the event, the reform is not confined to Judah and Benjamin but covers the whole of the central hill country, including Ephraim and Manasseh.

The destruction of the cultic installations of the indigenous Canaanite population and religion follows a conventional catalogue: the pillars and green trees, symbols of male and female deities; the high places representing the seats of deities and their claims to rival cosmic powers; the altars as the place of communication between the physical and spiritual worlds (2 Chron. 14.3).

The upshot of these reforms, undertaken 'with completeness' is the restoration of 'all the descendants of Israel', at least in principle, to an ideal state of primal equilibrium: the whole land at peace, divided out among all the families of Israel, each in its heritable possession in the LORD's land (1 Chron. 9.2; cf. on 2 Chron. 30.5).

Verse 2: The Organization of the Clergy
The personnel whereby Israel is enabled to attain holiness are organized (the verb as in 1 Chron. 6.31) in the perpetual sequence of their duty rosters (cf. 1 Chron. 23–26; 2 Chron. 8.14: Hezekiah is again the new David/Solomon): the priests and Levites in the adoration and integration effected through atonement cult and the affirmations and celebrations of the liturgy (1 Chron. 6). It is thus that Israel attains its destiny—in a state of perpetual mobilization as the war camps (1 Chron. 9.19; 12.22) of the LORD of Hosts (the archaic associations of the language, 'war camps', vividly conjure up the primal ideal).

Verses 3-6: The Payment of Dues

The payment of offerings in kind lies at the heart of C's conception of the practice of holiness. These offerings are at once the symbol (the dedicated part which sacramentally represents the whole) and the vehicle (the physical means whereby the whole range of religious life is expressed and realized).

The duty to pay these dues extends throughout the whole community. There is an 'allocation' (the word used by C only in vv. 3-4) required from the crown estates (1 Chron. 27.31; 28.1) for the maintenance of the whole stated round of the sacrificial cult, daily, weekly, monthly and yearly (the obligations are 'written in the Law of the LORD', v. 3, most conveniently in Numbers 28–29; for the annual amount see at 1 Chron. 29.21).

Every ordinary householder is responsible for the 'allocation' due to the priests and Levites; only so can the clergy be 'strong' (1 Chron. 11.10) in the Law of the LORD (v. 4), that is, devote themselves to their primary tasks in sanctifying the people. As soon as the word is promulgated (the vocabulary as in 1 Chron. 13.2), the people enthusiastically respond (vv. 5-6) with the transmission of 'holy things', firstfruits (Lev. 2.11-16; 23.9-21; Num. 15.19-21; 18.12-18; Deut. 18.3-4; 26.2) and tithes (Lev. 27.30-32; Num. 18.21-24; Deut. 14.22-29; 26.12-14), until they are piled, 'heaps upon heaps'.

Verse 7: The Accumulation of Dues

MT notes the payment of these 'holy things' in a separate paragraph, for they are the primary evidence for the realization of the main theme of C's whole work—the people's holiness. It is the shortfall in these 'holy things' that provides the primary index of unfaithfulness, *ma'al*. The payment this year begins in the third month, no doubt with the 'first-fruits' due at the wheat harvest (Exod. 34.22), and culminate with the tithes of oil and wine at the Festival of Tabernacles in the seventh month.

Verse 8: The Leaders' Blessing

The paragraph rounds off the section on the faithful response of the people. The evidence of the 'heaps' of payments due in kind is overwhelming that the system of holiness is perfectly in place. In grateful acknowledgment that the people have done everything required of them, Hezekiah and the other leading representatives of the people raise the prayer of 'blessing' (in the sense of 2 Chron. 30.27) to the LORD and his people.

2 Chronicles 31.9-21: The Reception of the Holy Things by the Clergy

The climax to the sections on the purification of Temple, city and land is the responsible use of these offerings of the people. As in 1 Chron. 9.17-32, it again at first sight seems a gross anticlimax that such mundane considerations should round off the spiritual exaltation of the reformation of Hezekiah's first year. But, as there, the whole point of the activities has been to set in place the mechanism by which the holiness of the people can be demonstrated, through the sacramental offering of 'holy things', and so the holiness be maintained.

Verses 9-10: The Question of the Disposal of the 'Holy Things'
The priests bear a heavy responsibility for the proper application of these offerings of the people in kind (cf. Lev. 22.1-16). By inappropriate action they can invalidate the gifts. Hezekiah, therefore, now turns to the clergy to require of them an account of the disposal of these heaps of 'holy things' (the thematic, term *drš* [1 Chron. 10.13-14], is now used with a preposition to indicate 'calling to account', 2 Chron. 24.6).

The chief priest (already in office under Uzziah, 2 Chron. 26.17), given here his full Zadokite title (1 Chron. 29.22) to underline his responsibility, replies on behalf of all the clergy with a certain pious disingenuousness: God has so greatly blessed his people that they cannot cope with the embarrassment of riches. Such has been the overwhelming response of the people that the priesthood has been swamped. They have eaten of their allotted portions of holy things to satiety and still there are vast quantities in surplus (*hāmôn*, the word used by David for his bountiful provision for the construction of the Temple, 1 Chron. 29.16).

> Azariah, the high priest, introduces the term *t^erûmâ*, for the offerings of the people (cf. 2 Chron. 30.24). It is used here in an all-purpose way as in Num. 18.8-32, which gives an idea of the scale of offerings the priests and Levites have to handle. It may have more specific uses, such as free-will offerings in kind (Exod. 25.2-3; 35.5, 21, 24), or—significantly in the context of the census in 1 Chronicles 21—the 'levy' imposed on the people when they are mustered for service (Exod. 30.13-15; cf. Num. 31.52).

Verses 11-21: Measures for the Storing and Disbursement of the 'Holy Things'

Hezekiah is not satisfied with the reply. Gratifying though the heaps of offerings are as evidence of the devotion of the people, they cannot be left lying about, but must be disposed of in an appropriate manner.

The final task is, therefore, the provision (the thematic term, *kûn*, 1 Chron. 14.2, is used twice in v. 11) of store-chambers (1 Chron. 9.26) in the Temple, where the priests and Levites can account for the offerings of the people, for they are the evidence of the people's dedication to ensuring that the LORD is given due priority in all things. It is unexpected that the word for the store-chambers in this context is not 'treasuries' but 'halls', the rooms around the periphery of the court where the communion sacrifice is consumed. The stress is thus not on the storing, but on the use to which these offerings of the people are put.

To the modern mind, the obvious application of such surpluses is that they should be redistributed among the needy in the community. This would be a misunderstanding. The 'holy things' are, indeed, about to be applied for the support of one of the traditional vulnerable groups within society, the Levites (as, e.g., Num. 18.23 insists). But the point of the superabundance of the contributions is not that the community is in any way impoverished by them. Quite the contrary: the ideal is that by the giving of the contributions the prosperity of the community is assured, so that there are no poor within the community (cf. Deut. 15.4).

Accordingly, a team of twelve Levites, two supervisors and ten assistants, answerable to king and High Priest (called here 'leader of the house of the LORD', 1 Chron. 9.11); cf. 2 Chron. 24.11), is commissioned for the tallying, storing and distribution of the 'holy things' (vv. 12-13) in the Temple itself. They act 'reliably' (1 Chron. 9.26; the word is repeated in vv. 11, 15 and 18; cf. 2 Chron. 34.12).

> Some of the names occur in other lists (e.g. Mahath, 2 Chron. 29.12), but identity cannot be established.

Most intriguing is their leader, Chananiah (*qere*; NRSV gives the *kethib* reading, 'Conaniah'). His name is very similar to that of Chenaniah, the Levite in charge of the capitation tax levied from all Israel when they are mustered as the LORD's host (cf. 1 Chron. 15.22; 26.29). Identity of function, if not of name, seems certainly to be implied by the specification of his duties in v. 13: he is assisted by 'overseers' in the 'muster' of the people by king and High Priest (both 'designated' and 'muster' [NRSV, 'appointment', seems too vague] come from the key root, *pqd*; cf. 1 Chron. 21.5). By this standing 'muster' of Israel in its state of perpetual mobilization (1 Chron. 27), every duty to king and to God is rendered and monitored: Israel is established and maintained as the LORD's sacramental host.

A further Levite (vv. 14-15), the gatekeeper in charge of the eastern gate (1 Chron. 26.14-28), the point of most traffic in the Temple (2 Chron. 23.5), assisted by a team of six, is to arrange the appropriate disbursing among the divisions of the priests and their families in the thirteen priestly cities (1 Chron. 6.57-60).

> Verses 16-18 give the technicalities of the registers (1 Chron. 4.33). The sequence of ideas, and, in part, the text, are rather obscure (cf. variations in the English Versions). The complexity arises from the fact that not only have the duty rosters of priests to be supplied, but their families as well. This requires the registering of dependants.
>
> The first phrase of v. 16 appears to be parenthetical: besides distributing the 'holy things' for the support of the priesthood in the priestly cities (v. 15), 'to each one who came to the house of the LORD as each day required to serve in their duty rosters [2 Chron. 7.6] according to their divisions' (v. 16aβb), the six thus undertook in addition the task of enrolling the males of the priestly families from the age of three (v. 16aα).
>
> Not only so: along with this task of enrolling the priests by family (v. 17aα), they undertook the enrolling of the Levites from the age of twenty upwards—all 'by their duty-rosters by divisions' (v. 17aβb).
>
> Thus it was that these six not only had to provide for the priests (v. 15b), but had also to enrol (the opening infinitive at the beginning of v. 18, picking up the opening infinitive at the beginning of v. 15b) all the dependants of the whole company of clergy (perhaps, rather, 'on behalf of the whole sacral assembly [of Israel]').

Thus it was (v. 18b) that, by the faithfulness of this team of six, the clergy were sanctified as regards the consumption of the 'holy things'. There were still further subordinate teams in these landward areas in the priestly and levitical cities to ensure the support of the clergy (v. 19).

The section ends with a final commendation of Hezekiah's opening year using the vocabulary of highest endorsement (vv. 20-21). His loyalty and scrupulousness in according to the LORD all that is due to him as defined by the Law, evidenced above all in the restoration of the Temple with its fundamental role of securing the holiness of the people, are summed up in the key term, *drš* (1 Chron. 10.13-14).

Undertaking it all with a perfect intention, he 'prospered' (1 Chron. 22.11).

2 Chronicles 32.1-8: Sennacherib's Invasion.
The Security of the Land

The final stage of the presentation of the reign of Hezekiah, as ideal monarch in the mould of his ancestors David and Solomon, now follows. The Temple, capital and land have been purified. All that remains is acknowledgment by the nations of the world.

The stakes could not be higher. The adversary is Sennacherib, the Assyrian emperor who has carried all before him. To the human eye, Jerusalem offers easy pickings, the final conquest on Sennacherib's way to world dominion.

> Historical relativities are immaterial. The substance in Sennacherib's claim is of as little concern to C as is the chronology of events. The date of the invasion is totally vague, so far as C is concerned: it is 'after these matters and display of constancy'. C has so far dealt with the first six months of Hezekiah's reign. The fact that Sennacherib invades in Hezekiah's fourteenth year, according to 2 Kgs 18.13, or in 701, according to the Assyrian sources, that is, more than twenty years after his succession, is of no moment to C. He is concerned to dramatize theology.

This section on the onslaught of the world of the nations begins (v. 1) in a way rather similar to 2 Chronicles 20, the equivalent section of the reign of Jehoshaphat: 'After these things...there came...'

Sennacherib lays siege to 'the fortified cities' of Judah with the intention of annexing them. Only Jerusalem is left and the attack cannot be long delayed (v. 2).

> For a brief moment C touches the Kings text (2 Kgs 18.13), but after less than a verse he veers off in his own direction. It is no part of his purpose to represent Hezekiah, as Kings does, as submitting to Sennacherib and being forced to pay him a huge indemnity, stripping the royal and Temple treasuries (2 Kgs 18.14-16).

Security becomes the urgent issue. But this is not simply a physical matter: as C has been arguing all through his work, and is now about to expound at length, security is fundamentally a theological question: wherein does strength lie? Thus in v. 5 the thematic term, on which Hezekiah's very name is a play (2 Chron. 29.1), is introduced: 'Hezekiah found himself established' (2 Chron. 1.1). Along the same line is Sennacherib's question in v. 10: 'On what do you rely?' (1 Chron. 5.20).

Hezekiah takes appropriate defensive measures. It is the role of the Davidic king as sacramental representative of the LORD on earth to undertake those defensive actions that appropriately express the protective power of God (compare the organizing of the citizen army, the fortifying of outposts, the strengthening of the defences of Jerusalem, undertaken by earlier kings, e.g. 2 Chron. 8.5). The battle belongs to the LORD, but the LORD's human host has to be perfectly in tune with his purpose (cf., e.g., 2 Chron. 20.17).

Accordingly, Hezekiah 'takes common counsel' (1 Chron. 13.1) with the leaders, including the military heroes (1 Chron. 1.10; 11.10), of his people (v. 3). The project is to block up the springs in the vicinity of Jerusalem. It is an obvious military strategy in a hot climate to deny the enemy water. But there is a profounder significance. Water is one of the potent symbols of the Jerusalem tradition of theology: as the waters of chaos were once ruled by God at creation, so he continues to rule the powers of chaos in nature and in history (e.g. Ps. 46; compare the use of the water of Shiloah as figure for divine blessing in Isa. 8.5-8, in contrast to the turbulent waters of Sennacherib's river, the Euphrates; the vocabulary of Isa. 8.8 is picked up here in v. 4 [in a rather different sense!]).

The leaders gladly co-operate ('help', v. 3; 1 Chron. 5.20) and the people fall to (v. 4; 'gather', 1 Chron. 11.1) with a will. The generalization of the incident is shown by the use of the plural 'kings' (as in 2 Chron. 28.16) of the Assyrians. Hezekiah reinforces the defences of the city (v. 5), where they had fallen into disrepair (under Ahaz?; Uzziah and Jotham had both undertaken defence works in Jerusalem, 2 Chron. 26.9; 27.3); he heightens the towers, constructs a new outer wall (on the northern side?) and consolidates 'the Millo' (1 Chron. 11.8, probably the terraces on the slopes of Mt Ophel on which the 'city of David' was built [KBS]). He organizes his army and arms his troops with the conventional weapons of the infantryman (1 Chron. 5.18).

Hezekiah then gathers this sacramental host and addresses them encouragingly ('to the heart', 2 Chron. 30.22) in the 'square at the gate of the city' (v. 6; 2 Chron. 25.23; 29.4?). His speech falls into two parts: exhortation in the imperative and jussive (v. 7a), followed by the reason for compliance, introduced by 'because' (vv. 7b, 8a).

The exhortation uses standard vocabulary: 'be strong and of a good courage', as of those succeeding to the role of the LORD's agents on earth; 'fear not and do not be dismayed', as in the prophetic oracle of victory (1 Chron. 22.13, for both phrases).

The ground for confidence is precisely Jerusalemite Immanuel theology: 'the LORD is with us' (1 Chron. 11.9; five times in nine words the preposition 'with' is used); it is in the power of the LORD of Hosts that the 'horde' (2 Chron. 13.8) of the nations of the world can be vanquished. The relative physical strength of the two sides is irrelevant to the theological power of right at play in the situation: the Assyrians only have 'the arm of flesh' (for the phrase cf. Jer. 17.5); Israel is vested with the power of the LORD. God is the true 'help' (cf. v. 3). The battle belongs to the LORD: 'our battles' are sacramentally his battles.

With exemplary faith, the people place absolute trust (the verb in this sense only here in C) in Hezekiah's words.

2 Chronicles 32.9-20: Sennacherib's Mockery of the Power of the LORD

This section of twelve verses represents a drastic reduction of the fifty-five verses of 2 Kgs 18.17–19.34. C's presentation follows Kings in general outline, but there are so many uses of words and phrases outside the sequence of Kings, that C is more of a pastiche than a parallel and amounts to a new version. The more sporadic uses of Kings will be noted in context below; the wider changes will be summarized at the end of the section.

(a) C treats the next section as a new episode—it begins with an 'after this' [not in 2 Kings 18.17] in similar fashion to v. 1. After Hezekiah is 'established', the onslaught of the nations against Jerusalem takes place.

Sennacherib is presently besieging Lachish in the lowlands some 45 km south-west of Jerusalem. Appropriately for the representative potentate of the nations of the world, he has 'all his dominion with him' (not in Kings). He sends his message by his servants (not in Kings; there is to be a play on the word in v. 16, where Sennacherib's servants are counterpointed to Hezekiah as servant of the LORD) to Hezekiah and his people (v. 9; it is as though 'all Judah' were cooped up with Hezekiah in Jerusalem). The onslaught is not just at the physical, but also at the psychological and theological levels: there is a sacramental dimension—the challenge is not just to Hezekiah but to the God whose representative he is.

Sennacherib's message opens with the 'messenger formula', 'Thus has Sennacherib spoken' (1 Chron. 17.4; C conflates 2 Kgs 18.19 and 29). It is formulated in classical two-part form, found also in prophecy: the description of the unsatisfactory present situation (vv. 10b-14), followed by the specific advice, introduced by 'so now' (v. 15; cf. 1 Chron. 17.7).

The description is made the more deadly by being couched in the form of rhetorical questions: these have the double effect of drawing the hearers into the interpretation of the message and of adding still greater emphasis to it. 'What are you relying on?' is the key issue (v. 10b). The continuation of the question supplies the surface answer: Jerusalem as fortress. But that focuses the question in still more specific terms. Wherein lies the strength of Jerusalem? Craftily, Sennacherib begins at the physical level (v. 11a): cooped up in Jerusalem they can only die a lingering death by hunger and thirst. Hezekiah has simply disastrously miscalculated his defence measures (the same verb is used of Hezekiah 'enticing' his people as has been used of Satan enticing David, 1 Chron. 21.1; cf. 2 Chron. 18.2). Sennacherib then moves to the theological level (v. 11b). Hezekiah's crazy strategic decision is based on the untenable traditional dogma of his royal house that Jerusalem is inviolable ('will be delivered', 1 Chron. 11.14; eight out of the twelve occurrences of this verb in C fall in this chapter in vv. 11-17) because it is the seat of the LORD the God of Israel.

Sennacherib now bids up the theological stakes. Confusingly for a people that may not be too sure of their theology (compare the actions of Joash, 2 Chron. 24.17-18, and Ahaz, 2 Chron. 28.2-4, and presumably the sectional support they could command, see 2 Chron. 33.17), Sennacherib relates the altars that Hezekiah has abolished to the worship of the LORD. By his reform, which has led to the affirmation of the sole legitimacy of the altar in Jerusalem as the place for the cult, Sennacherib suggests, Hezekiah has simply alienated his own Deity (v. 12)! In any case, how can the national God of Israel be any more successful in defending his people against the power of the Assyrians, than the national gods of any of the other nations whom the Assyrians have defeated down the years (v. 13)? Significantly, Sennacherib makes universal claims: his conquests have covered 'all the peoples of the lands' and have exposed the powerlessness of the 'gods of the nations of the lands'.

Sennacherib's challenge is fundamental: by his universal conquests he is established as truly the representative power of the nations of the world. These conquests he describes by the theological term of 'devoting to destruction' in honour of the deity who gives the victory (it was precisely Achar's failure in *not* devoting the spoils of victory to the LORD that was the archetypal failure of Judah, 1 Chron. 2.7: it has been Sennacherib's model devotion to his god that has brought him the victory; the phrase is brought forward from 2 Kgs 19.11). On the evidence of the powerlessness of the gods of the nations of the world, including, by implication, the God of Israel, he summons Israel to capitulate.

Sennacherib reaches his insolent summons (v. 15): do not let Hezekiah deceive or 'entice' you (the verb as in v. 11); do not 'rely' on him (the verb of the Jerusalemite tradition of theology, 2 Chron. 20.20). The reason is repeated in blasphemous polytheistic terms: as no god has been able to deliver his people from Sennacherib and his ancestors, so all the less will the gods of Israel (*sic*) be able to deliver them.

The sacramental force of such and other words of Sennacherib's servants is driven home in v. 16: what is said relates to both God and king. The theological confrontation is now put at its sharpest: Sennacherib backs up the spoken with the written word (v. 17); he sends to deride (the verb also has the overtone of 'challenge', as in 1 Sam. 17.10) the LORD, the God of Israel. As, in his oral message, Sennacherib had affected the standard two-part form of the prophetic oracle, so now, apeing one of the key roles of prophets all through C's work (Introduction to 2 Chron. 10-36), he seeks to validate that message in permanent written form. The message is expressed in substantially identical contumacious terms to those in vv. 13-15, using again the key term of the passage, 'deliver' (v. 11): 'as the gods of the nations of the lands could not deliver their people from my hand, so the god [now singular] of Hezekiah cannot deliver his people from my hand'.

C sums up the section by recapping on Sennacherib's argument. First, it is meant to undermine confidence in the physical defences of the realm (v. 18): it is addressed in Hebrew ('Judaean'), so that all may understand, to the defenders stationed, significantly, on the city

wall that Hezekiah has just fortified (v. 5). It is also meant to undermine morale by ridiculing the royal theology of the house of David. C
broadens out the expression to make absolute the assault of
Sennacherib on Jerusalem, as the assault of the nations of the earth on
the reign of God through his agent, and to make equally stark the col-
lision of theological systems: 'they spoke concerning the God of
Jerusalem [a formulation unique in the Hebrew Bible] as of the gods
of the peoples of the earth which are the handiwork of man [Adam,
the point of the whole work, 1 Chron. 1.1; the phrase is borrowed
from 2 Kgs 19.18]'.

(b) MT pauses to ponder Hezekiah's exemplary response in a separate, one sentence, sub-paragraph. Hezekiah turns the problem over to
the LORD, the one who is fundamentally the target of Sennacherib's
insolence. Isaiah, the chief prophet of the reign, adds his authority
(the only time in C's narrative that the prophet appears; he is otherwise noted simply as biographer in v. 32, 2 Chron. 26.22). Their cry
for help (1 Chron. 5.20) reaches the sky (see the refrain in Solomon's
prayer, 2 Chron. 6.23, etc.).

> The more significant of the larger interconnections between C and Kings
> may be briefly noted, if only the more sharply to highlight the distinctive-
> ness of C's presentation.
>
> Quite apart from the very substantial omissions (not least the content
> Hezekiah's prayer and Isaiah's lengthy oracle in 2 Kgs 19.15-34), C has
> broadened and flattened the Kings narrative. In the process, he has lost
> much of the vigour and inventiveness of the original. For example:
>
> – In v. 9, where 2 Kgs 18.17-18 gives a vivid list of the high officials
>   of state negotiating on both sides and circumstantial details about the
>   location of the negotiation, C has generalized.
> – In v. 11, C decorously reads that Hezekiah 'will put you to death by
>   hunger and thirst' for the vulgar 'the people who are living with
>   you...will have to eat their own excrement and drink their own
>   urine' of 2 Kgs 18.27.
> – Verse 13a, 'Do you not know what I and my fathers have done to all
>   the peoples of the earth', stands in place of itemized lists of nations in
>   2 Kgs 18.34; 19.12-13.
> – Verse 16 is a very generalized summary of the diplomatic exchanges
>   recorded in Kings and the panic they engendered.
> – Verse 17 suffices as summary of 2 Kgs 19.9-14.
> – The speaking in Hebrew (v. 18) has been transferred from the first
>   diplomatic negotiation in 2 Kgs 18.26.
>
> Deliberate changes to alter the sense of the Kings narrative are introduced.

For example:

- In the last phrase of v. 10: 'dwelling under siege [*māṣôr*] in Jerusalem' replaces the complex reference to reliance upon Egypt [*miṣrayim*] in 2 Kgs 18.20-21. It is striking that the word *māṣôr* occurs in 2 Kgs 19.24 as an alternative form of *miṣrayim*. It is perhaps important to observe that the word 'hand' in the next verse ('The LORD our God will deliver us from the hand of the king of Assyria', v. 11b) occurs in 2 Kgs 19.24, where it refers to the LORD's sovereign hand. It is just possible that vv. 10-11 thus represent a polemical application, against the pretensions of Sennacherib, of the affirmations about the power of the LORD against Egypt in 2 Kgs 19.24.
- In vv. 13-15, C adds five times the words 'be able [to deliver]' to 2 Kgs 18.33, 35: the point at issue for C is the LORD's ability to deliver his people over against the inability of the gods of the nations and Sennacherib's blind presumptuousness in not perceiving the difference between the two.
- The phrase, 'Do not believe in him' (v. 15), links with the Jerusalemite tradition of Isa. 7.9b.

2 Chronicles 32.21-33: Hezekiah's Deliverance, Lapse and Restoration

(a) In immediate response to the prayer of Hezekiah and Isaiah, the LORD sends deliverance. 'An angel' destroys 'every warrior, leader and general in the war camp of the king of Assyria' (v. 21). No clue is given as to the nature of this—presumably—supernatural agency. The 'war-camp' of the Assyrians is in contrast to the 'war camp' of Israel (cf. 1 Chron. 12.22), which stands in perpetual readiness for the battles of the LORD of Hosts (1 Chron. 27). Stripped of all his forces, Sennacherib, who has presumptuously defied the LORD of hosts and sacrilegiously equated him with the gods of the nations whose conquest he has attributed to his own and his ancestors' 'hand' (vv. 11, 13, 14, 15, 17), returns in humiliation to his homeland, only to be murdered there in the Temple of his god by some of his own offspring. His own sacramental pretensions are exposed as a sham.

Thus it was the LORD (v. 22), who delivered (1 Chron. 11.14) Hezekiah and the inhabitants of Jerusalem (appropriately stressed in view of the emphasis on Jerusalemite theology) from this 'hand' of Sennacherib—and from all others. Again these others are unspecified, but, since Sennacherib as representative power of the nations of the earth has been defeated, there can be no threat from any other quarter.

The last phrase of v. 22 is somewhat obscure. The verb is used primarily of the shepherd leading his flock to water (e.g. Ps. 23.2). If it means, 'he brought them back [as from captivity; 2 Chron. 28.15] from all around', then there is here an anticipation of that ideal future when all the dispersed of Israel go up to Jerusalem in the Return (2 Chron. 36.23). But there is much to be said for following the graphically similar reading implied by LXX: 'he gave them rest [*wayyānaḥ lāhem*, for *wayᵉnaḥᵃlēm*] on all sides' [*BHK* and *BHS*]. This reading would pick up the ideology of Jerusalem as the 'resting place' of the ark (1 Chron. 22.9) and, therefore, the focal point of peace on earth now realized under Hezekiah as ideal successor of David.

This idea is certainly continued in the next verse. In recognition of the status of Hezekiah as God's vicegerent on earth, now confirmed through the defeat of the Assyrians, 'many' nations of the world ('many' no doubt in the sense of 'the generality', e.g. Isa. 53.11-12) bring both their tribute (1 Chron. 16.29) to the LORD and precious gifts (2 Chron. 21.3) to Hezekiah. The ideal has again been realized: Hezekiah is 'exalted in the eyes of all the nations' (the same verb is used of the LORD himself, 1 Chron. 29.11). Through the sacramental status of her king, Israel has realized the primal relationship intended for Adam.

> Verse 21 is clearly the counterpart of 2 Kgs 19.35-37. But again there are very many differences: C suppresses the timing and the manner whereby the angel smites the Assyrians, the statistics of the dead and all the circumstantial details of the assassination of Sennacherib. There is no equivalent of vv. 22-23 in Kings.

(b) The episode of Hezekiah's illness and its aftermath now follow (vv. 24-33).

The benefits of the sacramental relationship, perfectly accomplished, are made real for Hezekiah personally. When he falls dangerously ill, in his plight he submits in prayer to the LORD, as he had done in the national emergency (v. 20). As then, so now the LORD graciously answers: he grants him a sign of his redemptive power (the word used, 'wonder', is that which occurs in, for example, Exod. 11.9-10 for the 'wonders' that God worked in Egypt in order to bring about the deliverance of his people; for Hezekiah too there has been an 'exodus' granted from his plague; see v. 31).

Again C drastically abbreviates Kings: material matching 2 Kgs 20.1a, 2b
is given, but no details about Hezekiah's illness nor the 'wonder' that he
is granted. It suffices C to note the bare sequence of events. The rest of
2 Kgs 20.1-19 is thus omitted (the role of Isaiah, in particular), though to
a degree (especially in v. 31) it is presupposed. Instead, C supplies his
own material in vv. 24bβ-31.

In a way not specified (v. 25), Hezekiah falls from grace. 'His heart
became inflated' (2 Chron. 17.6; 26.16); at the very least, the reader is
left to assume that that perfect submission as of a Solomon (cf. on
1 Chron. 29.23), which had just been evidenced in national and
personal crisis, is abandoned and Hezekiah falls into the temptation of
self-reliance. Instantly, in the dynamics of sacramental theology,
Hezekiah falls into alienation from God ('anger'; 1 Chron. 27.24);
and, since the king is also the representative of his people, that anger
falls on 'Judah and Jerusalem'.

Even so, Hezekiah's is a model response: he humbles himself (v. 26;
2 Chron. 7.14), the necessary first step in rehabilitation. At least in his
day the penalty is stayed—but with the implication that the inbuilt
self-destruction of the people is only delayed, not permanently
averted.

As befits his status Hezekiah enjoys 'wealth and honour' (v. 27), the
traditional tokens of respect accorded the Davidic house (1 Chron.
29.12). That 'wealth and honour' find physical expression in the
'treasuries': they are the appropriate means by which the duty owed to
the LORD's representative by offerings in kind by the peoples of the
world can be rendered (1 Chron. 9.26). Not the least of these tokens
are the 'shields' (2 Chron. 9.16) by which the nations recognize the
status of the Davidic king as leader of the LORD's host. The payment
of all the offerings in kind due from his subjects is equally monitored
by the 'storehouses' (v. 28; 2 Chron. 8.6). Hezekiah's standing is indicated by the stabling for his horses and the stalls provided for his
cattle (cf. Solomon, 2 Chron. 9.25), the cities he built and the size of
his flocks and herds (v. 29). Whether as a consequence of his actions
in blocking up the wells in the vicinity of Jerusalem (vv. 3-4) or not,
hydraulic works in connection with leading the waters from the spring
Gihon to the western side of the 'City of David' are credited to him as
a great feat of civil engineering (v. 30; cf. 2 Kgs 20.20a). In a word,
Hezekiah 'was successful' in all that he did (1 Chron. 22.11); his
'wealth and honour' signified the approval of the God in whose name
he ruled.

Another failure on Hezekiah's part is, nevertheless, noted (v. 31). This one is so obliquely referred to that the corresponding narrative in 2 Kgs 20.12-19 must be presupposed: Hezekiah's misjudgment in allowing emissaries from Babylon take note of all these tokens of his wealth, especially of his armoury. The failing in this case is that the Davidic king is associating himself with other monarchs in the world as though they were equals, thus compromising his status as the LORD's anointed (cf. 2 Chron. 10.1). C interprets the occasion as a test of Hezekiah's understanding of his position, engineered by God himself (cf. the role of Satan in 1 Chron. 21.1 or the lying spirit of prophecy in 2 Chron. 18.19-24).

Despite these shortcomings Hezekiah's reign is on the whole a success (marked by 'deeds of loyalty', v. 32), warranting (v. 33) the recognition of burial in the 'ascent' (not otherwise noted in the Hebrew Bible) to the royal tombs.

2 CHRONICLES 33.1-20: THE REIGN OF MANASSEH

The reign of Manasseh is a tale of two contrasting halves:

1. 2 Chron. 33.1-9: Manasseh the reprobate;
2. 2 Chron. 33.10-20: Manasseh the repentant.

C gives no clue as to where, chronologically, in Manasseh's exceptionally long reign (the longest of all the kings of Judah; see Introduction to 2 Chron. 10–36) the change takes place. Such matters are of total indifference to him.

> In vv. 1-9 C returns to a close shadowing of the Kings text (2 Kgs 21.1-9). The Kings text is marginally reduced in the number of points made, yet at the same time elaborated in some of the details. C suppresses 2 Kgs 21.10aβ-16 (prophetic oracle of doom and further outrages in a totally black presentation), and supplies, instead, his own material in vv. 10aβ-17, which gives a positive side to Manasseh's reign. At v. 18, C returns, with characteristic modifications, to the framework material of 2 Kgs 21.17-18.

2 Chronicles 33.1-9: Manasseh the Reprobate

The opening two verses reproduce unchanged from Kings elements (1), (2) and (4) of the standard framework (Introduction to 2 Chron. 10–36; element (3), the name of Manasseh's mother, Hephzibah, 'my pleasure is in her', supplied by Kings, is suppressed at the end of v. 1.

C is interested above all in the theological evaluation (v. 2a): 'he did what is evil in the eyes of the LORD'. For that Kings has given him copious materials, which he largely reproduces in vv. 2b-9.

The passage is carefully structured with matching opening and closing sections: Manasseh is condemned because he acts in the same abominable ways as the nations dispossessed by God in favour of Israel (v. 2b); indeed (v. 9) he made Judah and the inhabitants of Jerusalem do worse than these nations. In between, there is a list of these condemned practices (vv. 3-7a), followed by a commentary in the form of a divine speech in which the grounds for the condemnation are given (vv. 7b-8).

Manasseh's reign marks a reversion to the bad old days of Ahaz. His name, 'one causing to forget', no doubt in origin referring to how God causes the pain of childbirth to be forgotten in the joy of the birth of a son (see the folk etymology of the name Manasseh in Gen. 41.51), is grimly appropriate in the context: he, Manasseh, causes Israel to forget the reforms of Hezekiah and the well-being that flows from them. He commits (vv. 3-7bα) the abominations of which Ahaz was guilty (2 Chron. 28.2-4): he restores the high places of the age-old Canaanite worship that Hezekiah had torn down [Kings, 'destroyed'], rebuilds their altars and reinstates the symbols of the male and female deities [C reads the plural for the singular in Kings] (v. 3abα; 2 Chron. 28.2, 4 [C omits 'as had Ahab king of Israel' in Kings, perhaps because the influence of Ahab is considered over and done with by the time of Joash, 2 Chron. 24]); he reintroduces child sacrifice (v. 6aα; 2 Chron. 28.3; as there, C reads the plural, 'sons', for the singular in Kings and adds to Kings, 'in the valley of the son of Hinnom').

But Manasseh outdoes Ahaz. He also introduces a new cult (v. 3bβ), the astrological cult of 'all the host of heaven'. The rivalry from this new system to the worship of the LORD is obvious. The God of Israel is affirmed in tradition to be the 'LORD of Hosts' (1 Chron. 11.9); all the cosmic powers (including 'the stars in their courses', Judg. 5.20) are at his disposal and Israel's hosts are their counterpart in the historical realm. To single out one element of this system for worship, as in the astral cult, is to deify the creation at the cost of the creator and to honour the sign rather than the reality. It marks another attempt, like idolatry, to manipulate and control the Deity through visible manifestations and thus undercuts his revelation in the Law (cf. v. 8).

The fault is then compounded: Manasseh introduces these cults into the Temple alongside the worship of the LORD (vv. 4-5; the theological confusion on which Sennacherib played, 2 Chron. 32.12, was indeed real). The impossibility of associating any other deity with the God of Israel, who has made known himself by his Name (1 Chron. 13.6), and the abhorrence at attempting to portray him in any physical form are already clear from the Decalogue (Exod. 20.3-7; the same emphasis on the Name, in a similar transcription from Kings, is to be found in association with Rehoboam in 2 Chron. 12.13).

> Verse 4b anticipates the fuller citing of divine speech in vv. 7-8. In the last phrase in v. 4, 'my name shall be for ever', C has changed the 'I shall set my name' of Kings, which, in fact, as far as the verb is concerned, would anticipate the last phrase of v. 7 more closely. C's procedure here is the opposite to that which he has followed in 2 Chron. 6.20, where he replaced 'be' with 'set'. It is difficult, therefore, to see more than stylistic considerations in these changes.

The pertinacity with which Manasseh pursues this new cult is evident from the fact that he constructs altars for it in both courts of the Temple (v. 5; see sketch at 2 Chron. 23.5): it is mandatory for both priests and laity.

Not only so; Manasseh turns to other occult practices (v. 6aβ). It is an age of superstition: he engages in fortune-telling, divination, sorcery (this item not in Kings), necromancy and spiritualism. The exact force of some of these terms is uncertain (see KBS; the first is associated with the Philistines, Isa. 2.6; the second with the Egyptians, Gen. 44.5; the third with the Egyptians, Exod. 7.11, and Babylonians, Dan. 2.2; the 'witch of Endor', whom Saul consulted, possessed the last two in the list, 1 Sam. 28.3-9). But the point is that all of these are alternative attempts to gain knowledge from the unseen world; once again the fault in them lies in the fact that they bypass the revelation of God's will in the Law (for this reason they are forbidden in, for example, Lev. 19.26; Deut. 18.10-14). They include precisely the kind of resorting to other mediums and failure to rely on the LORD alone through which Saul incurred the archetypal guilt of *ma'al* (1 Chron. 10.13-14). In consequence, by this failure in the sacramental relationship, the LORD is in like measure 'vexed', provoked to anger (2 Chron. 28.25).

Manasseh's crowning outrage is to place an image in the Temple. The vocabulary used suggests that it was an object carved from wood or stone (the related verb is used in, for example, 1 Kgs 5.18, of masons), though what the image in itself represented is not made clear. The word C uses is rare, occurring outside this context only in Deut. 4.16 and Ezek. 8.3, 5, other passages condemning idolatry, where it appears to mean generally 'figure, representation'. 2 Kings 21.7 reads here 'asherah', that is, the image was one of the female deity. One cannot be sure whether C's change means that he is too scandalized by the Kings reading to reproduce it, or whether he wishes to broaden it to cover the prohibitions of the Decalogue.

This list of Manasseh's recidivist actions launches Kings and C into a statement of the grounds on which all of these practices are abhorrent and incompatible with normative worship of the LORD (vv. 7-8):

- The structure of v. 7 makes the fundamental point clear: the verb 'to put' both at the beginning and at the end of the verse contrasts the actions: 'he [Manasseh] put the image...I [the LORD] put my name'. The focus of life has to be the revealed nature of God ('the name', with all that that implies, 1 Chron. 13.6).

- The normative exposition of that revelation is the Law, as v. 8 insists: the Law as such in its entirety and as a system (Genesis–Deuteronomy, in whatever version was available to C); and the detailed prescriptions of the Law in its two main categories of statute (e.g. Exod. 21.12-17) and ordinance (e.g. Exod. 21.1-11).

- Further, the punctuation of v. 7 in both versions cuts across the syntax to place the Temple in great prominence: 'He put the image of the form which he made; (*sic*) in the house of God!, of which God said... "In this house and in Jerusalem which I have chosen...I will put my name for ever"'. The Temple is the sacramental expression of the force of that revelation, representing through its twin foci of altar and ark atonement and empowerment (1 Chron. 17–2 Chron. 7). C universalizes by reading (twice) the cosmic, 'God', in this context for the Israel-centred relational, 'the LORD' found in Kings.

- The combined weight of tradition is invoked: everything that was planned and achieved under David and Solomon (v. 7; 1 Chron. 17–2 Chron. 7) undergirds that claim. But all that David and Solomon achieved stands on a still more fundamental basis, the Law as revealed through the instrumentality of Moses (v. 8).

- The gracious deeds and promises of the LORD are recalled: it was by his own free choice that the LORD elected Jerusalem (v. 7; 2 Chron. 6.5-6); it is by his grace to their forefathers that Israel occupies the Land and has received the promise of continued possession of it (v. 8).

- But all is contingent. The continuing validity of both that election and that promise is conditional upon the observance of the Law (v. 8).

There are minor variations between the two versions of v. 8 (and the
beginning of v. 9): 'I will not again remove [Kings: 'cause to wander'
thinks of renewed exile from the land, rather than of forfeiture of it] the
foot of Israel from upon [Kings just 'from'] the land which I appointed
[1 Chron. 6.31] for [Kings: 'gave to'] their fathers, only provided they
observe to do [Kings adds 'in accordance with'] all that I commanded
them [Kings adds 'and'] as regards the Law and the statutes and the ordinances by the hand of Moses [Kings reads for 'and the statutes...
Moses', 'which my servant Moses commanded them (v. 9). But they did
not listen']. C adds weight to the reference to the Law by citing its main
components and emphasizes its divine origin.

The responsibility is placed squarely upon Manasseh (v. 9). It is he
who misled his people (C stresses 'Judah and the inhabitants of
Jerusalem'; Kings reads just 'them'). The insupportable weight of
wrongdoing is now manifest: Israel is now more culpable than the
nations whom the LORD destroyed (1 Chron. 5.25) to make way for
them. The practice of those abominations caused the destruction of the
Canaanites in the first place; the revival of these practices and worse
can only bring destruction for Israel itself ever closer. What hope can
there be for Israel (see the death of Achar for *ma'al*, 1 Chron. 2.7;
Manasseh's evil-doing is about to be termed *ma'al* in v. 19)?

2. 2 Chronicles 33.10-20: Manasseh the Repentant

'The LORD spoke to Manasseh and to his people' in warning (v. 10).

In the economy of his narrative C does not even pause to say that the message is communicated by prophets, as 2 Kgs 21.10 makes clear. In Kings
the purpose of the prophets is, by contrast, to announce the definitive end
of Judah.

The warning is not heeded. Therefore, immediate punishment is
inflicted (v. 11): the LORD sends 'the host which belongs to the king of
Assyria' against him. Again, the overtones of sacramental theology
(1 Chron. 17) are clear: the Davidic king is the leader of the LORD's
hosts on earth; when he fails in his mission, he becomes himself the
object of assault by the hosts of the nations (contrast the recognition
from the nations which Hezekiah gained by his reform, 2 Chron.
32.23). Manasseh is carried off to Babylon as a captive with 'hooks'
(like a fish carried home by its gills, Job 41.2 [KBS, or 'captured in
the rock crevices', cf. 1 Sam. 13.6?], hence 'manacles'? [JPSV, NRSV])
and chains but there he repents (v. 12) and is restored (v. 13).

In C's presentation, Manasseh thus becomes a model of exile and return for Israel. Though captured by Assyrians, he is taken, as Judah is to be, to Babylon; his being taken there 'in two bronze chains' anticipates the fate of Jehoiakim of the exilic generation (2 Chron. 36.6). 'In his adversity' (unlike Ahaz, 2 Chron. 28.22, where the same expression recurs), he seeks to allay the LORD's anger (the striking anthropomorphism, 'stroke the face' [KBS], only here in C, is, however, quite widely used in the Hebrew Bible with regard to God, for example, Exod. 32.11). He takes the first necessary step of admitting his guilt ('he humbled himself', 2 Chron. 7.14) and acknowledging the justice of 'the God of his fathers' (1 Chron. 5.25). Thus, when he prays (v. 13), he is given a hearing (1 Chron. 5.20); his plea for grace is granted and he is allowed 'to return to Jerusalem, his kingdom' (the vocabulary evokes that of Solomon's prayer in 2 Chron. 6: for example, v. 19, 'plea'; v. 23, 'hear/grant'; vv. 24-25, 'return'). The ideal outcome of this bitter experience turned to restoration is the fundamental confession: 'Manasseh knew (1 Chron. 14.2) that the LORD is God'.

Thereafter (v. 14), Manasseh turns to the appropriate activities for a Davidic monarch: the strengthening of the defences of Jerusalem and the fortifying and manning of cities throughout the land. As sacramental figure himself, he thus brings to sacramental expression the power of God to establish his reign (2 Chron. 8.5; it is notable, however, that C refrains from using the key term, hzq, 'be established', 2 Chron. 1.1, in connection with such an ambiguous figure as Manasseh). In particular, he builds another defensive wall on the slope below the eastern side of the city overlooking the Kidron valley above the spring Gihon (with all its associations as the place where the Davidic monarch is anointed, 1 Kgs 1.33-45, and as water-supply for Jerusalem, 2 Chron. 32.3-4). This is a truly massive structure, not only in its height, which C alludes to, but also in its length, which the reader is left to deduce: it runs from the Fish Gate, on the northern side of the city (see note on the topography of Jerusalem, 2 Chron. 25.23), all the way down the eastern side, to encompass Mt Ophel, the site of the original 'City of David', on the south (2 Chron. 27.3).

A purification of the Temple and city as under Hezekiah takes place: all the offensive cultic installations are thrown out of the city, presumably into the Kidron valley (v. 15; 2 Chron. 29.16; 30.14). In line with his confession of the sole deity of the LORD (v. 13), he totally removes the images ('the alien gods', cf. 2 Chron. 14.3) from the Temple and dismantles the altars he had installed at the beginning of his reign in the Temple and throughout Jerusalem. C uses here the archaic term, 'the mountain of the house of the LORD' (cf. 2 Chron. 3.1). The phrase is thoroughly central to the Jerusalem tradition of theology (Isa. 2.2-4; 66.20; Mic. 4.1-2). It refers to the traditional Canaanite conception of the mountain as seat of deities, which Manasseh had attempted to restore at the beginning of his reign; at the conquest of the land the LORD, the victor from Sinai, had dethroned these deities and had polemically appropriated their seats, titles and claims (e.g. Ps. 68).

After the purification, the cult in the LORD's name can recommence (v. 16; cf. the sequence in 2 Chron. 29–31). Manasseh 'rebuilds' (*qere*) or, probably the better reading, 're-establishes' (*kethib*; *kûn*, the key term of 1 Chron. 14.2) the altar of the LORD. Communion and thank offerings (2 Chron. 29.31) are brought, in reintegration of the community and in celebration of the restoration of throne and Temple. The command to Judah 'to serve' the LORD, refers primarily to the observation of the requirements of the cult but only because the cult is an expression of a way of life, which recognizes him as, indeed, 'the God of Israel'.

But Manasseh's reform is not complete (v. 17). Unlike Hezekiah (2 Chron. 31.1), Manasseh does not succeed in closing down the regional sanctuaries and thus in wholly purifying the land. Even though these sanctuaries are reformed to the degree that they become centres for the worship of the LORD alone, the unitary affirmation of the sole deity of the LORD through the sacramental sign of his one sanctuary in Jerusalem is not achieved, and the temptation for the populace at large to misinterpret these local sanctuaries as centres for the worship of Canaanite deities remains (cf. on 2 Chron. 32.12).

In vv. 18-20 C returns to the annalistic framework of 2 Kgs 21.17-18, but with customary modifications. Apart from the résumé of C's unique material on Manasseh's apostasy and repentance (the latter carried to further midrashic interpretation in the Prayer of Manasseh in the Apocrypha), the main addition is the standard reference to the prophetic midrash on the life of Manasseh. The prophet 'Hozai' (v. 19) should perhaps be read as *ḥôzāyw*, 'his seers' (cf. v. 18).

C reads (v. 20) that Manasseh was buried 'in his house' for the 'in the garden of his house, the garden of Uzza' of 2 Kgs 21.18 (so also for Manasseh's son, Amon, 2 Kgs 21.26, another detail which C suppresses). Perhaps this Uzza is the man who presumptuously touched the ark, 1 Chron. 13.7-11 (2 Sam. 6.3-8); his garden might then be thought of as providing a suitable burial place for a reprobate like Manasseh (and his son). With C's more positive account of Manasseh, such a reference may have been deemed less appropriate.

2 CHRONICLES 33.21-25: THE REIGN OF AMON

The brief reign of Amon—two years of unremitting evil—is dismissed by C in even briefer measure than in his parent text. As in the case of the immediately preceding reign item (3) of the standard framework (see Introduction to 2 Chron. 10–36), the name of Amon's mother, though present in Kings, is omitted. More unusually, items (5)–(7) are also suppressed—the prophetic commentary on the reign and the note on his burial and on his successor, all again available in Kings.

> It is possible that the last three items have been omitted by textual error (homoioteleuton): v. 25 ends with the phrase, 'Josiah, his son, in his place', the phrase with which item (7) ends in the Kings parallel (2 Kgs 21.26).
>
> In vv. 21-22a, 24-25 C is parallel to 2 Kgs 21.19-20, 23-24 (with the omission of item [3], and oddly retaining an unqualifiedly negative judgment on Manasseh, despite C's own material commending him in 2 Chron. 33.12-16). Verse 22b is analogous in substance with 2 Kgs 21.21, but uses different vocabulary.

C's independent material on Amon (ironically Amon's name probably means 'faithful' [KBS], rather than 'master-workman' [BDB]) in vv. 22b, 23 expounds the negative theological evaluation of the reign as evil in distinctive terms. His reign marks the revival of the 'images' that his father, Manasseh, had made in his first, reprobate period (v. 22b; 2 Chron. 33.7, 19).

This revival of idolatry provides C with opportunity to introduce two of his key themes, remorse and guilt (v. 23). In contradistinction to his father, Amon shows no sign of remorse at his reintroduction of idolatry, that acknowledgment of having done wrong which marks the first step in rehabilitation (2 Chron. 7.14). Because of his refusal to acknowledge wrongdoing, Amon 'multiplied guilt' (1 Chron. 21.3), the guilt in this case that arises from the failure to give to God the worship that is due to him alone.

His courtiers turn on him and assassinate him (v. 24; cf. 2 Chron. 24.25; 25.27). Their motives are given neither in C nor in Kings. The fact that the assassins in turn are sentenced to death by the 'people of the land' (v. 25; 2 Chron. 23.13) suggests that they are a reform movement without popular support. If so, the success of the impending reform measures of Amon's son and successor, Josiah, becomes all the more impressive. If the people of the land wished to retain the local sanctuaries, they were soon to be disappointed in their young new king.

2 CHRONICLES 34.1–35.24: THE REIGN OF JOSIAH

MT divides the presentation of Josiah's reign into five phases:

1. 2 Chron. 34.1-21: the purification of Judah, Jerusalem and the Temple;
2. 2 Chron. 34.22-28: the consultation with Huldah, the prophetess;
3. 2 Chron. 34.29-33: the covenant to keep the Covenant;
4. 2 Chron. 35.1-6: the preparation of the priests and Levites for the Passover;
5. 2 Chron. 35.7-24: the Passover and the negative Passover.

Sections 1, 2 and 5 are further sub-divided, as will be noted below.

C's account has a complex relationship to the parent text in Kings (2 Kgs 22.1–23.30a). The following table gives only a rough indication (there are many further modifications in detail):

2 Chronicles 34.1–35.24	2 Kings 22.1–23.30a
34.1-2	cf. 22.1-2
34.3-7	no parallel
34.8-12aα	cf. 22.3-7
34.12aβ-14	no parallel
34.15-32	cf. 22.8-23.3
no exact parallel	23.4-21
34.33-35.17	no exact parallel
35.18-20	cf.23.22, 23, 29
no parallel	23.24-28
35.21-24aα	no exact parallel
35.24aβγ	23.30a
35.24b	no parallel

1. 2 Chronicles 34.1-21: The Purification of Judah, Jerusalem and the Temple

Verses 1-7: The Purification of the Land in Josiah's Early Years
The section begins with the standard framework, the age at accession and the length of the reign (v. 1; see Introduction to 2 Chron. 10-36; C omits element [3], the name of Josiah's mother, as in the case of Josiah's two predecessors, Manasseh [2 Chron. 33.1] and Amon [2 Chron. 33.21]).

Once again, C retains in the framework an apparently positive theological evaluation of the reign from Kings (v. 2): Josiah (most likely the name means, 'May the LORD provide', compare 'Joash', 2 Chron. 22.11) 'walked in the ways of David, his ancestor' (2 Chron. 6.16). But that does not imply an overall favourable verdict on the reign: even Rehoboam was granted to have done the same, if only for three years (2 Chron. 11.17); Jehoshaphat (2 Chron. 17.3) and Hezekiah (2 Chron. 29.2) were measured by the same standard, but the reigns of both ended in disapproval. Josiah's reign is, indeed, to be brought to an abrupt conclusion in the final disaster of a 'negative Passover', which marks the end of the rule of the house of David in Jerusalem, and beginning of the exilic age. This disaster is due to Josiah's refusal to hear the word of God spoken through the Pharaoh Neco, and to trust the affirmations of his own Jerusalemite tradition of theology (see below, on 2 Chron. 35.20-21).

> It may be significant, then, that C drops the 'all' in 2 Kgs 22.2, which has, 'he walked in *all* the way of David'.

Josiah shows early resolve 'to seek the LORD' (v. 3a; for the key word *drš*, cf. 1 Chron. 10.13-14; for the description of Josiah as a 'youth'—here a sixteen-year-old—cf. Solomon, 1 Chron. 22.5; 29.1; but also Rehoboam, 2 Chron. 13.7). No doubt significantly, the practical steps to implement this resolve coincide with his reaching the age of twenty (v. 3b), the age of eligibility to be called up for military service (e.g. Exod. 30.14). For Josiah that enlistment can only be for service in the LORD's host (once again, the legislation of Exod. 30.11-16 for muster in the LORD's service is significant for the understanding of a passage in C; see v. 9, 1 Chron. 21.5). As for Hezekiah (2 Chron. 29–31), so now for Josiah the first step is to 'purify' (1 Chron. 23.28) the community.

The operation is in two phases: first Judah and Jerusalem (vv. 3b-5), then the north (vv. 6-7). The material on Judah and Jerusalem begins and ends with matching phrases: 'he began to purify Judah and Jerusalem' (v. 3b); 'so he purified Judah and Jerusalem' (v. 5). The direction of the purification is the opposite to that pursued by Hezekiah: whereas the latter began with the Temple (because of Ahaz's pollutions, but with Manasseh's reform that was presumably now unnecessary), and then worked out to city and land (and, in consequence, won the recognition of the nations round about), Josiah begins in the landward area with 'Judah and Jerusalem'. All the objectionable cultic installations re-erected by Amon are now once again removed ('high places', 2 Chron. 11.15; 'wooden posts', 2 Chron. 14.3; 'carved idols', 2 Chron. 33.7; 'cast idols', 2 Chron. 28.2; 'altars of Baal', 2 Chron. 23.17; 'incense burners', 2 Chron. 14.5; the verbs used, 'tear down', 'cut down', match the materials involved). At the beginning of v. 4 the verb is used in the plural, '*they* tore down the altars of Baal before him', as though in Josiah's triumphal procession through the land, his mere arrival is enough to precipitate irresistible action (the other verbs are singular, personalizing the action as Josiah's). It is difficult not to see in the note on the incense burners (which were 'above them [the altars]', $l^{e}ma'lâ\ m\bar{e}^{ia}l\bar{e}hem$) a double play on *ma'al*, the presumptuous denial of God of the worship due to him alone, one of the major themes of the work (1 Chron. 2.7). Furthermore, the representations of deity, whether as post or idol, are broken up and crushed and their fragments strewn over the graves, 'that is', the Hebrew runs, 'their worshippers': the pollution of idolatry is contained within, but at the same time doubly contaminates— one assumes for ever—the areas already polluted by the corpses of the dead idolaters. The altars of Baal are similarly profaned in perpetuity by burning, not offerings, but the bones of their own dead priests upon them (cf. 2 Chron. 23.17; 2 Kgs 23.16).

Josiah's crusade extends into the far north and the deep south: the remaining central highlands of Manasseh and Ephraim; Simeon in the farthest south; Naphtali in northernmost Galilee. The sequence Manasseh–Ephraim, only in this chapter in C (also v. 9), but common enough elsewhere in the Hebrew Bible (e.g. Gen. 46.20), gives a chiastic arrangement N → S → S → N, which well expresses comprehensiveness (Dan as elsewhere in C is missing; see on 1 Chron. 2.1-2; the comprehensiveness of Josiah's mission may be contrasted with the extent of the accession of northerners under Asa—only from Simeon to Manasseh, 2 Chron. 15.9,—and under Hezekiah—only as far as Issachar, 2 Chron. 30.18).

> The text at the end of v. 6 is obscure: the *qere*, 'with their swords [or: tools, Exod. 20.25] around' (or, with the change of a vowel, 'in their ruined settlements around' [cf. BDB]), at least makes better sense than the *kethib*, 'he chose their houses'. LXX and Syriac suggest, by an interchange of consonants, 'in their public places' (*BHK* and *BHS*).

A similar list of cultic institutions is destroyed in the north as in Judah (high places are not mentioned, nor cast images, perhaps merely because of economy of expression—though as trophies of war the latter might have been already carried off in one or other of the repeated invasions the north had to suffer; the verb 'beat to dust' is added with the idols). Josiah, having thus cleansed the whole land, north and south, returns to Jerusalem. There is no hint here of rejection by the north, such as Hezekiah suffered, let alone of opposition from the imperial power. If there were any political overtones in Josiah's action,[1] C is quite uninterested in them.

> In C this purification of the landward area precedes the finding of the book of the Law in the Temple; by contrast, in Kings it takes place later and as a consequence of the discovery of the Lawbook (2 Kgs 23.4-20). For C, it is, thus, a matter of conviction, not of mere obedience to the book.
>
> Nonetheless, there are echoes of 2 Kgs 23.4-20 in 2 Chron. 34.3-7: 'high places', 'tear down', 'graves', 'burn bones of priests', 'altars', 'crush', so that it would appear that 2 Chron. 34.3-7 is the intended utilization of 2 Kgs 23.4-20 (there is no parallel to it in the expected place at 2 Chron. 34.32).

Verses 8-21: The Restoration of the Temple in Josiah's Eighteenth Year
For the completion of the task of restoring the system of holiness, the Temple has to be purified. Verse 8 suggests that the mere removal of the objectionable cultic installations throughout Israel does not suffice: without the purification of the Temple the land itself remains unclean.

> The phrase, 'to purify the land and the house [of the LORD]', is C's addition.

---

1. Compare J. Bright, *A History of Israel* (London: SCM Press, 3rd edn, 1982), p. 317.

The procedure for gathering funds for the renovation of the Temple has already been described in connection with Joash (2 Chron. 24.8-14). A levy for the upkeep of the sanctuary is laid down for the community as a whole in Exod. 30.11-16. As the Lord's host in a state of perpetual mobilization (1 Chron. 27), it is Israel's duty to contribute this levy. Levites, as 'keepers of the threshold' (cf. 1 Chron. 9.12-32; 26.1-28), supervise the collection of this levy in a chest at the eastern gate of the Temple. At the notification by these Levites that the chest is full, the king sends his secretary, and the High Priest his designated official, to empty the chest. The king and the High Priest then transmit the necessary funds to the foreman in charge of the work on the Temple.

It is a recognizably similar practice that is followed here. The king delegates three of his highest officials to initiate the repair ('strengthening', the key term, *ḥzq*, 1 Chron. 11.10; so again v. 10) of the Temple: not only his secretary, Shaphan, but also the mayor of Jerusalem (2 Chron. 18.25) and the king's 'recorder'. The first and the last may well be Levites (see on 1 Chron. 18.15-16); only the highest suitably qualified religious and civil officials can suffice for the task of disbursing the redemption money of the community.

> The last two figures are added by C to the text provided by Kings and are unknown outside this passage. The mayor must be different from the personage mentioned in 2 Kgs 23.8. Shaphan is here, in contrast to Kings, shorn both of the name of his grandfather and of his title, 'scribe', perhaps for mere abbreviation. There is no doubt about his status later in the chapter (e.g. v. 15).

The Temple is called with all solemnity 'the house of the LORD his God' (cf. 2 Chron. 1.1) ['his God' added to Kings], in order to encapsulate a complete range of association and to express Josiah's standing as the Davidic monarch (1 Chron. 17).

These officials bring (v. 9) the money of the national levy to the high priest, Hilkiah ('The LORD is my portion'; he is listed in the genealogy of the high priests in 1 Chron. 6.13).

> C turns the command by Josiah to his officials to take the money, found in 2 Kgs 22.4, into a report of their carrying out of his command. He simplifies the rarish second verb of Kings, 'so that he may prepare [the silver]' into the straightforward 'they handed it over...' He is also at pains to emphasize the pan-Israelite response to the levy by developing the Kings text into an itemized list of the various regions of both north and

south from which the contributions were brought. At the end of v. 9, 'and
the inhabitants of Jerusalem' should be read with the *kethib*, not 'and they
[the Levites] returned to Jerusalem' with the *qere*: the Levites are 'keepers
of the threshold', not itinerant tax-gatherers (cf. on 2 Chron. 24.6).

But it is actually (v. 10) to the foremen (MT reads singular but the
following participle, 'duly appointed' [*pqd*, 1 Chron. 21.5], is plural;
Kings reads plural; cf. 2 Chron. 24.12) of the works that they hand
the silver over. They apply it to 'repair the breaches' in the Temple
and to renovate it.

2 Kgs 22.5 reads that the foremen in turn hand the silver over to the
craftsmen (C not till v. 11). It is curious that C, having suppressed the
2 Kgs 12.6-13 reading, 'breaches', in 2 Chron. 24.6-14, retains it here
but transposes it and puts it in verbal form.

A similar inconsistency is shown in v. 11. Whereas in 2 Chron. 24.12
'stone-masons' were included alongside 'craftsmen', here only the latter
are mentioned. Whereas there 'builders' were suppressed from Kings,
here they are retained. But C then suppresses 'wall-builders', while
retaining 'to purchase hewn stones', which occurs in both 2 Kgs 12.13
and 22.6, but with 'wood' added. C transposes the reference to 'wood'
and adds his own explanation, in a word that is peculiar to himself (also in
1 Chron. 22.3), 'for tie-beams'.

In v. 11b C adds an obscure reference to 'roofing the houses which the
kings of Judah had destroyed'. In the context of Temple renovation,
the reference is likely to be to parts of the Temple complex itself
(1 Chron. 28.11; a plural of 'local extension'). The point being made
is, however, a central one in C's presentation. 'Destroyed' is the key
word (1 Chron. 21.12) and refers to the 'negative Passover' brought
about by some of Josiah's predecessors (e.g. 2 Chron. 12.7; 22.4): by
Josiah's acts of renovation, the conditions are being prepared whereby
the true Passover can be celebrated, as is soon to be described in
2 Chron. 35.1-19.

C continues with his concern that the work progress in the hands of
those duly appointed (v. 12; the key term, *pqd*, again, as in v. 10). It
is vital that the redemption monies contributed as 'holy things' by
every Israelite for the maintenance of the sanctuary are properly
applied by those designated for the task. For that purpose, it is essential that it is all scrupulously monitored by the Levites. Thus, though
these men 'worked with honesty' (C quotes freely from Kings; oddly
again this Kings phrase was suppressed by C in 2 Chron. 24.12-14),
they were supervised by Levites (otherwise unknown) from the

branches of Merari and Kohath. As before at critical junctures, C incorporates a list of the names of the Levites actually involved (2 Chron. 29.12-14).

At the end of v. 12 is the note: 'As for the Levites, each one was skilled in musical instruments'. In context this appears to be a parenthesis singling out the *musicians* of Merari and Kohath for supervisory work, namely, Jeduthun and Heman (1 Chron. 6.31-48; see 1 Chron. 16.39-42 for their connection with the physical structure of the sanctuary). Verse 13 then continues with an additional category of workmen 'over' whom these Levites exercised their supervisory role: 'and over the porters'. Thus these musicians supervised the whole range of works of reconstruction and renovation in the Temple.

This stress on the function of the musicians in the Temple may explain why the branch of Gershon, specifically Asaph, is omitted in this context. According to 1 Chron. 16.7, 37, their particular function is in connection with the ark. But the ark is seemingly only now to be installed permanently in the renovated Temple (2 Chron. 35.3).

> By ignoring the 'and' at the beginning of v. 13 some English versions (e.g. NEB, JPSV, NRSV, even NIV) take the last phrase of v. 12 not as a parenthesis but as the beginning of a new statement continuing into v. 13. In that case the musicians merely supervise the porters, a statement which then stands in tension with the next statement that they 'supervised all workers of every task'.

As in 2 Chron. 29.12-17 the role of the musicians is remarkable. In the light of the definition of their role in 1 Chronicles 16 and 1 Chronicles 25, the whole task of Temple renovation is fundamentally one of reaffirmation and proclamation anew of the being and actions of God. It is a sacramental act through which the claims of the Jerusalem tradition of theology are once more reasserted.

At the end of v. 13 the role of the non-musicians among the Levites is then stated: any 'scribes, marshalls and gatekeepers' are provided by them also. The task of the Levites is to ensure that all contribute their due share in the work, whether in kind or in labour, and that in the course of the work none transgresses the sphere of the holy.

With v. 14 C constructs a link back to his parent source in Kings. As they apply the silver which has been brought by the people in obedience to the Law, Hilkiah the priest 'finds the scroll of the Law of the LORD at the hand of Moses'. Both the divine origin of the Law and the centrality of the Mosaic tradition are stressed in C's formulation.

Whence or how Hilkiah produces the scroll is not explained by C, nor what it contains (the fact that he reads parts 'in it', v. 18, rather than the whole of it, as in 2 Kgs 22.10, may imply that C assumes that it is the whole collection of the five books of the Law, which is too long to be read on one occasion; thus 'the scroll' is omitted in v. 19). What is significant is that it is within the context of all Israel fulfilling its duty to the LORD that its full tradition is recovered and becomes operational. Again, sacramental ideas are close to the surface.

Shaphan brought silver to the Temple (v. 9) but returns with the scroll of the Law (v. 15). To render what is due to God is to receive what God has to give (2 Chron. 15.2).

Shaphan reports back to Josiah (v. 16).

C has adjusted the reading of Kings to bring into greater prominence the bringing of the scroll of the Law to the king; in so doing, he has produced a less fluent text. He omits 'and he read it' at the end of v. 15: the destination of the scroll is the king not the intermediary. Similarly, at the beginning of v. 16 he reads, 'Shaphan brought the scroll [*et hassēper*] to the king', for the 'Shaphan the scribe [*hassōpēr*] came to the king' of 2 Kgs 22.9. Thus, the note on the bringing of the scroll precedes the reporting back to the king that the mission, on which he had sent them, has been accomplished and anticipates what is said in v. 18. C rather clumsily adds, therefore, an 'also': 'he *also* brought back the king word'.

Verse 16b is C's own adaptation from 2 Kgs 22.7. Whereas in Kings the silver was 'put into the hand' of the workmen, here it is stressed that 'everything that was put into the hand' of the king's emissaries ('servants', transposed from the beginning of v. 17) they have done. Similarly, in v. 17 to emphasize the punctilious supervision of the craftsmen by the Levites the word order has been changed: 'they have poured out the silver' not merely to 'those appointed to undertake the work', as in 2 Kgs 22.9, but to 'those appointed [i.e. as supervisors, v. 12]' *as well as* to 'those undertaking the work'.

Only then (v. 18) does Shaphan mention the scroll and read some of its contents to the king. Josiah's reaction (v. 19) is to 'tear his garments' (2 Chron. 23.13), in consternation at the gap between current practice and traditional requirement and in self-humiliation to avert the divine wrath. He dispatches a delegation of five of his high officials (v. 20), under the leadership of Hilkiah the priest, to consult (v. 21; the key word, *drš*, 1 Chron. 10.13-14) the LORD (through the prophetess, Huldah, v. 22).

For C the identity of these delegates is of less moment than for Kings, to judge from v. 22, where, instead of the sonorous repetition of the names found in 2 Kgs 22.14, he contents himself with 'Hilkiah and those of the king' (a verb may have fallen out of the text: for example, 'those whom the king had sent' [cf. *BHK* and *BHS*]). It is, nonetheless, striking that not only is Shaphan in the party, but also his son Ahikam, one of three sons of Shaphan to play a significant role in the story of Jeremiah (Jer. 26.24; cf. 29.3; 36.10), and who is, in turn, to be the father of Gedaliah, destined to be the Babylonian governor of Judah (2 Kgs 25.22). Shaphan's family will have long-standing reformist credentials. Abdon appears only here, but in the guise 'Achbor' he has a son who also occurs in the Jeremiah story (Jer. 26.22; 36.12). Asaiah bears the quite vague title 'servant of the king' (so, for example, Jeroboam to Solomon, 1 Kgs 11.26) and is not known otherwise. It is a curiosity that Achbor, 'mouse', and Huldah, 'mole', both bear animal names.

Josiah's message is two-fold (v. 21). First, there is a request for intercession by the prophet, implied by the words 'on behalf of'—on behalf of himself, as representative of the house of David, and on behalf of 'those who are left in Israel and Judah' (a more pointed description of Israel's parlous state than 'on behalf of the people and on behalf of all Judah', as found in 2 Kgs 22.13).

Confession is also implied—that humbling of oneself, which, C has insisted, marks the first step in restoration (2 Chron. 7.14), and which Josiah has already shown by tearing his garments. In the light of the contents of the scroll, Josiah has been brought to recognize how great the anger of the LORD (2 Chron. 12.7) must be that is 'poured out' on them (C has changed the verb from 'kindled' of Kings to make it match the first verb of v. 17; cf. v. 25). He confesses that the fault lies with 'our fathers'—earlier generations of the house of David, in the first instance, at least—who 'have not kept the word of the LORD to act in accordance with all that is written in this scroll'.

C's formulation is more relational than the objective reference in Kings to the written record: 'our fathers have not obeyed the words of this scroll to act in accordance with all that is written concerning us'.

C emphasizes the personal will of the LORD behind the objective formulation of Scripture. It is because of the LORD's relation with Israel that his anger has been provoked: it is not mere obedience that he craves, but the realizing of that quality of life in harmony with himself that is Israel's destiny. It is because of this relationship that he can be consulted: perhaps even now he may relent.

2. *2 Chronicles 34.22-28: The Consultation with Huldah, the Prophetess*

The section is divided into four sub-sections.

Verse 22: The Delegation Comes to Huldah
The delegates take their message to Huldah. Her husband, though he plays no further part in the narrative, is given some prominence and that prominence must have some significance. He is described as 'Keeper of the Garments', a title which occurs only in this context. One is left to surmise that 'the garments' are those worn by the priests, not least the High Priest (see, for example, Exod. 28.1-43; Lev. 8.7-9 for the garments themselves—the pouch, ephod, robe, tunic, breeches, turban, diadem and sash; and for changes of garment within ceremonies, Lev. 6.10, 11; 16.4, 23). If so, it is easy to imagine the commitment to the tradition of Moses and the Law of such a person, whose daily task it is to handle elaborate vestments with such powerful symbolism of Israel's dedication to God and to care for the changes of garment during the rites of national whole burnt offering and atonement. His role must surely also imply levitical status, and that may be why he is given a pedigree extending back for two generations, again genealogy functioning as legitimation of claim to standing (cf. 2 Chron. 20.14; nothing is otherwise known of his forebears). A connection between the wife of this key figure in the cult, ritual and liturgy and a book of the Law found in the Temple becomes comprehensible as does her sense of prophetic outrage at the violation of practice and of God's rights.

Another factor in Huldah's background is her place of residence. 'The second quarter', known only in this context and Zeph. 1.10, implies a secondary development of Jerusalem, probably the expansion to the western hill of the city, to accommodate in these unsettled times (2 Chron. 32.9) an increased population of Judaeans or of refugees—including Levites—from the north (2 Chron. 11.14). Here, too, in possibly less affluent circumstances, there would be a lively sense of the relevance of traditional stipulations for the care of the indigent and of the stark choice between tradition and modernity that had led to the fall of the north.

Verse 23: Introduction to Huldah's Prophetic Response
The MT arrests the progress of the narrative to make a series of short paragraphs for dramatic effect.

Huldah has two messages to convey, the first for the people as a whole, the second for the king himself. MT places them in separate paragraphs (vv. 24-25 and 26b-28; v. 26a marks the transition), each introduced by the 'messenger formula' (1 Chron. 17.4).

Verse 23 provides a solemn heading to Huldah's words. Once again the 'messenger formula' is used, not functionally as yet, since no words of the Lord are yet quoted, but to act as a formal introduction. What she says is not spoken by her own volition but by authority of 'the LORD, the God of Israel', the cosmic Deity in his particular relation to Israel. The subservience of even a king to the divine will is indicated by the unadorned way in which she refers to Josiah: 'Say to the man who sent you'. Status is a matter of obedience not of birth.

Verses 24-25: The Message to the People
The message to the people is constructed in the standard two-part prophetic oracle, consisting of verdict, the divine judgment on past life, and sentence, the penalty for that past (cf. 2 Chron. 12.5). In this case, the elements are reversed. First, the sentence is passed (v. 24); then the reason for that sentence is given (v. 25).

The sentence is that 'evil' is to come on 'this place and its inhabitants' (a formulation typical of Jeremiah; see, for example, Jer. 19.3, 12). C's definition of this 'evil' in terms of 'all the curses written on the scroll read in front of the king of Judah' (rather than 'all the words of the scroll which the king read', as in 2 Kgs 22.14) picks up the vocabulary of Deut. 29.11-20, though C may be envisaging the curses of the Law as a whole (e.g. Lev. 26.14-39).

To account for this sentence passed on his people, God uses the vocabulary of rejection (v. 25): 'they have forsaken me' (1 Chron. 28.9). That rejection is defined in terms of denying God his rights in the ultimate manner of replacing him with other gods, to which 'they have offered sacrifice'. Thus they have 'provoked' (2 Chron. 28.25) him 'by all the works of their hands' (possibly, meaning specifically, 'by all [the idols] that they have made', 2 Chron. 32.19). Therefore, the LORD's fury is 'poured out': the same verb is used as in v. 21 (replacing the 'kindled' of 2 Kgs 22.17, which, however, matches better the last phrase of the sentence, 'which cannot be put out').

Huldah now turns, speaking momentarily in her own words (v. 26a), to address Josiah's own situation. He at least has 'enquired [*drš*, 1 Chron. 10.13-14] of the LORD'.

Verses 26b-28: The Message to Josiah
Once again, the message falls into two parts, only this time it is a promise of blessing. First, in the classical sequence and with a classical introductory formula, 'because' (2 Chron. 1.11; 6.8), the reason is given for the promise (v. 27), then the promise itself (v. 28; in 2 Kgs 22.20 it is introduced with the matching classical formula, 'therefore'). But, dramatically, the message begins in v. 26b with the 'messenger formula' (normally to be expected at the beginning of v. 28 after 'therefore'), which is then followed by an arresting *casus pendens* (so also Kings): 'As for the words which you have heard', that is, the words read out of the scroll—the requirements of the Law and the curses that result because of non-compliance.

The reason for the promise of blessing for Josiah is that his heart is 'tender' ('susceptible'; compare Solomon, 1 Chron. 22.5; it is part of the fixed pair 'a youth and tender', the first element of which has just been used of Josiah in v. 3). He is open to correction and has 'humbled himself' in sincere lamentation before God (2 Chron. 7.14) in face of what he 'hears' about the fate of Jerusalem and its inhabitants. In true sacramental fashion, as Josiah 'hears', so does the LORD.

> For Kings, the word spoken 'against this place' was that it should become 'a desolation and a curse' (otherwise an exclusively Jeremianic formulation, e.g. Jer. 25.18); C replaces that with a second 'humble yourself'.

The specific promise to Josiah follows (v. 28). The crisis will be averted in his time; he will die in peace. In the light of the sequel, it is clear that this word is conditional. The promise of a long and happy life is no more unconditional than is the promise to David that his successors will sit on his throne in perpetuity or that the people will continue to inhabit the land (1 Chron. 28.7; C insistently adds here 'and on its inhabitants', to align this verse with v. 24). Josiah is about to forfeit that promise through his inability to rely on the affirmations of his theology in the face of the advance of the Egyptian king.

The section ends in v. 28b with a snatch of narrative: the delegation duly report back to the king.

3. *2 Chronicles 34.29-33: The Covenant to Keep the Covenant*

Josiah's response to Huldah's message is to bind the whole community in covenant to keep the terms of the newly discovered scroll, now called 'scroll of the covenant' (v. 30), rather than 'scroll of the Law', as it had been in v. 15. By observance of the covenant, the curse of the covenant will be averted.

The vocabulary here closely resembles that used on similar occasions: the covenants with David, 1 Chron. 11.1-3, and Joash, 2 Chronicles 23, and the covenants under Asa, 2 Chron. 15.10-15, and Hezekiah, 2 Chron. 29.10. The passage thus provides a convenient digest of C's thought and expression.

The standard vocabulary may be noted (vv. 29-31 are quite closely based on 2 Kgs 23.1-3):

- the dynamic response 'sent' stimulated by situation (v. 29; 1 Chron. 21.15);
- 'gather' (cf. David 1 Chron. 11.1-3 [in Kings the people 'gather themselves to him' in response to his summons]);
- the elders as representatives of the whole community (1 Chron. 11.3)
- in v. 30 where C reads, 'priests and Levites', Kings reads, 'priests and prophets'; compare the understanding of 'prophecy' in 1 Chron. 25.1;
- 'men of Judah and inhabitants of Jerusalem' is, apart from this parallel and Dan.9.7, another Jeremianic expression (e.g. Jer. 4.4);
- as in 2 Chron. 15.13, under Asa, the formulation 'small and great'—in that order as in Kings here—is used to embrace the whole community;
- Hezekiah stands 'on [or beside] his position' (v. 31), which is likely to be identical with the place where Joash stood in 2 Chron. 23.13;
- in contrast to 2 Chron. 29.10 the covenant is not made 'with the LORD' as partner but between the members of the community 'before the LORD' as witness (cf. 1 Sam. 23.18; Jer. 34.15). It is, of course, the covenant with the LORD that they are binding themselves to keep, but the formulation stresses the community's responsibility;
- 'to walk' (2 Chron. 6.16) after him, to give him his sole rights;
- the covenant is to observe the already existing covenant in all its variety of stipulations, 'commandments', 'testimonies' and 'statutes' (1 Chron. 29.19);

- 'with all his heart and with all his soul' (1 Chron. 22.19), the total commitment of mind and emotion. C personalizes by adding 'his' with both;
- there seems to be little significance in the variation between 'to do the words of the covenant' (v. 31; Deut. 29.8; Jer. 11.6, 8) and 'to realize the words of the covenant' (2 Kgs 23.3; Jer. 34.18; cf. Neh. 9.8), the former may (Jer. 11.8 may be influenced by v. 6) refer prospectively to commitment (but compare v. 32), the latter retrospectively to fulfilment (but in 1 Kgs 6.12 both verbs are co-ordinated);
- the unique 'all the people took their stand in the covenant' with which 2 Kgs 23.3 ends is turned into the equally unique causative at the beginning of v. 32, 'He made everyone stand', though with 'covenant' delayed till the next phrase with a change of preposition. It may be that the unexpected singling out of 'Benjamin' in the verse is a textual error for 'covenant' (*berît,* cf. *BHK* and *BHS*). The remainder of vv. 32-33 is C's own summary on Josiah's reform, substituting for 2 Kgs 23.4-20;
- 'the God of their fathers' (vv. 32-33), 1 Chron. 5.25;
- 'so he removed [2 Chron. 14.3] the abominations [2 Chron. 28.3]' (v. 33): this verse summarizes Josiah's achievements. His action marks the reversal in principle of the malpractice of Manasseh and his son (2 Chron. 33.2; cf. 2 Chron. 33.22);
- 'from all the lands of Israel [1 Chron. 13.2]': by the plural unique to C, Josiah is shown to be the true Davidic king who reunites the dispersed people in the one land in the ideal extent of their territory;
- thus he subjects all in Israel to the service (1 Chron. 28.9) of the LORD;
- as he 'removes' the abominations, so 'all his days they do not turn aside [same verb in the intransitive conjugation; 2 Chron. 8.15] from following the LORD'.

It is striking that the material omitted from 2 Kgs 23.4-20 after 2 Chron. 34.31 begins with the same phrase, 'And the king commanded' (2 Kgs 23.4), as 2 Kgs 23.21, with which the parallels resume in 2 Chron. 35.1 (though C has changed the formulation). It is just possible, therefore, that the MT of C omits a parallel to 2 Kgs 23.4-20 by a copyist's error (homoioarcton). That is, however, unlikely: see the echoes of 2 Kgs 23.4-20 noted above in 2 Chron. 34.3-7, which would appear to be the intended utilization of 2 Kgs 23.4-20. There are, also, points made in 2 Kgs 23.4-20 that do not suit C's presentation, especially the description of Solomon's polytheistic cult in v. 13 and the cross-reference in vv. 16-18 to the narrative in 1 Kings 13, which C has not reproduced.

4. *2 Chronicles 35.1-6: The Preparation of the Priests and Levites for the Passover*

Verse 1 functions as a double title for the next two sections: first, the general title, 'Josiah observed Passover in Jerusalem in honour of the LORD' (cf.2 Chron. 30.1); then a more particular title about the essential rite, 'they slaughtered the Passover victims on the fourteenth of the first month'. C expounds how the Passover can be celebrated acceptably only because the appropriate roles of priest and Levite are observed (vv. 2-7); then he records how the slaughter of the victims takes place (vv. 8-17).

> C's particular concerns are made clear by comparison with Kings. Verse 1a is a remote echo of 2 Kgs 23.21: 'The king commanded all the people, *"Observe Passover in honour of the* LORD *your God in accordance with* how it is written in this scroll of the covenant"'. The part italicized marks the only words in which the two versions coincide and even there the verbal form concerned is different. But C does not resume the continuation of the narrative in 2 Kgs 23.22-23 until v. 18: he has his own agenda about how the Passover is to be appropriately observed.

Verses 2-7 provide another 'flashback' (compare the structure of the account of Hezekiah's Passover in 2 Chron. 30.2-5). All this is possible because of the preparations Josiah has set in train. The role of the priests is somewhat summarily acknowledged in v. 2. The direct speech of the king to them is not reported, as it is about to be in the case of the Levites in vv. 3-6. The altar and the handling of the blood are not mentioned explicitly, but merely indirectly indicated by the rather vague statement that the king 'assigned them to their appointed duties [2 Chron. 7.6, with the same verb as here (cf. 1 Chron. 6.31); so of the Levites, 2 Chron. 8.14] and encouraged [the last occurrence in C of the theme word, *ḥzq*, 1 Chron. 11.10] them in the service [the sacrificial rites and liturgy, 1 Chron. 6.32] of the house of the LORD'.

It is the Levites who are C's major focus of attention—and the expected reason is stated at the outset (v. 3a): they are 'the instructors of all Israel, the holy ones of the LORD'. Their task is to be the teachers and monitors of Israel's practice of holiness, the according to God of all that is due to him.

But the reference to the ark is at first sight unexpected; it makes, however, a still more fundamental point. Sacral observance is not an end in itself but an expression of the sanctification of the whole of life.

The reason for building the Temple in the first place was to provide a place of rest for the ark, as a symbolical representation of the pacification of the world by the LORD (1 Chron. 28.2). The instruction here to the Levites not to carry the ark around any more is a reaffirmation of that divine pacification of the earth of which Israel by its holiness remains the agent. It is not the rites of the Temple that are important, not even the observation of the Passover, but what Israel is enabled thereby to become and to perform.

> The implication that the ark has *not* remained in the holy of holies in the Temple since the moment when it was deposited there in the time of Solomon (2 Chron. 5.9; cf. 1 Chron. 23.25-26) comes as a surprise (though cf. 2 Chron. 20.19). *BHK* and *BHS* list proposals that have been made to avoid this implication: for example, LXX at this point reads, not an imperative, 'Put the ark...in the Temple', but a historical statement, 'They put...' But the flow of the LXX narrative is somewhat different and, in any case, still refers to an action by the Levites in the time of Josiah. Given the following instruction not to carry a burden on the shoulders (as in 1 Chron. 23.26), the action of putting the ark in the Temple must be attributed to the Levites now. An alternative solution must be sought. The writing is probably highly ideological: it is likely that, along the lines of his 'timeless contemporaneity' (see on 1 Chron. 9.22), C is presenting Josiah's action as a rerun, that is, a reaffirmation, of what was achieved under Solomon.

What Solomon did, Josiah does. Solomon is given a list of sonorous titles, 'son of David, king of Israel', to emphasize the authority behind the action and to indicate that by his action Josiah is truly expressing his role as Davidic monarch in that succession (three times in this chapter the authority of David is invoked, vv. 3, 4, 15). The description of the ark as 'the holy ark' (unique in the Hebrew Bible, let alone C; cf. 2 Chron. 5.7) perhaps also reflects the view that its sole appropriate location is the 'holy of holies' in the Temple (though the Uzza narrative has already indicated its uncanny power, 1 Chron. 13.10).

The function of the Levites is, therefore, v. 3b, to 'serve [1 Chron. 28.9; cf. 2 Chron. 34.33] the LORD...and his people'. The service of the Levites links the LORD and his human agents here in a unique way; the sacramental relation of God and people is emphasized by the chiastically arranged co-ordinated titles, 'the LORD'–'his people', 'your God'–'Israel'.

To enable the slaughter of the Passover victims on the evening of the fourteenth day to be performed in the acceptable manner, Josiah now prescribes the appropriate procedures. He commands the Levites to organize themselves (reading with the *kethib* the form of the key term, *kûn*, 1 Chron. 14.2) in their roster duties by their families according to the plan (1 Chron. 28.19) drawn up by David (1 Chron. 23) and implemented by Solomon (v. 4; the written directions of Solomon are not referred to elsewhere, unless the prescriptive prophetic account of his reign is meant [2 Chron. 9.29]; the formulation may imply that the content was David's, while the writing down was Solomon's).

It is difficult to envisage precisely the procedures in mind (v. 5). The plan drawn up by David in 1 Chronicles 23 is presumably for the organization of the clergy in successive shifts for a whole year. It must be assumed that, on such an occasion of national pilgrimage as the Passover, when all Israel is present in Jerusalem, the normal rosters of duty are suspended and the whole force of the clergy is also in attendance to serve the needs of the whole community at one time (cf. 2 Chron. 23.8). Instead of coming to the Temple in successive shifts, the Levites are, accordingly, organized into corresponding teams now functioning contemporaneously. In the same way as the successive shifts of the Levites are here organized contemporaneously, so too the people, organized in 1 Chronicles 27 for monthly duty, are now brought together in these groups in one mighty assembly. This division of the Levites into teams thus matches the division of the populace into groups according to their households.

> It may be that the exceptional nature of the celebration (v. 18) accounts for the exceptional character of the vocabulary used to describe it. In addition to the normal word for 'rosters' (*maḥleqôt*), there is the related word, which occurs only here, from the same stem for the 'division' (*ḥaluqqâ*) of the Levites into teams. Equally the term for the division of the households of the ordinary Israelites into groups (*peluggôt*) is unique to this passage; so too the corresponding word in v. 12.

The comprehensiveness of the organization for this simultaneous celebration of Passover by the whole community, of one mind and in one place, marks in effective and appropriate fashion the beginning of the liturgical year (Exod. 12.1; Num. 28.16, in contrast to the agricultural year reflected in Exod. 23.16); the preparations for holding it necessarily involve the arrangements for the year as a whole, specifically, as v. 16 makes clear, the offering of whole burnt offerings (cf. under Hezekiah, 2 Chron. 30.16).

The warmth of the whole occasion is expressed by the term 'brothers' (v. 5); it is not on their own account but on behalf of the whole community that the Levites are functioning. Those who are termed 'brothers' are described by an unusual expression, 'the sons of the people' (four times in this chapter, vv. 5, 7, 12 and 13), which occurs elsewhere in the Hebrew Bible in contexts indicating fringe members of society, of little account or of dubious orthodoxy (2 Kgs 23.6; Jer. 26.23, where their graves are desecrated). This Passover is an expression of community solidarity from which not even the poorest and least regarded members are excluded.

In contrast to 2 Chron. 30.15-17, where the Levites slaughtered the Passover victim only of those who were not ritually pure, here, it seems, the Levites are commanded to undertake the slaughter on behalf of the whole community (v. 6a matches, in the imperative mood, the title in v. 1b). Josiah's concern must be that, at this moment of solemn reinauguration, no mischance befall the people. It is, therefore, the Levites who are 'to sanctify themselves' and 'to achieve' (the key term, *kûn*, again, as in v. 4) on behalf of their 'brothers' (who these 'brothers' are—the priests, the musicians and the gate keepers— is to be expounded at greater length in vv. 14-15). The section ends with the most solemn sanction conceivable: all is to be done in accordance with the revelation from the LORD, a revelation that has come through the mediation of Moses.

The procedures for observance of the Passover, again as in 2 Chron. 30.15-16, with their inclusion of the whole burnt offering of cattle, match the Temple rites of Deut. 16.1-8 rather than the domestic celebration of Exod. 12.1-13 (as in Deut. 16, Passover merges with Unleavened Bread; see v. 17): C is here exploring to its ultimate degree the potentiality of the Temple to act as vehicle and expression of the religious life of his people in the context of its primary religious ordinance, the Passover. The presentation about to be given is highly ideological: such huge numbers of victims involved and such a vast assembly of people all having their Passover sacrifices slaughtered, flayed and their blood presented and their flesh cooked and with Levites rushing to and fro to serve the people could hardly have been accommodated in the Temple on the single evening of Passover. But C's is an 'exilic' work: when king and Temple are swept away, the core of meaning in these ordinances enjoined by David and Solomon will have to be sought once more 'in the Word of the LORD by the hand of Moses' and realized in the home rather than at the Temple hearth.

5. 2 Chronicles 35.7-24: The Passover and the 'Negative Passover'

The final section on the reign of Josiah is divided into three sub-sections.

Verse 7: Josiah's Provision of Passover Sacrifices for the People

As the righteous king, like David, Solomon, and Hezekiah, Josiah supplies ('contributes the levy', cf. 2 Chron. 30.24; the verb recurs in vv. 8-9) from his own estate the Passover victims that enable people to fulfil their obligations. The royal estates are not private property, but the means whereby the power and prosperity of Israel as the LORD's host, focused on the LORD's anointed, are expressed. The provision of the Passover victims by the king is thus not an act of condescending charity but an empowering of the people's response and commitment (1 Chron. 27.31).

For an appreciation of the prodigious scale of Josiah's provision—30,000 sheep and goats and 3000 cattle—see the statistics at 1 Chron. 29.21. The large cattle, out of place in the domestic rite, Exod. 12.5, relate the occasion unambiguously to Temple sacrifice.

Verses 8-18: The Observance of the Passover

The leaders of the people are stimulated by the king's devotion to comparable acts of generosity (for the statistics, see again 1 Chron. 29.21). The leaders, at least those specified by name and gift, turn out to be only the priests and the Levites. The source of these sheep, goats and cattle provided by the clergy must be the priestly and levitical cities, where the clergy had the grazing rights (1 Chron. 6.54). While the same verb is used of the leaders' action as for the king's, theirs is termed a 'free-will offering' (1 Chron. 29.5-9). The free-will offering is, in general, a response in gratitude and praise to an experience of the special favour of God; here it is the expression of the zeal and commitment of the clergy at the rededication of the Temple, their joy that the means for discharging their basic task, the sanctification of the people, has again been reinstated. Thus, though their offerings are, in the event, only destined for the priests and Levites respectively (vv. 8-9), it is, nonetheless, 'for the people' in the first instance (v. 8) that their action is motivated.

From the statistics for the cattle, assuming a fixed rate per head, one might deduce that there was one priest for every ten of the laity and one Levite for every six, but the statistics for the sheep and goats for the priests do not quite fit such a calculation, and in any case the proportion seems rather high (compare 1 Chron. 23.3, where the adult male clergy amount to about one in thirty of the adult male population).

None of the three priests and six Levites named is known from other contexts, at least if one takes this episode historically as a distinct event in time. It is striking, however, that, for example, a Chananiah (with the same *qere* and *kethib* problem in the reading of his name) occurs in 2 Chron. 31.12, in connection with the people's contribution; compare 1 Chron. 15.22, a context in which a Jeiel occurs (gatekeeper–musician, 1 Chron. 15.18, 21; see the levitical scribe of that name in charge of the muster, 2 Chron. 26.11).

Verse 8 illustrates the frustrating lack of completeness of the evidence that C provides: whereas the High Priest has been called 'leader of the house of God' elsewhere (1 Chron. 9.11; cf. 2 Chron. 28.7), now not only is Hilkiah given that title, but the other two figures as well—but with no specification of their roles. Equally, no clue is given in v. 9 as to why the second and third named Levites are specified as the 'brothers' of the first, as though they were in some sense subordinate to him, nor in what sense these six were in any case the 'leaders' among the Levites (unless one engages in speculations as in the previous paragraph).

For other lists of named officials (outside the genealogies of 1 Chronicles 1–9 and David's organization especially in 1 Chronicles 11–12; 15; 23–27), see:

2 Chron. 17.7-9:	Jehoshaphat's teachers—5 lay, 9 levites, 2 priests;
2 Chron. 17.14-18:	Jehoshaphat's commanders—5;
2 Chron. 29.12-14:	Hezekiah's Levites to purify Temple—14;
2 Chron. 31.12-13:	Hezekiah's Levites connected with Temple stores—12;
2 Chron. 31.14-15:	Hezekiah's Levites connected with priestly cities—7;
and here	
2 Chron. 35.8-9:	Josiah's 3 priests and 6 Levites donating for Passover.

These lists are presumably in line with C's concern that only those with the requisite pedigree are entitled to observe the rites in the Temple, indeed, possess the requisite degree of holiness so as not to invalidate them.

Yet C gives other lists and these must have other purposes, which may not be absent here as well: the piling up of names for effect to emphasize the especial significance of the data. Thus he lists by name Rehoboam's fifteen fortified cities (2 Chron. 11.6-10), three out of eighteen of Rehoboam's wives (not to mention sixty concubines) and his seven sons

(2 Chron. 11.18-20), and six cities captured by the Philistines under Ahaz
(2 Chron. 28.18).

C does not apply his method consistently. A particularly noticeable
context in which a list might have been expected is in connection with
Solomon's dedication of the Temple in 2 Chronicles 5 and 7.

Thus, v. 10, the worship of the Temple is in readiness (the key note
verb, *kûn*, as in vv. 4 and 6 [and to come in vv. 14, 15 and 20]). The
same expression is to be picked up in vv. 15-16: it is through the
observance now to be detailed of these rites enjoined by the king in
connection with the Passover that the worship of the Temple is truly
re-established. 'The priests standing in their place' resumes v. 2; 'the
Levites in their divisions', v. 4.

This is how, then, 'they slaughtered the Passover victims', the
phrase in v. 11a picking up *verbatim* the title in v. 1b.

Verses 11b-13 then explain how the Passover, treated as a communion sacrifice, is observed with the utmost punctiliousness. The meal
is, as is required, shared three ways: the appropriate parts are burnt
on the altar to God; other appropriate parts are given as their due to
the priests; the remainder is available to the sacrificer and his house-
hold and, if need be, his neighbours (Exod. 12.3-4).

The process begins in v. 11b: the Levites slaughter the victims; the
priests receive the blood from their hand; the Levites flay the victims.

Verse 12 deals with the offering of the appropriate parts on the
altar to God. In line with 'what is written in the scroll of Moses' on
how the communion sacrifice is to be offered (specifically the legislation in Lev. 3.6-16 and 7.29-34), the portions of fat are first
'removed' (the verb at the beginning of v. 12 is the same as that used
in Lev. 3.10, 15), which are to be offered to God. These are 'given' to
the groups of households of the common people so that they may
'offer' them to be burnt by the priest on the altar (as a 'fire offering'
to the LORD, Lev. 3.9, 14). One must assume that, as the blood
equates with life (Lev. 17.14) and is thus dashed against the altar, so
the fat portions are burnt on the altar because they represent vitality
and are thus returned to God the giver of life.

It is crucial for the understanding of v. 12 that the word *'ōlâ*, used at the
beginning of the verse, is *not* taken in its normal technical sense of the
standard 'whole burnt offering', such as is legislated for in Leviticus 1 (so
NEB correctly, if freely, 'fat flesh' [cf. v. 14], and JPSV 'the parts to be
burnt'; the NRSV and NIV, on the other hand, rendering 'burnt offerings',
are to that extent misleading). Here it simply refers to the *parts* of the

communion sacrifice that are wholly burned on the altar, *not* the whole victim.

The 'cattle' at the end of v. 12 presumably refers to the whole burnt offerings, in the normal technical sense, which are sacrificed in addition to the Passover victims (cf. v. 16), rather than cattle as part of Passover rites themselves.

Cattle are indeed included in the permitted victims for Passover in Deut.16.1-8, but that is simply because the seven days of Unleavened Bread, in connection with which the sacrifice of whole burnt offerings is required (Num. 28.17-25), have been assimilated into 'Passover', now understood in global terms as a one-night-plus-seven-days festival.

Thereafter the priests and the people, the two other parties at the feast, may eat (v. 13). Choice cuts, defined in Lev. 7.28-34 and Num. 18.18, are reserved for the priests as 'holy things' (again 'holy things' functioning sacramentally to express the appropriate practice of the whole, 1 Chron. 6.49). The Levites then 'bring at the run to all the common people' their share in the Passover victims.

A point at issue is how these portions were cooked. There is no doubt that the portions for the priests were boiled: that is the normal meaning of the verb (e.g. Exod. 23.19); the vessels used, conventionally 'pots, cauldrons and pans [NEB, JPSV]', indicate the same, as do other passages in the Hebrew Bible on sacrificial practice (e.g. 1 Sam. 2.13-14). However, according the injunctions in Exod. 12.8-9, the Passover should be roasted; boiling is explicitly forbidden. Thus many wish to read in v. 13a, 'They roasted the Passover victim by fire according to custom' [JPSV, NIV, NRSV; NEB hedges, using 'cooked']. The difficulty with that interpretation is that the same verb is used in v. 13a as in v. 13b, and not the verb 'to roast'. Further, why should the priests alone, of all people, be in breach of the customary practice at Passover? It may, therefore, be more appropriate to envisage that the whole practice of this Passover is unique (as v. 18 acknowledges): it is here assimilated entirely to the sacrificial practice of the Temple, in the use of the clergy and the altar and in the mode of cooking the flesh (compare the recurrence of the verb in Deut. 16.7, where Passover and Unleavened Bread are conflated). In that case, 'according to custom' refers to normal sacrificial practice.

Given the preoccupation of the other clergy with their duties—the priests at the altar, the musicians to strike up at the appropriate points of the liturgy, the gatekeepers at each gate ensuring access only to those qualified—the Levites have the task of 'preparing' (the key word, *kûn*, again, vv. 14 [twice], 15, 16) the portions of the Passover for themselves and their colleagues. To emphasize division of labour and the precise definition of roles, the priests are explicitly defined as 'the sons of Aaron' (v. 14), and the musicians as the three orders of Asaph, Heman and Jeduthun (v. 15). Such is the scale of the task, that the priests have to work not just 'between the evenings' (Exod. 12.6) or 'at sunset' (Deut. 16.6) but, somewhat indeterminately, 'until night' (v. 14). The musicians are set in their places (1 Chron. 6.31). It is again striking how Asaph (because of special connection with the ark, 1 Chron. 16.7?) is given prominence (mentioned twice; in leading position). Jeduthun appears here to be given the title, 'king's seer', which was attributed to Heman in 1 Chron. 25.5 (in view of that variation the suggestion [*BHS* on the evidence of the versions] should probably be followed of reading the plural, 'king's seers'). In C, the musician is the prophet, par excellence: such is the assimilation of ideal to institution, that prophecy, the proclamation of the impending act of God, is identified with the hymn of the choir celebrating the realization of that act (1 Chron. 25.1).

Verse 16 acts as a summary, resuming v. 2, while v. 17 recapitulates v. 1. It is now acknowledged explicitly for the first time that this celebration of Passover has in fact merged with Unleavened Bread, as the narrative has already signalized and as the stipulations of the Law demand (cf. v. 6).

C has now expounded in his own terms the revolutionary nature of the Passover celebrated in Josiah's eighteenth year (v. 18): never before had any such Passover been held in which the clergy, in particular the Levites, had enabled Temple worship to be reinstated with all its potentiality to affirm the LORD's sovereignty over the world and to express Israel's duty in recognition of that sovereignty.

In v. 18abα, C returns briefly to his parent text in 2 Kgs 23.22-23, but with his own distinctive emphases. C begins by marginally strengthening the expression of uniqueness: 'No Passover like it had been observed in Israel' for Kings: 'For there had not been observed such a Passover as this'. He redefines the history of Israel's observance as 'from the days of Samuel', rather than 'from the days of the judges who ruled Israel', as in Kings: C's interest is in the monarchy as means for Israel to realize her destiny; Josiah is going beyond even the guidance of Samuel to David (cf. 1 Chron. 9.22). The distinction in Kings between the monarchs of Israel and Judah is then suppressed—it is Israel in its completeness that is of importance to C. To confirm these points he adds, 'they [all the kings of Israel] did not observe such a Passover as Josiah observed'—and gives a new exhaustive list of the components of Israel after the king: 'priests and Levites, all Judah and Israel', adding poignantly, 'that survived', 'and the inhabitants of Jerusalem'.

Verses 19-24: The 'Negative Passover'

C now begins a new subsection. The resumption of 'Josiah's eighteenth year' (v. 19; cf. 2 Chron. 34.8) is not so much by way of a summary but the platform from which the final episode of Josiah's reign is launched.

> Kings, by contrast, continues the preceding assessment of Josiah's unparalleled reformation with a linking 'only'. C omits 2 Kgs 23.24-27: apparently, the assessment in Kings, that there was none like Josiah before or after, does not suit C's presentation either with regard to the ideal achieved under David and Solomon, or with regard to the sequel, which for him is the start of the exile—there are no later kings worthy of the name who can be compared with Josiah; the explanation for the exile in Kings in terms of Manasseh's provocations does not fit either C's account of the repentance of Manasseh or the reason he gives for the exile, namely, Josiah's failure.

A more radical reformation could not have been put through: what blessing could now be expected?—surely some new recognition by the world of the nations of the sovereignty of God and of the status of his vicegerent on earth, the Davidic king. But instead of that new recognition, C has now to turn to trace how, despite all these reforms and the expectations they must arouse, Josiah—almost immediately, it seems, but, chronologically, it is thirteen years later—is killed and leaves his people at the mercy of the Egyptians. How can these things have happened?

C begins with a portentous 'after all this' (v. 20), somewhat in the manner in which he introduces the final historical section of Hezekiah's reign (2 Chron. 32.1, 9). With masterly economy, he juxtaposes in successive phrases what Josiah has done to restore (key word, *kûn*, v. 4, yet again, but now for the last time in the work, unless one includes the ironical use of the name, Jehoiachin; 2 Chron. 36.8-10) the Temple and the menacing advance of the Egyptian army.

C tells us nothing about the occasion that led the Egyptian Pharaoh Neco to do battle 'at Carchemish on the Euphrates'. Kings informs the reader—indeed, reads instead of that phrase—that it was to attack 'the king of Assyria'. It is the period of the terminal decline of Assyria and the emergence of Babylon as the new imperial force in

Mesopotamia. One may make educated guesses about the competing economic and imperial interests of the Egyptians and the Mesopotamian powers, but it is not such factors in the international situation that interest C.

With a third terse phrase, C adds, 'Josiah advanced to meet him'. The words are laden with meaning. 'To advance' is the verb C uses as early as 1 Chron. 1.12, to describe the onslaught of the nations, in that case specifically the Philistines, but within the wider context of Cush and Nimrod (1 Chron. 1.10). It is precisely between Cush and Nimrod, the rival powers of the earth of west and east, that Josiah is caught at this moment.

> It may be that it is for that reason that C has changed the verb from the more neutral, 'went' of Kings, which carries straight into the fatal conse-quences: 'he put him to death at Megiddo when he saw him' (2 Kgs 23.29). C now adds independent material in vv. 21-24aα.

But for C there is a further level of meaning. Josiah's sallying forth to intercept the Egyptian king is as ill-conceived and ill-fated as the venturing forth of predecessors of Josiah's into the international arena: Rehoboam's going to Shechem (2 Chron. 10.1); Asa's hiring of Benhadad (2 Chron. 16.2); Jehoshaphat's alliance with Ahab (2 Chron. 18.2); Ahaziah's alliance with Jehoram (2 Chron. 22.5); Amaziah's challenge to Joash (2 Chron. 25.17); Ahaz's appeal to Tiglath-pilneser III (2 Chron. 28.16); Hezekiah's entertainment of the Babylonian spies (2 Chron. 32.31). In each of these cases, the fault is the compromising of Jerusalem theology. The LORD is enthroned as cosmic ruler and his Davidic king in Zion is his agent among the nations of the earth. The LORD's ark is at rest in the holy of holies; the resting of that ark sym-bolizes the pacification of the nations of the world. It is that funda-mental theological statement that Josiah himself has just reaffirmed by his instruction to the Levites in v. 3 that there is now no need to transport the ark. Josiah's failure is that he ignores the reaffirmation of the pacification imposed by God represented by the ark at rest just lately permanently installed at his own instruction in the Temple.

The Pharaoh tries to prevent the inevitable tragedy, first at the level of sheer military fact (v. 21): 'What have we to do with each other?', the rhetorical question expressing in a still more forceful way the statement, 'We have nothing to do with one another'. Neco's objective has nothing to do with Judah, but with Egypt's traditional Assyrian rival.

The Pharaoh then moves on to the theological plane, in words full of recognition of Jerusalem's theological claims, at least to the limits of his capacity: it is none other than God himself who has 'alarmed' Neco (2 Chron. 32.18, may be better than the standard English versions understanding of the verb, 'speeded' him on his way, though that fits with the next phrase), so that he will have nothing to do with Josiah. He, too, is on a divine mission; to resist him is to resist God. Then, with words that add the full pathos to the confrontation, Neco adds, 'Lest he destroy you'. Here is the basic vocabulary of the 'negative Passover' (1 Chron. 21.12): in the original exodus from Egypt, God had sent 'the destroyer' to slay the first-born of the Egyptians, so that Israel his first-born might be delivered. Now, in the mouths of Egyptians, the same vocabulary is used: if Josiah does not heed the warning issued by God through the Egyptians, he will bring down upon his own people the very destruction by God from which it was the purpose of the exodus to deliver them.

There is yet a further irony. In situation after situation of crisis, God has sent his prophetic figures to warn (cf. Introduction to 2 Chron. 10–36). Here is the ultimate irony: it is these 'messengers' (one of the traditional titles of God's own prophets; 2 Chron. 36.15-16), of Israel's longest standing traditional enemy, who convey the word of salvation to God's own people. Once again, God has not left himself without a witness.

Josiah refuses to heed the warning (v. 22a). Like the defiant, yet profoundly insecure, Ahab, he 'disguises himself' (2 Chron. 18.29; if that is the correct reading—*BHK*, for example, reads, 'he was determined to fight with him') for the battle, as though by that act he could escape the determinate purpose of God.

Battle is engaged at the strategic site of Megiddo (v. 22b) at the north-west corner of the central hill country, where the coastal route crosses into the Valley of Jezreel. Josiah, despite his disguise, is shot by the archers (v. 23), is removed from his war chariot and transported mortally wounded to Jerusalem, where he dies (v. 24).

In Kings Josiah dies at Megiddo itself (2 Kgs 23.30). C has modified the tradition to make a significant point: he, who should have reigned victoriously seated on the LORD's throne in Jerusalem, is instead brought back there in powerlessness, because of his failure to rely on his own theological tradition, to perish at the very site of his loftiest claims.

Josiah is the last of the kings of Judah to be buried in Jerusalem, according to C's presentation. The period of independence of the house of David is at an end: the following kings are installed and removed by Egypt or Babylon and all die in exile. The exile has effectively begun. All the people of Judah and Jerusalem are in mourning for Josiah and for all that his death must now mark in the history of his people.

By the notice of the burial (v. 24), C has promoted item (6) of the standard framework out of its due position (it should follow 2 Chron. 35.26). By this very change in the framework C is signalling that a radical break has now occurred in the presentation of the monarchy. MT confirms this break by the strong paragraph marker inserted at the end of v. 24 and by the way in which the next paragraph is defined as running from 2 Chron. 35.25–36.4. The account of kings who die in exile has now begun.

2 CHRONICLES 35.25–36.23: EXILE AND RETURN;
GUILT AND ATONEMENT

To understand the last phase of C's presentation of Israel's history, it is, as has just been noted, once again imperative to heed the paragraph markers of MT. A major paragraph marker is inserted at the end of 2 Chron. 35.24, four verses before the end of the material on Josiah; but the next marker does not occur until the end of 2 Chron. 36.4, the conclusion of the material on Josiah's successor, Jehoahaz. In other words, C now breaks across the logic of a merely historical account to integrate the final elements of the framework of Josiah's reign (elements [5] and [7] in 2 Chron. 35.26–36.1; element [6] has already been treated, out of sequence, in 2 Chron. 35.24) with the whole of the reign of his successor (2 Chron. 36.2-4). Why should this be?

The account of the end of Josiah's reign is thus made to introduce the final phase of Israel's life. This final phase is presented in five sections —the four last kings of Judah, followed by the opening to the future represented by the Edict of Cyrus:

1. 2 Chron. 35.25–36.4: the transition from Josiah to Jehoahaz;
2. 2 Chron. 36.5-8: Jehoiakim;
3. 2 Chron. 36.9-10: Jehoiachin;
4. 2 Chron. 36.11-21: Zedekiah;
5. 2 Chron. 36.22-23: the call to immigration.

Sections 4 and 5 are each subdivided into two.

Whereas the logic of the succession of kings' reigns is thus cut in C's presentation, it is striking that one, non-monarchical, figure binds the whole of this final part of C's history together, namely, the prophet Jeremiah (2 Chron. 35.25 in section 1; 2 Chron. 36.12 in section 4—that is, in the first and last sections dealing with Davidic kings; and 2 Chron. 36.22, in Section 5, inaugurating the Return). The whole of this part is thus predicated on the prophetic word of Jeremiah and ends with the fact that Israel is poised at the moment of the fulfilment of his word. The specific word to be fulfilled is his prophecy that the exile will last for seventy years (Jer. 25.11-12; 29.10). This prophecy, and the function of Jeremiah in this whole final part of his work, make it clear why C has so arranged these final sections. The edict of Cyrus marking the end of the exile and the beginning of the Return, and, thus, the fulfilment of Jeremiah's prophecy, is conventionally dated in 538 BCE.[1] The 'seventy years' of exile takes the reader back, therefore, to 608, almost precisely the year of the death of Josiah—conventionally dated 609.[2] The word of Jeremiah imposes a unitary framework of exile and the end of exile on the presentation of the final phase of Israel's history.

The reason for C's breaking across the historically logical limits of the presentation of the reign of Josiah is now clear. With the death of Josiah the new phase of exile has now begun for Israel. Each of the four kings who now follows is carried off into exile; for the sake of this pattern, Jehoiakim, too, suffers an exile otherwise unknown in the Hebrew Bible (2 Chron. 36.6; there is an eloquent silence from Bright on that one—as on the whole of 2 Chron. 36). Each of the sections 1–4 thus has an exilic destination: Egypt (2 Chron. 36.4); Babylon (v. 6); Babylon (v. 10); Section 4 is subdivided precisely to repeat in each of its subsections the exilic destination, Babylon (v. 18); Babylon (v. 20). Cush and Nimrod (1 Chron. 1.10) have triumphed.

But there is a still more far-reaching reason why C treats this last phase as all one period, integrated through the prophetic word of Jeremiah. With the integrated presentation of Israel from the death of Josiah to the edict of Cyrus, C has created a single, uniform 'exilic' generation. This 'exilic' generation is the fiftieth from creation. (There are ten generations from Adam, the father of humankind, to Noah, the second father of humankind; there are ten further generations to Abraham, 'the father of a multitude of nations' [1 Chron. 1.1-4, 24-27]. Israel's history has been presented in terms of fifteen generations from Abraham to Solomon [1 Chron. 1.34; 2.1, 4-5, 9-12, 15; 3.5], the realization in monarchic terms of the ideal of Israel's existence, and a further fifteen from Rehoboam to Josiah [2 Chron. 10.1–35.24], the end of the monarchy in *ma'al*-induced failure. Given that Abraham figures twice in these calculations, there are thus 49 generations from Adam to Josiah.) It is in this fiftieth, exilic generation, that the edict of Cyrus is proclaimed; the exilic generation is the

---

1.   Bright, *History of Israel*, p. 361.
2.   Bright, *History of Israel*, p. 324.

generation that hears the summons to return, to immigrate into the land.

Cyrus's edict thus represents the proclamation of jubilee in the fiftieth generation. C accounts for the exile in terms of *maʿal* (2 Chron. 36.14) and of the rest which the land requires because of the sabbaths that it has been denied during Israel's occupancy of the land (2 Chron. 36.21), in the manner of Lev. 26.40, 43. Likewise, after the manner of Lev. 25.8-11, he interprets the Return from exile in terms of the proclamation of jubilee in the fiftieth year (cf. Introduction to Volume I).

The relationship between the relevant parts of C (2 Chron. 35.25–36.21) and Kings in these sections is particularly complex. The following table is merely a preliminary overview:

2 Chronicles	2 Kings
35.25	no parallel
35.26-27	cf. 23.28
(cf. already at 35.20, 24)	23.29-30a
36.1-2	23.30b-31a
no parallel	23.31b-32
36.3-4	cf. 23.33-34
no parallel	23.35
36.5	cf. 23.36a, 37
no parallel	23.36b
36.6a	cf. 24.1a
no parallel	24.1b-4
36.6b, 7	no parallel
36.8a	cf. 24.5
no parallel	24.6a
36.8b	24.6b
no parallel	24.7
36.9	cf. 24.8a, 9a
no parallel	24.8b, 9b-16
36.10a	no close parallel
36.10b	cf. 24.17a
no parallel	24.17b
36.11	24.18a
no parallel	24.18b
36.12a	cf. 24.19a
36.12b	no parallel
no parallel	24.19b, 20a
36.13aα	cf. 24.20b
36.13aβ-21	no close parallel
no close parallel	25.1-30

A striking feature of C's narrative is its compression. This final section is only twenty-six verses long (twenty-four, if one omits 2 Chron. 36.22-23 which lies outside the period dealt with in Kings), as opposed to the some fifty-eight verses of the equivalent section in Kings; in particular the thirty verses of 2 Kings 25, on the fall of Jerusalem under Zedekiah and its aftermath, are condensed into four (it is notable how the material from 2 Kgs 25.12 onwards is ignored). In line with the argument above about the function of this final period in C's presentation—to present the exilic age in concerted fashion—this concentration is not surprising.

Only a rather broad profile of events is, in general, retained. Notable omissions in C are the depredations of the successive foreign invaders, Neco and, especially, Nebuchadnezzar; the macabre details on the fate of the kings—C is interested in their exile, not their deaths; the governorship of Gedaliah; the release of Jehoiachin from prison. For C, exile is a continual, cumulative and, ultimately, total process, not limited and not in two main phases (the details of the exile under Jehoiachin, for example, are largely suppressed).

On the other hand, notable additions in C are the figure of Jeremiah and the theological evaluation in 2 Chron. 36.13-16, 21.

There is a marked reduction of the framework, within which the reigns of these last four kings of Judah are set (Introduction to 2 Chron. 10–36). That reduction is to be explained by C's purpose not only to compress the data but to present these reigns as the initial stages of the exile: only elements (1) and (2), the age at accession and length of reign are consistently given; element (3), the mother's name is consistently suppressed; element (4), the theological evaluation—the main point of the discussion—is retained for Jehoiakim, Jehoiachin and Zedekiah; element (5), the record of the reign, occurs only for Jehoiakim; element (6), burial in Jerusalem is, naturally, missing from all; element (7), the succession of the son, is given in its standard form only for Jehoiakim.

1. 2 Chronicles 35.25–36.4: The Transition from Josiah to Jehoahaz

The story of Israel now passes from monarchy to exile. Israel's life had started in Egypt; to Egypt, in the last word of 2 Chron. 36.4, its first exiled monarch returns.

In place of the celebration ('joy', the key word *śimḥâ*, 1 Chron. 12.40), which should mark the response of the people as they hail the triumph of God's purposes, the closing phase of the life of God's people is inaugurated with its polar opposite, lamentation, *qînâ* (v. 25).

Three times the doleful root, *qîn*, is sounded in the opening verse of the section. Jeremiah raises the dirge over the dead king.

The root *qīn* is indeed characteristic of Jeremiah (7.29; 9.10, 17, 20); see also Jeremiah's lamentation over successive kings of the house of David, Jer. 21.11–23.8, where, however, there is only a fleeting reference to Josiah himself (22.10): there the mourning for Josiah is as nothing compared with the lamentations to come.

That dirge is taken up by the professional singers, male and female (for the latter in contexts of mourning, see, again, Jer. 9.17). The practice of commemorating disasters in the life of the people seems to have been commonplace in this period (cf. Zech. 7.3, 5). It has thus become a 'statute' for the people, a memorial, required perhaps on a stated annual occasion, of the tragedy that has happened and an expression of longing for what might have been.

As in the case of the prophetic word, composition passes through two stages: first, the laments are cast in literary form to ensure memorability in order to perpetuate the content as valid 'to this day'. The 'day' is the contemporary moment of C, the writer; it is also the unspecified present of any audience, among whom C counts himself, who share the memory and hope of the generations of the past whose song they sing.

The second stage is the recording in writing and inclusion within the corpus of scripture, as part of the whole stock of authoritative writings of the community.

> Whether this composition is now to be found in the canonical book of Lamentations, traditionally associated with Jeremiah (see the subtitle, 'of Jeremiah', in RSV, dropped, however, in NRSV), can only be uncertain (as it is uncertain how much, if any, of the prophetic midrash, to which C has made constant reference [v. 27; see Introduction to 2 Chron. 10–36], is contained within the present prophetic corpus in the Hebrew Bible). It is notable that Lamentations concerns, rather, the fall of Jerusalem; the references to monarchy are relatively, perhaps, even, surprisingly, few (cf. Lam. 2.6, 9; 4.20). The basis of hope is, however, shared, whatever the literary connection may in fact be or not be: *the* throne is the throne of the LORD (Lam. 5.19; cf. 1 Chron. 28.5). Lamentations at the very least contains examples of the genre, if not the very words composed in response to the death of Josiah.

Element (5) of the framework (Introduction to 2 Chron. 10–36) adds here a unique element that heightens the poignancy of the contrast between ideal and actuality. Alone of the kings of Judah, it is said that 'the remainder of the acts of Josiah and his deeds of loyalty were in accordance with what is written in the Law of the LORD' (v. 26).

Apart from faltering once on the occasion of Neco's advance, Josiah has been a paragon of compliance with the Law. The one act of mistrust in the LORD, as defined by his own royal theology, has brought down the dynasty. There is already an indication here of the sole basis on which life can safely be constructed—not monarchy, but the Law alone as mediated through Moses.

> 'And his deeds of loyalty' C reads for the colourless 'and all that he did' in 2 Kgs 23.28.

In face of the crisis—the sudden death of the king still under the age of forty, perhaps before he had arranged the succession (cf. 2 Chron. 11.22), and the land at the mercy of the Egyptian Pharaoh and his army—'the people of the land' (2 Chron. 23.13; cf. 'the sons of the people', 2 Chron. 35.5), those under immediate threat and for whose sake the monarchy exists, have to take what appropriate action they can. They make Josiah's younger son, Jehoahaz, king (2 Chron. 36.1).

The interrelationship of these last kings of Judah (and the variations between C and Kings) can be conveniently indicated by the following family tree:

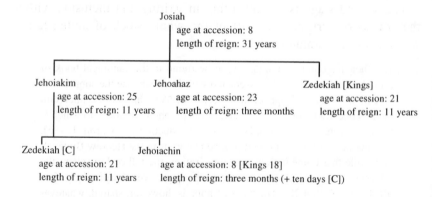

Apart from the variations in the data on Jehoiachin, the major discrepancy between C and Kings is on the relationship of Zedekiah to Jehoiachin: according to C he is a brother (v. 10), while in Kings he is an uncle.

On these figures, the following are the ages of the fathers at the birth of the respective sons:

Jehoahaz was born when his father was 16;
Jehoiakim when his father was 14;
Jehoiachin when his father was 28 [C; 18, Kings]
Zedekiah when his father was 15 [C; 29, Kings]

Merely to judge by the general pattern, Kings is more likely for Jehoiachin, C for Zedekiah. But the names of the mothers, consistently suppressed by C but given by Kings, show that Zedekiah is a full brother of Jehoahaz (both are sons of Josiah by Hamutal, daughter of Jeremiah of Libnah), and that Jehoiakim is a half-brother of them both (son by Zebidah). In strictly historical terms Kings is therefore to be preferred in both variations.

> If it is accepted that the year of Josiah's death is 609, the following are the regnal years of these last kings of Judah, according to the figures in the above genealogy:
>
> Jehoahaz: 609;
> Jehoiakim: 609–598;
> Jehoiachin: 598;
> Zedekiah: 598–587.

C does not delay to analyse the motives of 'the people of the land' in their choice of Jehoahaz ('The LORD has upheld'; cf. 2 Chron. 22.2; 28.1). It is not made clear whether the reason for the choice was merely palace intrigue or because he was regarded as the more nationalist of the two. Certainly, Jehoahaz is immediately forcibly removed by the Egyptians, which would support the latter view (compare Zedekiah, his full brother, who gives the impression, for example, by his private consultation with Jeremiah [Jer. 38.14], of being a reluctant pro-Babylonian and a would-be independent at heart). They 'make him king' as once the representatives of Israel had made David king (1 Chron. 12.38). Perhaps C's addition of 'in Jerusalem' at the end of the verse is a conscious echo of the way in which David was once king 'in Hebron' and 'in Jerusalem' (1 Chron. 29.27; but C suppresses the 'and anointed him' of Kings, despite retaining it for David in 1 Chron. 11.3 and for Joash in 2 Chron. 23.11).

In line with his suppression of macabre detail, C simply notes (v. 3) that Neco 'removes' (*way^{e}sîrēhû*) Jehoahaz.

> 2 Kgs 23.33 has the more graphic, similar-sounding, verb, 'bound him in chains' [*wayya'as^{e}rēhû*], and adds 'at Riblah in the land of Hamath'.

The land has laid upon it an indemnity of one hundred talents of silver and a talent of gold. For the comparative amounts, see 1 Chron. 29.4: one hundred talents of silver represents precisely double the redemption money for the army of Judah and Benjamin (see 2 Chron. 25.6).

24

So far from the armies of Israel being mustered as the LORD's host to fight the LORD's battles, they are neutralized and enlisted in the service of Egypt.

Now it is no longer the volition of the people of the land that matters: it is 'the *king* of Egypt' (Kings again names him; C heightens the play on the following verb) who 'makes *king*' (v. 4; compare v. 1. The verb tolls ominously through this chapter, recurring in v. 10, where Nebuchadnezzar is the subject).

Neco's choice of replacement is Jehoahaz's older brother (again, C wastes no time in discussing any adventitious political considerations in the choice). To underline the merely local, Israelite, character of his new puppet ruler, as he thinks, Neco changes his name from Eliakim, 'El [the supreme, universal deity] shall establish', to Jehoiakim, 'The LORD [the local, national name of the God of Israel] shall establish'. In the verbal element in Jehoiakim's name, 'he shall establish', there is a melancholy play on the verb 'to establish' (*hēqîm*) that was part of the LORD's promise to David to perpetuate his descendants on the throne after him (1 Chron. 17.11), a promise renewed through Solomon (2 Chron. 6.10; 7.18). Nothing could more sharply underline the conditional nature of the promise to the monarchy than the fate of the bearer of this name and of his sons, about to be noted. Meanwhile, Jehoahaz, as the first in line, is removed as a captive to Egypt.

> 2 Kgs 23.34 adds, 'and he died there'. C is again interested in recording the fact of exile, not the ultimate fate of the individual king.
>
> Twice in the verse C emphasizes that Jehoahaz and Jehoiakim are brothers, in preference to the note in Kings that Jehoiakim is the son of Josiah, and stresses that Jehoiakim is king only over Judah and Jerusalem. C thus underplays the succession, and reminds the reader, not of the glorious reign of the father, but of the vulnerability of his heirs.

2. 2 Chronicles 36.5-8: Jehoiakim

There is a change of overlord in Jehoiakim's reign. The subordination of a replacement Davidic king as vassal of Egypt is bad enough; much worse is to follow. Jehoiakim is deported in chains to Babylon; the Temple is plundered and some of its holy vessels are carried off as spoils of war. These vessels consecrated to the worship of the LORD of Hosts are placed in triumph in the national temple in Babylon in acknowledgment of the victory given to Nebuchadnezzar by his god.

No doubt C wishes the reader to expect that this act of sacrilege will bring its own destruction on the impious emperor; the desecrated holy vessels lie there in Babylon like a ticking time-bomb, as Daniel 5 vividly portrays.

Again, C provides no international military or political explanation for the change of overlord (the final victory of Babylon over Assyria, followed by successes on the field of battle by the Babylonians over the Egyptians, notably at Carchemish in 605, which opened the way for Babylonian sovereignty over Syria and Palestine;[3] these events are alluded to in 2 Kgs 24.1-2, 7). For C, all is sufficiently explained in terms of the fact that 'Jehoiakim did what is evil in the sight of the LORD his God' (v. 5; for the theological, not the military, explanation, cf. 1 Chron. 10.13-14). In what way he did what is evil is not divulged: v. 8 includes simply the conventionalized 'abominations' (so, v. 14), such as were practised under Ahaz (2 Chron. 28.3) and subsequent kings.

> 2 Kgs 24.2-4 adds atrocities reflecting the instability of the times: the shedding of innocent blood in Jerusalem.
>
> C's material on the captivity of Jehoiakim is unsubstantiated historically: his purpose is to portray a recurrent pattern of exile. The terms in which Jehoiakim's captivity is described are reminiscent of those already used in connection with Manasseh (2 Chron. 33.11), which in turn reflect the account of the deportation of Zedekiah in 2 Kgs 25.7, that C has not reproduced. A deportation of Jehoiakim also stands in tension with the smooth transition to the reign of his son, Jehoiachin (v. 8b), which C has preserved from 2 Kgs 24.6. The carrying off of Temple vessels at this time is also unique to C and must again be regarded as part of his patterning of events (cf. v. 10, where it is again added to the underlying text of 2 Kgs 24.1, and v. 18).

3. *2 Chronicles 36.9-10: Jehoiachin*

Jehoiachin bears the programmatic name, 'The LORD shall establish'; as it happens, the verbal element in the name, 'he shall establish', is derived from precisely the key root, *kûn* (1 Chron. 14.2), which expresses the sacramental status and function of the Davidic house. It is by bringing the divine will into effect that the Davidic king is himself established.

---

3.   Bright, *History of Israel*, p. 326.

The brevity of the reign of the little boy expresses with all harshness the stark conditions which attach to that status. The penalty that falls on Jehoiachin seems, viewed in personal terms, far beyond the evil that an eight-year-old is capable of committing in a hundred days. Indeed, 'woe to you, O land, when your king is a child' (Eccles. 10.16). But that is hardly the point in C—after all, Joash was a seven-year-old, 2 Chron. 24.1, and Josiah an eight-year-old, 2 Chron. 34.1! The extreme youth of the lad makes the point at issue all the more sharply (stressed, indeed, by C's 'eight-year-old' for 'eighteen-year-old' as in 2 Kgs 24.8): Jehoiachin is enmeshed in a situation, not of his creating but one from which he cannot escape (just as in Kings all the kings of the north, as such, could not be other than guilty of 'the sin of Jeroboam which he caused his people to sin', 1 Kgs 14.16, and elsewhere, so Jehoiachin, in a phrase equally derived from Kings, 'did evil in the eyes of the LORD'). Despite its high theology, the monarchy as an institution has failed to bring to realization the true character and function of Israel. Jehoiachin may be a Davidic king, but he is so in name only. In appearance he belongs to the last generation of the line to sit on the throne, but in reality he is already in a condition of exile, totally at the mercy of the world empire of the time.

Thus it may be quite intentional that the short paragraph on Jehoiachin is modelled quite closely on that on Jehoahaz in vv. 1-4. The pattern, from which there is no escape, laid down in the first 'exilic' generation of the house of David, continues inexorably into the second and last. Once more a king is crowned by local choice, the younger of two brothers. Once more, just when there might have been thought of independence regained, the overlord intervenes to deport the king ('he brought him to Egypt/Babylon') and appoints his older brother in his place as king 'over Judah and Jerusalem' (vv. 4, 10; both phrases are added by C to his underlying in Kings text). It may be that it is to mark the failure of Israel as cumulative and progressive, that C makes Zedekiah now the brother of the deposed king, not his uncle. 'At the return of the year', the conventional time in the drier weather of the spring when armies are on the march (1 Chron. 20.1), Nebuchadnezzar 'sends' (again that verb of provoked response, 1 Chron. 21.15) the punitive expedition.

C emphasizes more strongly the deliberate policy of Nebuchadnezzar, as opposed to 2 Kgs 24.10-11 where he appears after his forces have taken the initiative. Kings has a much longer text on the process of the siege, the capitulation of the king, the plundering of the treasuries of Temple and palace, and the initial exiling of thousands of the leading members of the community.

As under Jehoiachin's father, so now under himself, the Temple is again raided and still more of the precious utensils (again a phrase inserted by C; it is used in 2 Chron. 32.27 in connection with Hezekiah) are added to that stock of desecrated articles in Babylon, the tyrannical power whose time will surely come.

4. *2 Chronicles 36.11-21: Zedekiah*

Zedekiah bears the awesome name, 'The LORD is my righteousness'. This name and the reign of the king who bears it provide C with the appropriate climax to his presentation of the failure of Israel. Human righteousness (1 Chron. 18.14) is conformity with the norms laid down in the Law, the punctilious rendering to God of all that is due to him; God's righteousness is his all-prevailing vindication in the life of the world of the norms he has laid down. At their own invitation, by the naming of their sons, the house of David have invoked the participation of the LORD in their affairs. It was with a rightly motivated reticence that Israel perceived that there were occasions when it was appropriate *not* to invoke the name of God (Amos 6.10).

The reign is presented in two paragraphs.

Verses 11-19: The Destruction of Jerusalem
C first stresses Zedekiah's own culpability (vv. 12-13). The general condition of 'doing what is evil in the eyes of the LORD', into which these 'exilic' Davidic kings are locked, is brought to its fearsome fruition by the personal failings of the king.

First (v. 12), C stresses, 'the LORD is *his God*' [C's addition to 2 Kgs 24.19]: everything that happens is personalized in terms of the relationship between king and God.

'Humbling oneself' (2 Chron. 7.14), the confessing that one is in the wrong which is the first essential step in rehabilitation, is beyond Zedekiah's capacity. Zedekiah bears full responsibility for the consequence: he received warning from the LORD, through Jeremiah (2 Chron. 35.25), the final, climactic figure of the succession of the prophets (Introduction to 2 Chron. 10–36).

The whole of v. 12b with these distinctive concepts has been added by C.

The specific trigger of the catastrophe is Zedekiah's attempt to revolt against Nebuchadnezzar (v. 13). Again, C is not in the least interested in the military factors in the equation—the colossal gamble that Zedekiah takes, in withholding his tribute, on non-reprisals on the part of the Babylonians, despite their overwhelming military might.

> Kings, though it, too, is not fundamentally concerned with the military situation, adds much further information on Nebuchadnezzar's punitive response. At this point, apart from general adherence to the profile of events and the occasional verbal echo (especially v. 17, 'against them', 'Chaldeans'; compare 2 Kgs 25.1, 4; 'they burned down the house of God and tore down the wall of Jerusalem', v. 19, compare 2 Kgs 25.9-10; 'he deported those who were left', v. 20, compare 2 Kgs 25.11), C takes final leave of Kings.

For C, the fundamental flaw is theological (1 Chron. 10.13-14) and this at two levels. The surface level is the breaking by Zedekiah of a covenant of allegiance solemnized by oath before God. No matter how inappropriate the contractual arrangements may be that have had to be entered into with alien nations, because of failure on the part of God's people to represent his sovereignty on earth, God's people are not entitled unilaterally to withdraw from these binding obligations (one of the expressions of *ma'al*, Lev. 6.3, 5). It is not thus that God's people repossess their true status. That can only come through patient, faithful living in the way of God.

Thus the deeper level is failure to trust in God. That failure is not this time expressed in terms of Jerusalem theology (though cf. v. 23); more fundamentally still, it is couched in terms of resisting the Law, specifically 'stiffening the neck' (2 Chron. 29.6), as in, for example, Exod. 32.9; Deut. 10.16 (the following phrase, 'he made his mind inflexible' is unique, but see 2 Chron. 13.7, where the same verbal root is used of intransigent resistance to Rehoboam).

This failure on Zedekiah's part is then defined in C's classic terms of *ma'al* (1 Chron. 2.7). The stiffening of the neck and the refusal to repent have both been already related to *ma'al* in 2 Chron. 30.8.

But, v. 14, the failure is not Zedekiah's alone. At this point the specific failures of Zedekiah merge with the history of failure on the part of the whole people from beginning to end of its occupation of the land.

> The gap in the standard Hebrew texts, *BHK* and *BHS*, *after* v. 14, as though a new paragraph begins at v. 15, is tendentious and quite

unwarranted. Already in v. 14 the narrative is being broadened out to include the culpability of past generations.

The leadership of the whole community, in particular the priests, whose role at the altar represents the central responsibility of those charged with the faithful response of Israel (1 Chron. 6.49), and the community itself have been guilty of manifold deeds of *ma'al*, as C's whole history has endeavoured to expound.

This failure to accord God his due is expressed in three of its particular aspects. Israel has surrendered its status by becoming conformed to the 'abominable practices' (2 Chron. 28.3) of the nations of the world. These have involved the 'pollution' (2 Chron. 23.19), the desecration of the Temple. This Temple has been 'consecrated' as the central expression and manifestation of Israel's holiness, which consists in her rendering of her duty in every aspect of life (1 Chron. 6).

C does not record the personal fate of Zedekiah—he is not even mentioned after this point; it is the destiny of the people that is C's ultimate concern. First, the divine long-suffering is emphasized: it is because of the pity (the verb is used only here and in v. 17 in C) for his people and for his 'dwelling place' (the Temple as sacramental expression of his cosmic dwelling, 2 Chron. 30.27), that the LORD, 'the God of their fathers' (the divine title that expresses length and continuity of tradition, 1 Chron. 5.25), has sent (the verb of the LORD's response by means of his messengers, 1 Chron. 21.15), at earliest opportunity and continually his prophets (cf. the double continuity of the prophetic role, Introduction to 2 Chron. 10–36). But equally continually (v. 16; C uses the past tense of the verb 'to be' with the participles of three verbs to express the continuousness of the action), the people have been ridiculing the LORD's messengers until his anger (2 Chron. 12.7) has been provoked past the point of recovery ('healing', that is, restoration after acknowledgment of sin, 2 Chron. 7.14).

The response of Babylon is now resumed (v. 17) from v. 13. Once again, C's discourse is on the theological plane. Nebuchadnezzar is no longer mentioned by name; he is described impersonally as the 'king of Chaldeans'. He is but a cypher in the hand of God. It is not on his volition that he launches the punitive expedition; it is the LORD's doing. Grammatically speaking, it is even possible that the LORD is the subject of all the verbs in the sentence. It is so for the first and the last verbs, 'He brought up the king of the Chaldeans...he delivered everything into his hand'. There is no indication of change of subject for the intervening verbs, 'he slaughtered their youths...and did not spare [picking up the verb of v. 15] young man or virgin...': the English versions take the first of these with 'the king of the Chaldeans' (for example, NRSV, 'who killed their youths'; 'youths' probably has here the technical meaning 'flower of the army', given that the same word is repeated in the singular in co-ordination with 'virgin').

Nothing could express more pointedly or starkly the rejection by God of his own people, than the slaughter of his own worshippers in his own sanctuary. The rites of atonement are designed specifically to secure the lives of the worshippers; these rites no longer avail. The requirement of a sacrificial death for the sin and guilt of the community can no longer be satisfied by a substitutionary victim (Lev. 4.1–6.7); it must be met by the life of the wrong-doers themselves. No atonement is for the moment possible.

Nothing could express more horrifically the pollution of the sanctuary: the shedding of the blood of its own worshippers in it is the most extreme form of desecration conceivable (2 Chron. 23.17). None of this is Israel spared: the word 'all' is repeated five times in vv. 17-19.

The sack of Jerusalem marks the culmination of the process begun under Jehoiakim (v. 18; cf. vv. 7, 10). Now all the furnishings of the Temple that the earlier lootings have left are removed; the treasuries of Temple and palace are pillaged. The inversion of the normal word order, with the *casus pendens*, indicates the ultimate character of the disaster: 'As for all the vessels...all these he brought to Babylon' (again there is no grammatical reason why 'God' should not be regarded as the subject of the verb). These vessels and treasuries had been the symbols of the sovereignty of God exercised through the Davidic king and the host of Israel under his command (e.g., 1 Chron. 26.27). By their removal Israel's role is worse than nullified; it is usurped by the chaotic power of the gentile emperor. All that Israel was called to achieve on behalf of the nations of the world has been totally reversed.

The point is made once again in v. 19 with all sharpness, using the alternative language of the 'negative Passover' (1 Chron. 21.12): 'destruction', the disaster that the original Passover was designed to avert, stands now in climactic position. All security is destroyed: the fundamental security offered by God, sacramentally represented by the Temple and the defences of the city, and by the wealth of its possessions. The question of security, which had dominated the reign of the first king after Solomon (2 Chron. 11-12), is now posed in ultimate terms.

Verses 20-21 The Exile to Babylon
In contrast to the statistics in 2 Kings 24–25 for repeated deportations in the 590s and 580s and implication that by far the larger proportion of the population remained in the land, C insists on the total exile of the entire population (v. 20): 'He took into exile to Babylon those who had survived the sword'. Nebuchadnezzar (again unnamed) is unambiguously the subject, in view of the next phrase: 'they became his sons and slaves'. The expression, 'sons and slaves' expresses the condition of total surrender of status and subjection to the overlord (see 2 Kgs 16.7 [not in C] for Ahaz's acknowledgment of dependence upon Tiglath-pileser).

But this is not in perpetuity. Liberation from this exile comes with the rule of the Persians. Yet once more, C provides no information of a military or political nature for the triumph of the Persians.[4] On the contrary, all is governed 'in order to fulfil the Word of the LORD' (v. 21), the determinate plan of God as announced through prophet and Law.

It is Jeremiah who provides the temporal framework (v. 21aα, bβ): the release is to come after seventy years of exile (Jer. 25.11-12; 29.10, as noted in the Introduction to this section). But the content of the expectation is provided by Leviticus (v. 21aβ, bα; the operative vocabulary here does not occur in Jeremiah). The seventy years are to endure, 'until the land receives satisfaction for its sabbaths; all the years when it lies in devastation it will enjoy a sabbath rest'.

The vocabulary is derived from Lev. 26.34-35, 43 (the only other passages in the Hebrew Bible where the infinitive of the passive causative of the verb 'to devastate' occurs). The passage in Leviticus is of crucial importance for C's presentation. As in C (1 Chron. 2.7), the course of Israel's history, its exile and hope of return are all interpreted in terms of *ma'al* and its expiation (specifically, Lev. 26.40). Israel has defrauded God of all that is due to him. That fraud is symbolized by non-payment of 'holy things', the offerings in kind (Num. 18, especially), which express Israel's acknowledgment of its dependence upon God and of its role in his purposes. The penalty for this

4. For an account, see Bright, *History of Israel*, pp. 351-54, 360-62.

fraud is forfeiture of the land that has produced the offerings in kind. After seventy years of sabbath rest the land will have had repaid to itself, and thus to God the giver, the debt of payments in kind. As the fraud in holy things has symbolized the total fraudulence of way of life, so the satisfaction paid for the fraud in 'holy things' symbolizes the possibility of the restoring of the normal relations envisaged by God between himself and his people. Through the forfeiture of the land the way to restoration to the land is now opened.

5. 2 Chronicles 36.22-23: The Call to Immigration

These verses are virtually identical to Ezra 1.1-3aβi (for comment on the significance of the parallel, see the Introduction to Volume 1).

The jubilee of the fiftieth generation from the creation of the world and of humankind has arrived (Lev. 25.8-13; see Introduction to this section). Now is the moment of the restoration of the relationship with humanity originally intended in Adam. Now is the moment of return to ancestral lands, to the ideal envisaged since the beginning of time. Central to this purpose is Israel. After all the vicissitudes of Israel as the finally designated agent of the restoration of the relationship, the moment has come for Israel when she will be enabled to fulfil her role and realize her destiny among the nations of the world.

To allow full trenchancy to the proclamation of the return, C divides the section into two paragraphs.

Verse 22: The Making of the Proclamation
Again, any motives of political self-interest that Cyrus may have had are beside the point. Cyrus's edict is first and last 'to fulfil the Word of the LORD in [Ezra, 'from'] the mouth of Jeremiah'. It is the LORD who 'stirred up the spirit of Cyrus, king of Persia': this is an inspiration of a truly prophetic character (1 Chron. 5.26). Cyrus 'sends a proclamation throughout the whole of his kingdom', not only orally 'but also in writing': the decision is final and as canonical as any other Scripture (cf. Ezra 1.1-4; 5.13-15; 6.1-5).

Once again, the connection with Leviticus should be noted—the legislation on the Jubilee in Lev. 25.9: there the same verb is used (twice) as here for 'sending round' the trumpet that announces the inauguration of the jubilee on the Day of Atonement, and there, too, it is 'throughout the whole' of your land (compare the interim realization under Hezekiah, 2 Chron. 30.5; 31.1).

Verse 23: The Content of the Proclamation
Cyrus's proclamation opens with a confession of faith (cf. Huram, 2 Chron. 2.12): 'The LORD, the God of heaven, has given me all the kingdoms of the earth'. This is a truly astonishing statement. The gentile emperor acknowledges that the LORD, the personal God of Israel, is truly the cosmic deity. As cosmic deity there is nothing that can hinder the onward progress of his power on earth. The seat of his dominion he has given into the power of an earthly world figure who is carrying out nothing but his bidding. The LORD as cosmic deity has appointed Cyrus his vicegerent on earth. The kingdoms of the whole earth are, therefore, involved in this act as once they paid tribute to David (1 Chron. 29.30; cf. Solomon, 2 Chron. 9.22-23).

Then comes the specific proclamation. The LORD has 'enjoined me to rebuild for him a Temple in Jerusalem'. The verb, 'enjoin', picks up precisely the language of the muster for sacral duty (*pqd*, 1 Chron. 21.5). The building of the Temple is once again a sacramental act by which the power and the authority of the Deity, in whose name the Temple is constructed, is acknowledged (e.g., 1 Chron. 22.9).

C's whole work ends with an invitation to 'go up'.

By abbreviation and by the change of one word, C provides a different version of Cyrus's edict from that in Ezra 1.3-4. In Ezra, the edict runs: 'Whoever there is among you who belongs to his people, may his God be with him and let him go up to Jerusalem...and rebuild the Temple'. C reads the first part as a statement, not a wish, and curtails the second: 'Whoever there is among you who belongs to his people, the LORD is with him, so that he may go up'. The statement reaffirms the 'messianic' preposition 'with' of the old Jerusalemite theology (cf. 1 Chron. 11.9). The promises of God to David are now reaffirmed to his people.

The final phrase, 'so that he may go up', uses the verb from the same root as the word *ᶜᵃliyyâ*, which in post-biblical Hebrew acquires the sense, 'pilgrimage to Jerusalem, immigration to Israel'. Thanks to the providential ordering of God, the whole of God's people stand poised at the moment of Jubilee for Return to their land. But, strikingly, C does not include 'Jerusalem' as the goal of the 'going up'. He deliberately stops short of the version of the edict in Ezra in order to end on an eschatological note: he still writes 'in exile'; the definitive Return has not yet taken place. In the light of the exposition of guilt and atonement in Lev. 26.40-45, that Return awaits the final act of restoration in the mercy and good pleasure of God. Israel, in the meantime, is in the interim of waiting.

But Israel is not left in a vacuum. The placing of the Levites centrally in the life of the people (1 Chron. 6), above all as teachers and monitors of holiness, provides Israel with the form and shape of life within which to ensure that all duty to God is honoured. It is to that honouring of God that 'one may go up', to which one may aspire even now. It is in that honouring of God that the quality of the life of the Return in the jubilee can be anticipated. The promises of God to David have indeed been reaffirmed to his people, but now in the fundamental mode of the Law of Moses.

It is through the practice of holiness as laid down by that Law that the definitive means for the restoration of the relationship between God and Adam has now been provided.

BIBLIOGRAPHY

This bibliography is far from being an exhaustive list of the secondary literature on C and its related questions. It is more of an account of works used in the process of writing the commentary and some further leads, which themselves provide substantial bibliographies.

A commentary is written not because the interpreter knows, but because he or she needs to know. It has to be the inductive description of the material in the work itself, written with as few preconceptions as possible about what the theme or themes may turn out to be. The Hebrew text has to be patiently read with, as chief tool, the Hebrew concordance to enable the main interconnections of language within the work and between the work and the rest of the Hebrew Bible to be traced. This is the policy I have tried to follow. I apologize to my predecessors for the inevitable occasions where insights are duplicated, with earlier work unacknowledged. My conclusions have been reached, for the most part, independently: where I am conscious of indebtedness, I have tried to acknowledge it.

Fuller discussion of individual topics has also to be left on one side. I have offered studies of some special areas elsewhere, noted below.

The commentary has been drafted on the basis of the Hebrew Text (*BHK* and *BHS*) and with extensive use of the Hebrew concordance, both manual (Mandelkern, on the whole for single words) and computerized (macBible™, Zondervan Electronic Publishing, Grand Rapids, 1990, usually for combinations of words and phrases). Where access to a range of informed scholarly opinion has been required, I have used the standard lexica (BDB, KBS), and representative modern English Versions (NEB, JPSV, NIV, and NRSV; where the rendering differs from NRSV, it is my own, unless otherwise stated). For geographical matters, I have used Grollenberg's atlas (occasionally J.B. Pritchard's 'Times', 1987, but on Jerusalem, the main crux, it provides little help); for historical, Bright's *History of Israel*, not because I always agree with it, but because it has been a standard textbook, which, simply because I do disagree with much of it, helps to provide a certain degree of objectivity. Where proper names have not been sufficiently differentiated by Mandelkern (e.g. under Mattithiah, '*nonnulli viri*'), I have consulted the standard Hebrew–English Lexicon, BDB. For technical terms (such as discussion of identification of precious stones or architectural features), I have consulted the review of opinions in KBS.

The secondary literature on C is growing rapidly. The mention of, perforce, only a fraction gives, perhaps, sufficient leads into the extensive discussion.

While within the confines of this commentary it is not possible to engage in debate with the work of one's predecessors, I have reviewed some of the commentaries available up to 1989 in 'Which is the best commentary?: The Chronicler's Work', *ExpTim* 102 (1990–91), pp. 6-11 (E.L Curtis, A.A. Madsen, ICC, 1910; J.M. Myers, Anchor, 1965; P.R. Ackroyd, Torch, 1973; R.J. Coggins, Cambridge, 1976; H.G.M. Williamson, New Century, 1982; J.G. McConville, Daily Study, 1984; R. Braun, R.B. Dillard, Word, 1986-87).

Since then, a number of commentaries have appeared: S.J. de Vries, *1 and 2 Chronicles*; S. Japhet, *I & II Chronicles*, which complements her, still essential, earlier work, *The Ideology of the Book of Chronicles and its Place in Biblical Thought* (I have offered a critical appraisal of some of her conclusions in my essay, 'The Use of Leviticus in Chronicles', noted below); M.J. Selman, *1 and 2 Chronicles*.

The most magisterial commentary of all to date will be T. Willi, *Chronik* (in progress).

An overview of issues and proposals in interpreting Chronicles is provided by: P.R. Ackroyd, *The Chronicler in his Age* (a collection of essays written over some thirty-five years) and, especially, G.H. Jones, *1 and 2 Chronicles*. Studies of special features are to be found in the monographs by: Gray, Kleinig, Riley, Kalimi, Steins, Weinberg and Kelly.

Ackroyd, P.R., *The Chronicler in his Age* (JSOTSup, 101; Sheffield: JSOT Press, 1991).
Bright, J., *A History of Israel* (London: SCM Press, 3rd edn, 1981).
de Vries, S.J., *1 and 2 Chronicles* (FOTL, 11; Grand Rapids: Eerdmans, 1989).
Douglas, Mary, 'Sacred Contagion', in J.F.A. Sawyer (ed.), *Rending Leviticus* (JSOTSup, 227; Sheffield: JSOT Press, 1996), pp. 86-106.
Graham, M. Patrick, Kenneth G. Hoglund, McKenzie, Steven, *The Chronicler as Historian* (JSOTSup, 238; Sheffield: Sheffield Academic Press, 1997).
Gray, J., *The Biblical Doctrine of the Reign of God* (Edinburgh: T. & T. Clark, 1979).
Grollenberg, L.H., *Atlas of the Bible* (London: Nelson, 1956).
Japhet, Sara, *The Ideology of the Book of Chronicles and its Place in Biblical Thought* (Frankfurt: Peter Lang, 1989).
—*I & II Chronicles* (London: SCM Press, 1993).
Johnstone, W., 'The Signs', in H. Frost (ed.), *The Marsala Punic Ship* (Rome: Notizie degli Scavi, Accademia dei Lincei, 1981), pp. 191-240.
—'Guilt and Atonement: The Theme of 1 and 2 Chronicles', in J.D. Martin and P.R. Davies (eds.), *A Word in Season: Essays in Honour of William McKane* (JSOTSup, 42; Sheffield: JSOT Press, 1986), pp. 113-38.
—'Reactivating the Chronicles Analogy in Pentateuchal Studies, with Special Reference to the Sinai Pericope in Exodus', *ZAW* (1987), pp. 16-37.
—'Justification by Faith Revisited', *ExpTim* 104 (1992–93), pp. 67-71.
—'Solomon's Prayer: Is Intentionalism such a Fallacy?', *ST* 47 (1993), pp. 119-33.
—'The Use of Leviticus in Chronicles', in J.F.A. Sawyer (ed.), *Reading Leviticus* (JSOTSup, 227; Sheffield: Sheffield Academic Press, 1996), pp. 243-55.
Jones, G.H., *1&2 Chronicles* (OTG, Sheffield: JSOT Press), 1993.
Kalimi, I., *Zur Geschichtsschreibung des Chronisten: Literarisch-historiographische Abweichungen der Chronik von ihren Paralleltexten in den Samuel- und Königsbüchern* (BZAW, 226; Berlin: de Gruyter, 1995).

Kelly, B.E., *Retribution and Eschatology in Chronicles* (JSOTSup, 211; Sheffield: JSOT Press, 1996).

Kleinig, J.E., *The LORD's Song: The Basis, Function and Significance of Choral Music in Chronicles* (JSOTSup, 156; Sheffield: JSOT Press, 1993).

Mandelkern, S., *Concordance to the Old Testament* (repr.; Tel Aviv: Schocken Books, 1962).

Milgrom, J., *Cult and Conscience: The Asham and the Priestly Doctrine of Repentance* (SJLA, 18; Leiden: Brill, 1976).

Neusner, J., *Between Time and Eternity* (Encino: Dickenson, 1975), p. 52.

Riley, W., *King and Cultus in Chronicles: Worship and the Reinterpretation of History* (JSOTSup, 160; Sheffield: JSOT Press, 1993).

Selman, M.J., *1 and 2 Chronicles* (London: Tyndale Press, 1994).

Steins, G., *Die Chronik als kanonisches Abschlussphänomen: Studien zur Entstehung und Theologie von 1/2 Chronik* (BBB, 93, Weinheim: Beltz Athenäum, 1995).

Weinberg, J.P., *Der Chronist in seiner Mitwelt* (BZAW, 239; Berlin: de Gruyter, 1996).

Westermann, C., *Basic Forms of Prophetic Speech* (trans. Hugh Clayton White; London: Lutterworth, 1967).

Willi, T., *Chronik* (BKAT, 24; Neukirchen–Vluyn: Neukirchener Verlag, 1991–in progress).

INDEXES

Reference	Pages
22.8	131
22.9	11, 60, 61, 104, 136, 219, 275
22.11	56, 62, 102, 145, 164, 212, 220
22.12-13	10
22.12	39, 80, 204
22.13	29, 36, 54, 56, 66, 80, 86, 94, 100, 122, 150, 154, 189, 214
22.18	182
22.19	35, 67, 245
23–27	251
23–26	207
23	248
23.1	24
23.2	42, 194
23.3	251
23.13	206
23.25-26	247
23.26	247
23.28	69, 233
23.32	55
234.30	244
24.3	135
25	238
25.1	196, 254
25.5	38, 254
25.16	99
26.1-28	236
26.1-3	101
26.4	161
26.8	161
26.14-28	211
26.14	101
26.15	161
26.20-26	44
26.24	33
26.26	140
26.27	272
26.29-30	166
26.29	210
26.30	138
27	79, 81, 113, 218, 236, 248
27.1-15	62
27.1	82, 123
27.16	33, 94
27.24	92, 94, 144, 191, 220
27.25-29	44
27.25	33
27.31	208, 250
27.32-33	117, 158
28.1	82, 208
28.2	52, 104, 137, 192, 247
28.4	24
28.5	9, 54, 97, 263
28.7	243
28.9	34, 39, 42, 43, 56, 65, 67, 111, 144, 180, 191, 194, 202, 242, 245, 247
28.11-19	191
28.11	237
28.12	64
28.13-16	55
28.17	195
28.18	167
28.19	248
28.20	29, 36, 54, 142
29.1	54, 233
29.4	265
29.5-9	250
29.5	55, 197, 198
29.10	206
29.11	97, 219
29.12	220
29.14	57, 106
29.16	209
29.19	11, 69, 80, 94, 151, 244
29.20	101, 144, 197
29.21	67, 195, 197, 198, 208, 250
29.22	11, 24, 39, 209
29.23	32, 93, 220
29.24	202
29.27	265
29.28	74, 78
29.30	9, 275

2 Chronicles

Reference	Pages
1.1	36, 46, 58, 66, 73, 77, 109, 122, 152, 165, 173, 174, 186, 189, 212, 227, 236
1.8	24
1.9	24
1.11	24, 92, 243
1.14	41
2.2	24
2.4	55
2.6	57
2.10-11	106
2.10	172
2.11	92
2.12	204, 275,
2.17	24
2.18	24
3.1	146
3.15-17	126
4.7	55
4.8	55
4.9	96
4.22	142
5	252
5.5	191
5.7	247
5.9	103, 247
5.10	103
5.11	127
5.12-13	56
5.12	193

INDEX OF SELECTED KEY TERMS

(words are listed in the order of the Hebrew alphabet, vowelled forms first)

JOURNAL FOR THE STUDY OF THE OLD TESTAMENT
SUPPLEMENT SERIES